A BLUE RIBBON
Poultry
COOKBOOK

FAVORITE RECIPES OF ®
HOME ECONOMICS TEACHERS

Dear Homemaker

The imaginative preparation of poultry is the second of our Blue Ribbon Cook book series. America's home economics teachers share their favorite recipes with you and demonstrate their remarkable versatility with chicken and other poultry. A rich and diversified harvest of exciting poultry recipes teach marvelous new ways to fry, roast, braise and broil. Here are recipes truly worth of the "BLUE RIBBON" Award.

Our sincere thanks are extended to the teachers who entered their home-tested recipes in the 1973 Blue Ribbon Food Fair. Their enthusiastic participation made this award-winning edition possible.

Thank you for your interest and confidence in the Favorite Recipes of Home Economics Teachers Cookbooks. We feel certain that the many reliable poultry recipes in this volume will become your family favorites too. Remember, in purchasing this cookbook, you are supporting your school's home economics department. Thank you.

Sincerely yours,

Mary Anne Richards

© Favorite Recipes Press MCMLXXIII
P. O. Box 3396, Montgomery, Alabama 36109
Library of Congress Catalog Card No. 73-82897
ISBN 0-87197-047-3

Preface

Remember holidays when the house was filled with the aroma of a
roast turkey in the oven; the smell beckoning family members into the
kitchen to ask when dinner would be ready? Appetizing, nutritious,
and economical, poultry is a favorite main dish in most homes,
not only on holidays but every day.

The second edition in the Blue Ribbon Cookbook series is dedicated
to the exploration of new dimensions in the preparation of chicken,
turkey, duck, capon, quail, pheasant and Cornish hen — drawing
upon the experience of home economics teachers from all parts of the
country. Hundreds of recipes for savory poultry dishes were entered
in the annual Blue Ribbon Food Fair, and judged by a panel of
food experts. Entries were evaluated primarily on recipe accuracy,
excellence of eating quality, originality and creativity. Flavor, texture
and appearance were also important.

On the basis of these factors, the "best of the best" were chosen to fill
the pages of this unique cookbook. In addition you will find sections
featuring tried and proven tips on how to choose poultry, how to clean
and store it, which kitchen utensils are needed — all the essentials
to prepare flawless, Blue Ribbon dishes for your own family.

Donna Roy

Linda Bailey

JoAnn Bailey

Margaret Bruce

Robbie Strom

Contents

Ruth Stovall
Branch Director
Program Services Branch
Division of Vocational-
Technical & Higher
*   Education*
Alabama Department
*   of Education*

Jeanne Voltz
Food Editor
Woman's Day Magazine

Highlights

of the Blue Ribbor

Food Fair

In mid-April of this year, five home economics teache
received air mail, registered letters announcing that th
were finalists in the 1973 Blue Ribbon Food Fair! The
with husbands, would be flown to Chicago for a whirlwi
weekend, all expenses paid by Favorite Recipes Press. T
weekend would culminate in awarding $5000 in pri
money. Although they had never met, the five were soon
share a thrilling and memorable experience.

There was the immediate excitement of school farewell p
ties and the congratulations of principals, students a
friends. The interest of well-wishers made the finalists f
very honored and special; but that was to be only the beg
ning. A great adventure lay ahead in the "Windy City."

On Friday, May 11th, the finalists — JoAnn Bailey, Lin
Bailey, Margaret Bruce, Donna Ray and Borghild ("Bobbie
Strom — arrived at Chicago's O'Hare Airport. Upon arri
in the city they were whisked directly to the downto
Holiday Inn where the hotel marquee read, "Welco
Favorite Recipes Food Fair." A bountiful tray of fr
awaited each teacher in her room, and exclamations
can't believe all this!") were heard as they stepped to
windows overlooking beautiful Lake Michigan.

After a short rest, everyone was off to lunch at the Ma
Pan restaurant, noted for its exotic crepes. Then it was ti
to visit the test kitchens of the People's Gas Company
Chicago.

Sue Spitler
Food Editor
Sphere Magazine

Vy Catt, Rose Rybowiak and Pat Matheny of the Gas Company had made all the advance preparations for the cook-off. When the ladies arrived, Pat showed them to the modern test kitchens where they tested equipment and practiced preparing their winning recipes.

Dinner that night was a festive affair at the Kon Tiki Ports restaurant, where everyone equally enjoyed Polynesian food and conversation. There was a sense of warmth among the participants, although they had met only hours before. To finish off the evening, they visited the top of the John Hancock Center in the heart of Chicago, towering ninety-six stories over the city. Through floor-to-ceiling glass, they viewed the brilliant lights of the pulsating, fast-moving metropolis below.

Saturday was the big day . . . the 1973 Blue Ribbon Food Fair would soon begin. As the participants entered the test kitchens where they had practiced the day before, the atmosphere seemed electrified with anticipation. A professional photographer (as well as proud husbands!) snapped pictures as the finalists donned their personalized aprons, gift mementos from Favorite Recipes Press.

Margaret Bruce accepts a $2,500 First Place check from Marilyn Black for her winning Pheasant Muscatel recipe.

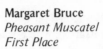

Margaret Bruce
Pheasant Muscatel
First Place

Quiet tension and excitement settled upon the room as the teachers began to prepare their poultry creations, with tantalizing aromas filling the air. Each lady realized there would be only one chance to produce her recipe at its best, and each took care that everything was just right. By noon the cooking was finished, and the judges' work began. The decision rested upon three women, each prominent in the food industry: Sue Spitler, Food Editor for Betty Crocker's *Sphere* magazine; Ruth Stovall, Program Services Branch Director, Division of Vocational-Technical and Higher Education of the Alabama Department of Education; and Jeanne Voltz, Food Editor for *Woman's Day* magazine.

While the panel of judges tasted and scored the entries, tension of the teachers was, for the time being, relieved as they and their husbands set off to tour sites of interest in the bustling city. Afterwards, they rushed back to the hotel to dress for the awards banquet. Entering the room, each lady was thrilled to find a large, beautiful white orchid to adorn her gown that evening. "When it comes to taking care of people, they certainly know how to do it!" one exclaimed.

And now the climax of the weekend, and the culmination of weeks of planning by the Favorite Recipes Press staff was at hand as everyone entered the banquet room of the

Borghild Strom
Chicken with Orange Rice
Second Place

Linda Bailey
Hot Chicken Salad
Third Place

elegant Drake Hotel. Soon the outcome would be known! Doubtless, each teacher relived in her mind the events of the past weeks and particularly this unbelievable weekend, as Favorite Recipes Press president Jim Perkins asked them how they had felt when notified of their selection as finalists.

Marilyn Black then stepped to the podium to give the banquet address. A past vice president who had been with Favorite Recipes Press since its inception, Marilyn explained that the Blue Ribbon Food Fair is a national awards program designed to recognize and honor America's home economics teachers and their schools. The excitement and tension mounted as she spoke, for the awards presentation was approaching. Finally the moment arrived to announce the awards. Anxiously, the five finalists watched and listened in attentive silence as the sealed envelopes were opened in Bert Parks' fashion: "Fourth runner-up, JoAnn Bailey's Tutti Frutti Chicken; third runner-up, Donna Ray's Turkey Supreme; second runner-up, Linda Bailey's Hot Chicken Salad." Two teachers remained, one of whom would receive the grand award of $2,500. "Bobbie Strom's Chicken with Orange Rice is the first runner-up. The Blue Ribbon winner is Margaret Bruce's Pheasant Muscatel!" Tears of happiness filled Margaret's eyes as her minister-husband hugged her; then she rose and accepted the award. The Blue Ribbon was hers!

The sentiments of one of the finalists echoed the feelings of everyone when she said, "Thank you for everything from the moment we arrived — from the welcome cup of coffee at the Holiday Inn, to the beautiful tray of fruit, the delicious meals in special places, the gorgeous view from our room. I'll always remember this weekend as one of the most exciting times of my life."

A month prior to the National cook-off in Chicago, food editors at Favorite Recipes Press selected 100 of the best entries from over 700 submitted by home economics teachers across the country. A week of test-cooking and judging at Favorite Recipes Press headquarters in Montgomery, Alabama, narrowed the entries to the five most outstanding recipes. The five finalists who participated in Chicago were the best of the hundreds of recipes submitted. Together, they shared the adventure that will not soon be forgotten . . . the 1973 Blue Ribbon Food Fair.

Donna Ray
Turkey Supreme
Fourth Place

JoAnn Bailey
Tutti-Frutti Chicken
Fifth Place

Buying and Storing

Poultry

Chicken is popular with homemakers not only because it has a delicious, mild flavor but because it also is one of today's best buys. Although low in price, chicken is high in protein, niacin, and iron . . . an important consideration for nutrition-minded women.

In choosing chicken, look for birds with short legs, plump bodies, and unbruised skins. They should have a good fatty layer. If pre-packaged, the packages should be unbroken. Almost all poultry sold is inspected and is rated Grade A. Under the latest legislation, chicken-packing plants are continuously inspected for your family's protection.

Broiler-fryers are the most popular type of chicken. They are an excellent buy from May until September. These young, tender chickens weigh between 1 1/2 to 3 1/2 pounds and come ready to cook. They are perfect for roasting, simmering, baking, frying, grilling, or broiling.

Capons are large chickens, usually weighing from 4 to 7 pounds. They yield a large amount of white, flavorful meat. They are most often roasted, although they may be baked, fried, or broiled.

Roasters are large — 3 1/2 to 5 pounds — tender birds and are an excellent buy from September to January. Usually sold ready to cook, they are delicious when stuffed and baked in the oven.

Stewing chickens are mature, less tender birds weighing from 2 1/2 to 5 pounds. They are priced lowest from October to January. These fatty birds are cooked in a large amount of liquid. One stewing chicken will usually yield enough meat for a chicken pie plus a salad, with plenty of rich broth left over.

Cornish game hens are the smallest and youngest members of the chicken family. Weighing 1 1/2 pounds or less, they are excellent for roasting, broiling, or frying. They are also the most expensive of all chickens.

Chicken roasts generally come in two-pound sizes. They are made of uncooked chicken, boned, rolled, and covered with skin. They are just right for small family meals, luncheons, or in buffet service when you want pieces of uniform size.

The amount of chicken you buy will depend on how many people you are serving. In general, allow 1/4 to 1/2 a bird per person for broiling or frying.

If roasting or stewing, allow 1/2 pound per person (3/4 pound for hearty eaters). Allow one Cornish hen per person. If you are serving chicken roasts, plan on 1/3 pound per serving.

BUYING TURKEY

The same general rules for buying chicken apply in buying turkey. Your best buy in turkeys is the 16- to 24-pound birds — they yield more meat per pound. If this size is too big for your family, ask the butcher to split it: freeze half and use it later.

Like chicken, turkey is available in boned and rolled roasts. These roasts come in 2 1/2 to 10-pound sizes. Also available are rolls — three to ten pounds of fully cooked turkey not covered with skin. These rolls are perfect for sandwiches or casseroles.

In buying turkey, you'll want to calculate how many people you can serve per pound. For a 5- to 12-pound turkey, allow 3/4 to 1 pound per person. A 12- to 24-pound turkey will give you 1/2 to 3/4 a pound per serving. For uncooked boneless roasts, allow 1/3 pound per person.

STORING CHICKEN AND TURKEY

Chicken and turkey you are going to use within a day or two can be safely kept in the refrigerator. Giblets and liver should be used within 24 hours. Ready-to-cook, whole chicken will keep in the refrigerator for two to three days; cut-up chicken will keep two days. Whole turkey will keep for four to five days. To prepare for refrigeration, remove any wrapping around the poultry as soon as you get home from the store, wash the bird, separate the giblets and liver (usually wrapped separately), and wrap both bird and giblets and liver loosely in transparent paper or foil.

Turkey and chicken may be kept in the refrigerator's freezing compartment or your home freezer. All poultry should be frozen at zero degrees or less. To prepare for freezing, remove all wrapping and rinse the bird thoroughly under cold running water. Pat dry and wrap tightly in transparent wrap, foil, or freezer paper. Try to squeeze out as much air as possible. Whole chickens can be kept frozen for 12 months, cut-up chicken and whole turkeys for 6 months. Never freeze stuffed poultry — the dressing will sour.

To store cooked poultry, remove the stuffing and cooked meat from the bones as soon as possible. Chill both the stuffing and the meat thoroughly. Both may be frozen or kept in the refrigerator. Cooked poultry with liquid will keep in the refrigerator for two days or in the freezer for six months. Poultry without liquid keeps in the refrigerator for two days and in the freezer for one month. Gravy and stuffing may be kept in the refrigerator for three to four days or in the freezer for two months.

Methods of Preparing Poultry

Roasting takes place in an oven preheated to 325 degrees. Poultry to be roasted should be rubbed thoroughly with softened butter and placed on a rack in a shallow roasting pan. Turn the bird breast-side up for the last 15 minutes of cooking time for added color and a crisper skin. Covering the roasting pan with a tent of foil will not only ensure good color and crispness but will keep grease from spattering your oven surfaces. When the drumstick moves easily, the bird is cooked.

Barbecuing is a traditional southern way of preparing poultry. Place broiler-fryer quarters or halves, skin-side up, on a grate about six inches away from glowing coals. Brush with your favorite barbecue sauce — you'll find many delicious sauces in the following pages. Turn frequently and brush often with sauce. The meat will cook in 45 minutes to one hour depending on the size of your pieces.

Broiling is a dry-heat cooking method. Preheat your broiler with the oven temperature set at 350 degrees. (Hotter than this and the poultry will singe.) Brush your broiler halves or quarters with melted butter — you may want to try seasoning the butter for added flavor. Place broiler pan as far away from the heat as possible and broil for 20 minutes on each side, brushing with melted butter frequently. After 40 minutes, prick the chicken with a skewer. If the juices run red, additional cooking time is needed.

Of all the cooking methods of poultry, none is more southern than *frying*. Cover the cut-up pieces of your fryer with seasoned or plain flour. Meanwhile, heat 1/2 inch oil or shortening in a skillet. Beginning with the larger pieces, place chicken skin side down in the pan of oil over moderate heat. Turn and brown other side. Reduce heat and cook for 15 to 25 minutes on each side.

Braising is much like frying, but the cooking is done in oil plus another liquid. To braise, season cut-up pieces of chicken and place them, skin-side down, in a skillet with 1/4 cup oil. Brown over high heat to seal in all the juices. Reduce heat and add 1/2 cup broth, consomme, vegetable juice, or other liquid and cook, covered, for 30 minutes or until tender.

Stewing is a good method to use with older poultry. Place chicken in a large kettle with water to cover. Add your favorite seasonings — celery, onion, peppercorns, salt, and parsley are nice. Cover and simmer for one to three hours, or until the meat comes away from the bones easily. Cooking time will depend on the age and size of your bird.

SPECIAL METHODS FOR GAME

Both waterfowl — ducks and geese — and upland birds — grouse, pheasant, quail, pigeons, doves, woodcock, snipe, and wild turkey — should be well larded before cooking. Larding is the process of adding fat to the poultry by placing strips of bacon over it or by inserting fat into the flesh with a larding needle. Roasting is the preferred cooking method for most game birds.

Quail is the notable exception. It is almost all white meat and can be cooked like domestic chicken. It may be sauteed, broiled, stewed, or roasted. Whatever the cooking method, quail should be thoroughly larded.

13

Roasting Charts

GAME BIRDS

GAME BIRDS	READY-TO-COOK WEIGHT	OVEN TEMP.	ROASTING TIME	AMOUNT PER SERVING
Wild Duck	1-2 lbs.	350°	20-50 min.	1-1 1/2 lbs.
Wild Goose	2-4 lbs. 4-6 lbs.	325°	1-1 1/2 hrs. 1 1/2-2 1/2 hrs.	1-1 1/2 lbs.
Partridge	1/2-1 lb.	350°	30-45 min.	1/2-1 lb.
Pheasant	1-3 lbs.	400°	1-2 1/2 hrs.	1-1 1/2 lbs.
Quail	4-6 oz.	375°	15-20 min.	1/2-1 lb.
Squab	12-14 oz.	350°	30-50 min.	12-14 oz.

DOMESTIC BIRDS

DOMESTIC BIRDS	READY-TO-COOK WEIGHT	OVEN TEMP.	ROASTING TIME	
			UNSTUFFED	STUFFED
Chicken	1 1/2-2 lbs. 2-2 1/2 lbs. 2 1/2-3 lbs. 3-4 lbs.	375° 375° 375° 375°	3/4 hr. 1 hr. 1 1/4 hrs. 1 1/2 hrs.	1 hr. 1 1/4 hrs. 1 1/2 hrs. 2 hrs.
Capon	4-7 lbs.	375°	2 hrs.	3 hrs.
Turkey	6-8 lbs. 8-12 lbs. 12-16 lbs. 16-20 lbs. 20-24 lbs.	325° 325° 325° 325° 325°	3 1/2 hrs. 4 hrs. 4 1/2 hrs. 5 1/2 hrs. 6 1/2 hrs.	4 hrs. 4 1/2 hrs. 5 1/2 hrs. 6 1/2 hrs. 7 1/2 hrs.
Foil-Wrapped Turkey	8-10 lbs. 10-12 lbs. 14-16 lbs. 18-20 lbs. 22-24 lbs.	450° 450° 450° 450° 450°	2 1/4 hrs. 2 1/2 hrs. 3 hrs. 3 1/4 hrs. 3 1/2 hrs.	2 1/2 hrs. 3 hrs. 3 1/4 hrs. 3 1/2 hrs. 3 3/4 hrs.
Domestic Duck	3-5 lbs.	375° then 425°	1 1/2 hrs. 15 min.	2 hrs. 15 min.
Domestic Goose	4-6 lbs. 6-8 lbs. 8-10 lbs. 10-12 lbs. 12-14 lbs.	325° 325° 325° 325° 325°	2 3/4 hrs. 3 hrs. 3 1/2 hrs. 3 3/4 hrs. 4 1/4 hrs.	3 hrs. 3 1/2 hrs. 3 3/4 hrs. 4 1/4 hrs. 4 3/4 hrs.
Cornish Game Hen	1-1 1/2 lbs.	400°	1 1/2 hrs.	1 1/2 hrs.
Guinea Hen	1 1/2-2 lbs. 2-2 1/2 lbs.	375° 375°	3/4 hr. 1 hr.	1 hr. 1 1/2 hrs.

Cooking Aids

ABBREVIATIONS USED IN THIS BOOK

Cup	c.	Large	lg.
Teaspoon	tsp.	Small	sm.
Tablespoon	tbsp.	Package	pkg.
Pound	lb.	Pint	pt.
Ounce	oz.	Quart	qt.
Gallon	gal.	Square	sq.
Minutes	min.	Slice	sl.

EQUIVALENTS

3 tsp. = 1 tbsp.

2 tbsp. = 1/8 c.

4 tbsp. = 1/4 c.

8 tbsp. = 1/2 c.

16 tbsp. = 1 c.

5 tbsp. + 1 tsp. = 1/3 c.

12 tbsp. = 3/4 c.

4 oz. = 1/2 c.

8 oz. = 1 c.

1 oz. = 2 tbsp. fat or liquid

2 c. fat = 1 lb.

2 c. = 1 pt.

2 c. sugar = 1 lb.

5/8 c. = 1/2 c. + 2 tbsp.

7/8 c. = 3/4 c. + 2 tbsp.

1 lb. butter = 2 c. or 4 sticks

2 pt. = 1 qt.

1 qt. = 4 c.

A few grains = less than 1/8 tsp.

Pinch = as much as can be taken between tip of finger and thumb

Dash = less than 1/8 tsp.

OVEN TEMPERATURE

Temperature (°F)	Term
250-300	Slow
325	Moderately slow
350	Moderate
375-400	Moderately hot
425-450	Hot
475-500	Extremely hot

First Place

PHEASANT MUSCATEL

3 1 1/2-lb. pheasants, split in half
1/2 lemon
Salt and pepper to taste
1/3 c. butter, softened
3 oranges, halved
1 c. white raisins
1 tsp. grated lemon peel
1/3 c. muscatel
1 c. chicken broth

Rinse pheasants with warm water; drain well. Rub the inner sides with lemon; season with salt and pepper. Place, skin side up, in baking dish. Spread with butter. Squeeze juice from oranges, reserving shells for cups. Combine the orange juice with remaining ingredients; pour into baking dish. Bake at 350 degrees for 45 minutes, basting with pan juices at 10 minute intervals.

Nutted Rice In Fluted Orange Cups

2 c. chicken broth
1 c. rice
2 tbsp. butter
2/3 c. chopped pecans
2 tbsp. minced parsley
Salt to taste

Mrs. Margaret Bruce
Redwood High School
Larkspur, California

Flute the edges of the reserved orange cups. Combine the broth and rice in a saucepan; bring to a boil and stir. Cover and cook for 14 minutes. Remove from heat; stir in butter, pecans and parsley. Season with salt. Spoon rice into orange cups and serve with the pheasant.

This edition of the Favorite Recipes of Home Economics Teachers cookbook series contains hundreds of exciting poultry recipes submitted for the Blue Ribbon Food Fair. Beautiful full-color photographs, chosen by editors of Favorite Recipes Press, expand the book into other food subject areas. Located throughout the volume, the photographs — along with their accompanying recipes — offer menu ideas to add to your cooking enjoyment.

Cornish Hen

The following pages are filled with excellent recipes for preparing
those juicy, mild-flavored, domestic birds called Cornish hens.
(You may find them in your supermarket entitled Cornish game
hen, Cornish Rock hen or Rock Cornish hen.) These birds are delicious
served in a variety of ways, including stuffed, baked or barbecued.
They are especially good served with wild rice or bread stuffing.

Because of the small size of Cornish hens, you must plan on one per
person. You'll find them individually wrapped in the frozen meat section
of the supermarket, either stuffed with wild rice dressing or unstuffed
with only the giblets. If you are lucky enough to have access to
a Cornish hen farm, you'll be able to get them fresh.

There is something exotic about a Cornish hen dinner, and once
you've tried the delicious recipes in the following section, you'll be
anxious to serve Cornish hens to family and guests.

SPANISH-ROASTED GAME HENS

4 Cornish game hens
Salt and pepper
1 lb. small fresh mushrooms
Whole pimento-stuffed olives
2 slices bacon, halved
1/2 tsp. paprika
4 tbsp. butter or margarine
1/3 c. chopped filberts
1/3 c. finely chopped onion
1 c. rice
2 c. cold chicken broth or stock
1/2 c. grated Swiss cheese
1/4 c. chopped pimento-stuffed
    olives

Sprinkle insides of Cornish game hens with salt and pepper. Toss mushrooms with 2/3 cup whole olives; stuff body of hens. Fasten openings with poultry pins; tie legs together. Place 1/2 slice bacon on each hen; place hens in roasting pan. Roast in 450-degree oven for 20 minutes; remove bacon. Combine paprika with fat in roasting pan; brush on hens. Reduce oven temperature to 350 degrees; roast for 30 minutes longer or until hens are lightly browned and tender. Melt 2 tablespoons butter in heavy saucepan. Add filberts; saute until lightly browned. Remove filberts with slotted spoon; reserve. Add remaining butter, onion and rice to saucepan; cook, stirring occasionally, until rice turns opaque. Add stock; bring to a boil. Cover pan tightly; simmer for 12 to 14 minutes or until rice is tender and all liquid is absorbed. Stir in cheese, chopped olives and reserved filberts. Place rice mixture on serving platter; arrange hens on top. Garnish with whole olives. Serve sauce from pan with hens and rice. Yield: 4 servings.

Photograph for this recipe on page 18.

APRICOT-STUFFED CORNISH HENS

4 Cornish hens
Flour
Salt and pepper to taste
1/2 c. butter
1 c. rice
14 dried apricot halves,
    chopped
4 tsp. minced onion
4 tsp. minced parsley

Simmer giblets in 4 cups water until tender. Combine 1/2 cup flour with salt and pepper; coat hens with flour mixture. Brown hens on all sides in butter in Dutch oven or large heavy skillet. Remove from skillet; cool slightly. Combine rice, apricots, onion and parsley; mix well. Stuff hens with rice mixture; truss securely. Return hens to skillet; add giblet broth. Season with 1 teaspoon salt and additional pepper to taste. Cook, covered, over medium heat for 1 hour. Remove hens to warm platter. Thicken pan gravy with 1 tablespoon flour combined with 1/4 cup water, if desired.

Kathryn Frazior
Nederland High School
Port Neches, Texas

CEOLA CORNISH HENS

2 tbsp. slivered almonds
2 tbsp. finely chopped onions
1/3 c. uncooked long grain rice
3 tbsp. butter
1 chicken bouillon cube
1 tsp. lemon juice
1/2 tsp. salt
1 3-oz. can chopped mushrooms
4 Cornish hens

Saute almonds, onions and rice in butter in small saucepan for 7 to 10 minutes, stirring frequently. Add 1 cup water, bouillon cube, lemon juice, salt and mushrooms to rice mixture. Bring to boil, stirring to dissolve bouillon cube. Reduce heat. Simmer, covered, for 20 minutes or until liquid is absorbed and rice is fluffy. Stuff Cornish hens with rice mixture; truss. Arrange in shallow baking pan. Bake at 325 degrees for 45 minutes or until browned and tender.

Jessye Jacobs
Hyannis High School
Hyannis, Nebraska

CORNISH HENS IN ORANGE AND HONEY SAUCE

1 pkg. wild rice
2 Cornish hens
Salt to taste
Butter or margarine
4 slices bacon, halved
1/2 c. honey
1/2 c. concentrated orange juice
1 tbsp. lemon juice

Cook rice according to package directions. Sprinkle hens inside and out with salt. Stuff hens with rice; truss securely. Rub hens with butter. Place bacon in glass baking dish; arrange hens over bacon. Preheat oven to 350 degrees. Bake hens for 1 hour. Combine honey, orange juice and lemon juice. Baste hens with half the orange sauce; turn hens. Baste for 5 minutes longer. Turn hens; baste. Return to oven. Bake for 15 minutes; add remaining sauce. Bake for 15 minutes longer. Remove hens and bacon; arrange hens on warm platter. Drain off excess fat from sauce; serve over hens. Bacon may be served as a side dish.

Beverly Schneider
Halsey Annex 296 School
Kew Gardens, New York

CORNISH HEN CASSEROLE

Salt
6 Cornish hens, split
Flour
1/2 c. Wesson oil
Paprika
3 c. instant rice
1 c. wild rice
1 can celery soup
1 can chicken soup
Parsley flakes
1 pkg. frozen English peas

Salt hens; flour lightly. Brown in oil; add paprika while turning. Combine rice in buttered large, shallow casserole. Combine celery and chicken soup with 2 cans water; bring to a boil. Pour soup over rice; stir until well mixed. Place hens on rice, cut side down; sprinkle with parsley flakes. Bake at 300 degrees for 1 hour and 30 minutes. Bring peas to boil in water according to package directions; drain well. Arrange peas around edge of casserole. Bake for 30 minutes longer. Garnish with parsley, if desired.

LaVerne Stokes
Jefferson County School
Lakewood, Colorado

CORNISH HENS AND RICE

1 c. long grain rice
1 env. Italian salad dressing mix
1 can cream of chicken soup
2 frozen Cornish hens, thawed
Salt and pepper to taste (opt.)

Preheat oven to 350 degrees. Spread rice in 3-quart shallow baking dish. Bake for 15 minutes or until golden, stirring occasionally. Combine salad dressing mix with 2 1/2 cups boiling water and soup; stir into rice. Cut hens in half lengthwise; season with salt and pepper. Place, cut side down, on rice; cover tightly with foil. Bake for 1 hour. Uncover; bake for 30 minutes longer or until rice and hens are tender.

Beverly Cederstrom
Chicago Lakes Area School
Lindstrom, Minnesota

CORNISH HENS WITH WINE SAUCE

6 Cornish hens, halved
Salt to taste
6 tbsp. red wine
1/4 c. melted margarine
4 tbsp. lemon juice

Season Cornish hens with salt; place in baking pan. Cover with heavy-duty foil. Mix wine, margarine and lemon juice. Bake hens at 325 degrees for 1 hour, basting frequently with sauce until all is used. Uncover; bake for 30 minutes longer.

Earle H. Vallentine
Edisto High School
Cordova, South Carolina

CORNISH HENS WITH RICE-MUSHROOM STUFFING

2 Cornish hens
Salt to taste
Lemon-pepper seasoning to taste
1 lg. stalk celery, chopped
2 tbsp. chopped onion
4 fresh mushrooms, chopped
1/4 c. melted butter or margarine
1 c. cooked rice
1/4 c. chicken broth
Pepper to taste

Rinse hens; pat dry. Sprinkle inside and out with salt and lemon-pepper seasoning. Saute celery, onion and mushrooms in 3 tablespoons butter until just tender; combine with rice and broth. Season with salt and pepper; mix well. Stuff hens lightly with rice mixture; truss. Brush hens with remaining butter; arrange hens in shallow roasting pan. Bake at 350 degrees for 1 hour and 30 minutes or until hens are golden brown and tender.

Doris A. Weinberg
Houston Technical Institute
Houston, Texas

CORNISH HENS WITH SAGE DRESSING FOR TWO

2   14-oz. Cornish hens with giblets
1 qt. boiling water
1 1/4 tsp. salt
3/4 c. finely chopped onions
1/2 c. finely chopped celery
2 c. soft bread crumbs
1 egg
1/2 tsp. sage
1/2 c. butter or margarine
1/2 tsp. rosemary
1/8 tsp. garlic powder

Place giblets in boiling water with 1 teaspoon salt; simmer, uncovered, for 1 hour or until tender. Chop giblets; reserve broth. Mix 1/4 cup onions, celery, bread crumbs, egg, 1/2 cup reserved broth, sage and remaining salt. Add giblets; mix. Rinse Cornish hens; stuff cavities with dressing. Tie legs together with string or use skewers. Melt butter in saucepan. Brown remaining onions in butter; add rosemary and garlic powder. Place Cornish hens in small roasting pan; pour onion mixture over hens. Cover. Bake at 375 degrees for 45 minutes. Uncover; bake for 15 minutes longer, basting with pan drippings frequently.

Barbara Cerotsky
Pilot Butte Junior High School
Bend, Oregon

CURRANT GO-GO CORNISH HENS

2 Cornish hens, split
2 tsp. salt
1/2 c. currant jelly
1 tbsp. lemon juice
1/2 tsp. paprika
1/4 c. rose wine

Sprinkle hens with salt. Arrange hens, skin side up, on grill over glowing charcoal, 8 to 10 inches above coals. Grill hens for 30 minutes, turning once. Combine jelly, lemon juice, paprika, 1/4 cup water and wine in saucepan; simmer, stirring constantly, for 3 minutes. Brush hens with sauce; grill for 5 minutes longer. Turn hens; brush with additional sauce. Grill for 5 minutes longer. Serve hens with remaining sauce.

Harriette McDowell Holton
Shelby Senior High School
Shelby, North Carolina

HONEY-GLAZED CORNISH HEN

2 c. croutons
1/2 sm. onion, chopped
2 stalks celery, chopped
2 Cornish hens
1/2   6-oz. can frozen orange
*   juice*
3 tbsp. honey

Combine croutons, onions, celery and 3/4 cup water; mix well. Stuff hens lightly; truss. Arrange hens in shallow roasting pan. Bake at 400 degrees for 45 minutes. Combine orange juice and honey; blend thoroughly. Bake hens for 15 minutes longer, basting every 5 minutes with honey mixture.

Eileen Gerald
Senior High School
Newport, Minnesota

DELMIRES BRANDY-GLAZED CORNISH HEN

1 box long grain and wild rice
3 Cornish hens
Salt and pepper to taste (opt.)
5 tbsp. apricot brandy
1/4 c. dry-roasted sunflower seed
1/2 c. finely chopped dried
 apricots
2 eggs, well beaten
2 tbsp. melted butter or
 margarine
3 tbsp. apricot jam

Prepare rice according to package directions. Season hens inside and out with salt and pepper. Mix rice, 4 tablespoons brandy, sunflower seed, apricots and eggs; spoon into hen cavities. Truss. Place, breast side up, on rack in shallow roasting pan; brush with butter. Excess fat from hens may be placed on breasts for self-basting instead of using butter, if desired. Roast, uncovered, in oven preheated to 350 degrees for about 50 minutes, basting frequently with additional butter or pan drippings. Mix apricot jam and remaining brandy; brush on hens. Increase oven temperature to 375 degrees; roast for 10 minutes longer or until brown and tender.

Mrs. Lois M. Summersgill
North Hills School
York, Pennsylvania

DELICIOUS ORANGE-GLAZED CORNISH HENS

4 1-lb. Cornish hens
Salt
Melted butter
1 c. orange juice
1/2 c. raisins

1 1/3 tbsp. cornstarch
1 8-oz. package chicken-flavored
 rice

Preheat oven to 350 degrees. Rub cavities of hens with salt. Arrange hens, breast side up, on rack in shallow roasting pan; brush with butter. Bake for 50 minutes, brushing frequently with butter. Increase oven temperature to 400 degrees. Bake for 10 minutes longer or until browned and tender. Combine orange juice and raisins in saucepan; bring to a boil. Reduce heat; simmer for 5 minutes. Dissolve cornstarch in 1/4 cup water; stir into orange mixture. Cook, stirring constantly, over medium heat until sauce is clear and thickened. Prepare rice according to package directions. Arrange hens on bed of rice on heated platter; top with orange glaze. Garnish with orange slices and parsley if desired.

Joanne Weber
East High School
Green Bay, Wisconsin

ORANGE-GLAZED CORNISH HENS WITH RICE

4 Cornish hens
Salt to taste
1 pkg. wild rice
Pepper to taste
2 c. orange juice
2 c. corn syrup

Clean hens thoroughly; salt cavities. Prepare rice according to package directions for partially cooking. Stuff hens lightly; truss. Salt and pepper hens; arrange in shallow roasting pan, breast side up. Combine orange juice and corn syrup; pour half the syrup mixture over hens. Cover with foil. Bake at 350 degrees for 1 hour. Drain pan drippings; reserve. Pour remaining syrup mixture over hens. Bake at 300 degrees for 1 hour and 30 minutes, basting every 20 minutes. Reserved pan drippings may be used to baste if needed.

Marianne Blanchard
Southeastern Junior High School
Battle Creek, Michigan

FLOWERING PLUM CORNISH HENS

4 Cornish hens, split
1 tsp. seasoned salt
2 lg. oranges, sliced
1/4 c. margarine, melted
1/4 c. diced onion
1 tsp. ginger
1 tsp. Worcestershire sauce
1 1/2 tsp. mustard
1/3 c. chili sauce
1/4 c. soy sauce
1 6-oz. can frozen lemonade,
  thawed
1 1-lb. can purple plums,
  pureed
1/4 c. shredded coconut

Sprinkle hens with seasoned salt. Arrange orange slices in shallow roasting pan; place hens, skin side up, over oranges. Bake at 350 degrees for 45 minutes. Combine margarine, onion, ginger, Worcestershire sauce, mustard, chili sauce, soy sauce, lemonade and plums in saucepan; blend well. Simmer, stirring frequently, for 15 minutes. Pour plum sauce over hens. Bake for 20 minutes longer, basting frequently. Arrange hens on heated platter; top with pan drippings. Sprinkle with coconut. Yield: 4-6 servings.

Mrs. Frances Baratz
Clark Lane Junior High School
Waterford, Connecticut

INDOOR-OUTDOOR BARBECUED CORNISH HENS

2 Cornish hens
1/2 c. catsup
3 tbsp. brown sugar
2 tbsp. vinegar
1 tbsp. soy sauce
1 tbsp. prepared mustard
1/4 tsp. paprika
1/4 tsp. garlic powder
1/4 tsp. onion salt
1/2 c. water

Cut Cornish hens into halves or quarters; wipe dry. Arrange, skin side up and close together, in baking dish. Mix remaining ingredients in order listed; pour over Cornish hens, coating each piece well. Bake at 325 degrees for 20 minutes; turn. Bake for 20 minutes longer. May be barbecued on grill over hot coals, brushing frequently with sauce. Chicken, cut into serving pieces, may be substituted for Cornish hens; sauce may be made several days before using and refrigerated.

Mrs. Paula Scutt
Kelowna Secondary School
Kelowna, British Columbia, Canada

NG KA PY CORNISH HEN CASSEROLE

4 Cornish hens
1/2 c. sesame oil
1 garlic clove, finely chopped
Ng Ka Py, Chinese liquor
2 tbsp. finely chopped shallots
1/4 c. wine vinegar
1 c. fresh tomato puree
1/2 c. cognac
1/2 c. (firmly packed) dark
  brown sugar
1 c. heavy cream
1/4 c. water
1 c. tomato sauce
1/4 c. finely chopped green pepper
2 tbsp. finely chopped onion
2 tbsp. finely chopped pimentos
1/4 c. sliced water chestnuts
1/2 c. sauteed fresh mushrooms
1/4 c. drained pineapple chunks
3 tbsp. flour

Clean and quarter hens; place in large bowl. Mix oil, garlic, 2 tablespoons Ng Ka Py, shallots, vinegar, tomato puree, cognac and brown sugar; pour over hens. Marinate for 24 hours in refrigerator, turning hens occasionally and basting with marinade. Remove hens from marinade; place in lightly buttered 13 x 9-inch baking dish. Combine 1 teaspoon Ng Ka Py and remaining ingredients; pour over hens. Bake at 350 degrees for 1 hour and 15 minutes. Serve hot with rice.

Mrs. Millicent L. Riggs
Claremont High School
Claremont, California

RICE-STUFFED CORNISH HENS

1/2 c. butter
1 lb. fresh mushrooms, sliced
1/2 c. chopped onions
1/2 c. minced parsley
1 c. chopped celery
3 c. cooked brown rice
Salt and pepper to taste
4 Cornish hens

Melt butter in heavy skillet; add mushrooms. Cook mushrooms for 5 minutes; remove from skillet. Stir onions, parsley and celery into remaining butter in skillet. Cook, stirring frequently, until onions are golden; stir in rice, mushrooms, 1 teaspoon salt and 1/8 teaspoon pepper. Mix thoroughly; remove from heat. Stuff hens with rice mixture; truss. Rub outside of hens with additional salt and pepper. Arrange hens in shallow roasting pan. Bake at 325 degrees for 15 minutes per pound; allow 30 to 40 minutes longer when stuffed. Baste with pan drippings every 30 minutes. One 8-ounce can sliced mushrooms may be substituted for fresh mushrooms.

Mrs. Marlene Figone
Manteca High School
Manteca, California

ROCK CORNISH HENS ON BAKED STUFFING

6 Cornish hens
Celery
1 oz. brandy
1 No. 2 1/2 can peach slices
1/2 tsp. grated lemon rind
Butter, melted
3 c. cooked long grain and
    wild rice mixture
1/2 sm. onion, minced
1/2 tsp. rosemary
1/2 tsp. sweet basil
1/2 tsp. thyme
1/4 tsp. ginger
1/2 tsp. salt
1 1/2 tbsp. cornstarch
1/4 c. wine vinegar
Spiced crab apples
Parsley

Clean hens. Place small piece of celery and 1/2 ounce of brandy in cavity of each bird; truss. Place hens on rack in shallow roasting pan. Drain peach slices, reserving syrup. Combine reserved syrup with lemon rind, ginger and 2 tablespoons butter; blend well. Pour syrup over hens. Bake at 400 degrees for 45 minutes or until browned and tender. Chop peach slices; reserve several for garnish. Combine peaches, cooked rice, onion, seasonings and 1/4 cup melted butter; mix lightly. Place in 1-quart greased baking dish. Bake, covered, at 400 degrees for 30 minutes. Arrange hens on platter over stuffing; keep warm. Pour pan drippings into saucepan. Blend cornstarch and 1/4 cup water; stir into drippings. Cook, stirring constantly, until clear and thickened. Add vinegar; heat through. Pour over hens and stuffing or serve separately. Garnish platter with reserved peach slices, crab apples, and parsley. Yield: 6 servings.

Sharlene Sivertson
Washington Junior High School
Ely, Minnesota

SAUCY CORNISH HENS

2 to 4 tbsp. soy sauce
1 sm. can tomato sauce
2 tbsp. instant minced onion
1/2 to 1 tsp. grated candied ginger
1/2 tsp. curry powder
1/2 tsp. garlic salt
Salt and pepper to taste
2 Cornish hens, split

Combine soy sauce, tomato sauce, onion, ginger, curry powder, garlic salt, salt and pepper. Allow to stand at room temperature for 15 minutes. Arrange hens in shallow roasting pan. Bake at 350 degrees for 30 minutes; turn hens. Bake for 30 minutes longer or until tender. Baste occasionally with sauce. Serve over rice.

Mrs. E. L. McCleary
West Junior High School
Waco, Texas

25

ROCK CORNISH HENS WITH ORANGE SAUCE

1 6-oz. can frozen orange juice
3/4 c. butter or margarine
3 tbsp. soy sauce
1/4 tsp. dry mustard
3 tbsp. sugar
2 tbsp. minced instant onion
4 Cornish hens
1/2 c. melted butter

Combine orange juice, 3/4 cup water, butter, soy sauce, mustard, sugar and onion in saucepan. Bring to a boil; cool. Refrigerate overnight. Brush hens with melted butter; arrange in shallow roasting pan. Bake at 350 degrees for 30 minutes; brush with sauce. Bake for 30 minutes longer; brush with sauce at 5-minute intervals.

Jodie R. Cannon
R. O. Gibson Junior High School
Las Vegas, Nevada

ROCK CORNISH HENS WITH CELERY STUFFING

1 8-oz. package herb-seasoned
   stuffing mix
1 tsp. sage
1 c. chopped celery
1/2 c. chopped onion
1 can consomme
1/4 c. butter or margarine,
   melted
Salt and pepper to taste
4 1-lb. Cornish hens
1/4 c. light corn syrup

Combine stuffing mix, sage, celery and onion in medium bowl; mix well. Reserve 1/4 cup consomme. Combine remaining consomme with butter; heat, stirring to blend. Add consomme mixture to stuffing mixture; toss lightly. Salt and pepper hens. Stuff each hen lightly with 1/2 cup stuffing; reserve remaining stuffing. Arrange hens, breast side up, on rack in shallow pan; brush with additional butter. Roast at 400 degrees for 45 minutes or until tender. Bake reserved dressing in foil packet. Combine reserved consomme and corn syrup; blend well. Bake hens for 15 minutes longer; baste frequently with syrup mixture. Yield: 4 servings.

Evelyn B. Willey
Gates County High School
Gatesville, North Carolina

ROCK CORNISH HEN WITH SOUTHERN DRESSING

1/4 c. raisins
1/2 c. sauterne
3 tbsp. chopped onion
Butter or margarine
2 c. crumbled corn bread
1/2 tsp. salt
1/8 tsp. pepper
1/8 tsp. poultry seasoning
2 eggs, beaten
3/4 c. chopped pecans
4 Cornish hens

Soak raisins in sauterne overnight. Saute onion in 1/3 cup butter until golden. Combine onion, corn bread, salt, pepper, poultry seasoning, eggs and pecans in large bowl; mix well. Stir in raisins and sauterne. Stuff hens lightly, topping dressing with 1 teaspoon butter under breast. Arrange hens on rack in shallow roasting pan. Bake at 350 degrees for 1 hour; baste with additional butter every 15 minutes. Serve with wild rice, if desired.

Mrs. Mary Ada Parks
Anna-Jonesboro High School
Anna, Illinois

ROCK CORNISH HEN WITH RICE

2 1 1/2-lb. Cornish hens
Salt and pepper to taste
Melted butter
1/2 c. wild rice
2 tbsp. minced onion
1 tbsp. minced green pepper
1 2-oz. can sliced mushrooms,
   drained
1/2 can cream of mushroom soup

1/2 c. heavy cream
1/8 tsp. dried marjoram
1/8 tsp. dried basil
1/8 tsp. dried tarragon
1/4 tsp. curry powder

Preheat oven to 350 degrees. Sprinkle hens with salt and pepper; arrange in shallow roasting pan. Bake, basting frequently with butter, for 45 minutes or until golden brown and tender. Prepare rice according to package directions. Combine 1 tablespoon butter, onion, pepper and mushrooms in saucepan; saute until onion is golden. Stir in soup, cream, marjoram, basil, tarragon, curry, 1/4 teaspoon salt and 1/8 teaspoon pepper; blend well. Simmer for 10 minutes, stirring constantly. Stir in rice; heat through. Arrange rice on heated platter; top with hens. Garnish with fresh dill sprigs. Yield: 2 servings.

Mrs. Janet Mead
Hortonville High School
Hortonville, Wisconsin

SPICY CHICKS

1 c. syrup from spiced fruits
2 tbsp. maraschino cherry juice
2 tbsp. wine vinegar
1 c. sauterne
1 tsp. powdered ginger
2 Cornish hens, split in half
1 tsp. salt
1/2 tsp. pepper
1/4 c. melted margarine
1 tbsp. cornstarch
2 c. spiced or pickled fruits
1/4 c. maraschino cherries

Preheat oven to 450 degrees. Mix fruit syrup, cherry juice, vinegar, sauterne and ginger. Rub hens with salt and pepper; place in 9 x 13-inch baking pan. Brush with margarine. Bake in 450-degree oven for 10 minutes. Reduce temperature to 350 degrees; baste hens with syrup mixture. Bake for about 1 hour or until hens are tender, basting frequently with syrup mixture. Place hens on ovenproof platter; return to oven to keep warm. Skim excess fat from pan juices.

Measure 1 cup pan juices; place in small saucepan. Bring to a boil. Mix cornstarch with small amount of cold water; stir into pan juices. Cook until thickened; add more sauterne, if desired. Pour over hen halves; garnish with spiced fruits and cherries. Spiced or pickled apples, watermelon, cantaloupe, peaches, pears or any combination may be used. Yield: 4 servings.

Mrs. Melva Houtcooper
Nova High School
Ft. Lauderdale, Florida

STUFFED ROCK CORNISH HENS

1 1/2 c. wild rice
1 sm. onion, finely chopped
1/4 c. finely chopped green pepper
1/2 c. finely chopped water
   chestnuts
1/2 c. finely chopped celery
1 c. finely chopped fresh mushrooms
Melted butter
1 tsp. poultry seasoning
Salt and pepper to taste
3 1-lb. Cornish hens
1/4 c. lemon juice
1 c. seedless green grapes
2 tbsp. sliced almonds

Wash rice thoroughly. Simmer in 3 cups water for 30 minutes or until tender; drain well. Saute onion, green pepper, water chestnuts, celery and mushrooms in butter over medium heat for 5 minutes. Stir in poultry seasoning, 1 teaspoon salt and 1/4 teaspoon pepper. Add rice; mix well. Season hens, inside and out, with additional pepper and salt. Stuff each hen with 1/2 cup rice mixture; truss securely. Reserve remaining rice mixture; keep warm. Place hens on rotisserie spit. Combine lemon juice with 1/3 cup butter. Baste hens with lemon juice mixture occasionally while roasting over low flame for 45 minutes or until browned and tender. Place rice mixture on warm platter; top with hens. Garnish with grapes and almonds.

Mrs. Frances Eldridge
Central High School
Clifton, Illinois

ROCK CORNISH HENS TERIYAKI

2 c. seasoned packaged croutons
1/4 c. butter, melted
1/4 c. diced mandarin oranges
4 1-lb. Cornish hens
1/4 c. soy sauce
1 clove garlic, crushed

Preheat oven to 400 degrees. Combine croutons, butter and oranges; mix lightly. Stuff hens with crouton mixture. Line shallow pan with roasting wrap. Arrange hens in pan over wrap. Combine soy sauce and garlic; brush hens with sauce. Wrap; seal securely. Bake for 40 minutes. Remove from wrap; arrange on warm platter. Yield: 4 servings.

Mrs. Richard Vaughan
Fairfield Community High School
Fairfield, Illinois

STEAMED CORNISH HENS

2 Cornish hens
2 c. milk
Salt to taste
1 c. flour
1 tsp. pepper
Garlic salt
Monosodium glutamate
1 egg, beaten
3 c. salad oil
1/2 c. butter, melted
1 tsp. cornstarch
1 tsp. grated lemon rind
1/4 c. lemon juice
1/3 c. pineapple syrup
2 tbsp. chopped onion
2 tsp. soy sauce

Arrange hens on rack in Dutch oven or heavy saucepan. Add milk; cover tightly. Steam over low heat for 30 minutes; remove from heat. Drain well; cool. Sprinkle hens with salt. Combine flour with 1 teaspoon salt, pepper, 1 teaspoon garlic salt and 1 teaspoon monosodium glutamate; blend well. Roll hens in egg; coat with flour mixture. Heat oil in heavy saucepan or deep fat fryer to 300 degrees. Brown hens slightly in oil; drain. Arrange on platter; keep warm. Combine butter with cornstarch in saucepan; stir in lemon rind, lemon juice, pineapple syrup, chopped onion, soy sauce, 1/4 teaspoon monosodium glutamate and 1 teaspoon garlic salt. Simmer for 5 minutes, stirring constantly. Serve with hens.

Oliva Villena
Mayerthorpe Junior and Senior High School
Mayerthorpe, Alberta, Canada

YELLOW AND GREEN STUFFED CORNISH HENS

1 pkg. frozen spinach
1/2 c. butter
3 c. cooked rice
1 c. milk
4 eggs, beaten
4 c. grated Cheddar cheese
2 tbsp. chopped onion
2 tbsp. Worcestershire sauce
1 tsp. marjoram
1 tsp. rosemary
1 tsp. thyme
1 tsp. oregano
1 tsp. salt
1/2 tsp. pepper
4 Cornish hens
5 peach halves
2 c. cranberry relish
5 lettuce leaves

Preheat oven to 425 degrees. Cook spinach according to package directions; drain. Melt 1/4 cup butter; add to rice. Add milk to eggs; add cheese. Add spinach; mix well. Stir in onion, Worcestershire sauce and seasonings; set aside. Rub cavities of Cornish hens with part of the remaining butter; stuff with rice mixture. Melt remaining butter; brush on hens. Place hens in 13 x 9 1/2 x 2-inch pan, breast side up. Roast for about 1 hour, basting frequently. Stuff peach halves with cranberry relish; place on lettuce leaves. Place hens on platter; garnish with peach halves on lettuce. Serve immediately.

Janet Marr Currie
Springfield High School
Bergholz, Ohio

STUFFED BAKED CORNISH HEN

2 Cornish hen livers, finely
   chopped
1/4 c. finely chopped onions
1/2 c. finely chopped ham
2 tbsp. chopped mushrooms
1 c. butter
1 tsp. chopped parsley
2 c. bread crumbs
1/2 tsp. salt
1/4 tsp. pepper
1/2 tsp. poultry seasoning
1 egg, slightly beaten
2 1 1/2-lb. Cornish hens
4 slices bacon
1/2 c. dry white wine

Saute liver, onions, ham and mushrooms in 1/2 cup butter in large saucepan. Cool; remove to large bowl. Stir in parsley, bread crumbs, salt, pepper, poultry seasoning and egg; blend well. Stuff hens with bread mixture; truss securely. Arrange hens on rack in roasting pan; crisscross breasts with bacon strips. Bake at 400 degrees for 1 hour. Combine remaining butter with wine; blend well. Baste hens frequently with wine mixture. Serve on wild rice seasoned with pan drippings. Yield: 2 servings.

Connie Schlimgen
Edison Junior High School
Sioux Falls, South Dakota

WILD RICE TOSS WITH CORNISH HENS

1/3 c. sliced almonds
1/3 c. chopped green onions
1/3 c. wild rice
2/3 c. long grain rice
2/3 c. butter
4 c. water
4 chicken bouillon cubes
1 1/2 tbsp. lemon juice
1 1/2 tsp. salt
1 8-oz. can chopped mushrooms

4 Cornish hens
Melted butter

Place almonds, onions, rice and butter in 4-quart saucepan; cook for 10 minutes, stirring frequently. Add water, bouillon cubes, lemon juice and salt; cover. Simmer for 25 minutes or until rice is tender and liquid is absorbed. Stir in mushrooms. Place in cavities of Cornish hens; place hens in roasting pan. Brush with melted butter. Bake, uncovered, at 400 degrees for 30 minutes. Cover; bake for 45 minutes to 1 hour or until golden brown and tender. Yield: 4 servings.

Susan Kusnier
Lee M. Thurston High School
Detroit, Michigan

STUFF 'N SUCH HENS

4 Cornish hens with giblets
1 med. onion, chopped
2 stalks celery, chopped
1 pkg. Stuff 'n Such
1 4-oz. can mushrooms stems
   and pieces, drained
Dash of sage
Dash of poultry seasoning
Salt to taste
1/4 c. butter
Pepper and garlic salt to taste

Cover giblets and necks with water; add onion and celery. Cook until tender. Prepare Stuff 'n Such according to package directions for stuffing fowl, using stock from giblets in place of water. Chop giblets; add to Stuff 'n Such. Add mushrooms, sage and poultry seasoning. Wash Cornish hens; dry thoroughly. Season cavities with salt. Stuff each with 1/4 of the dressing mixture; skewer. Place on rack in roasting pan, breast side up. Melt butter; stir in salt, pepper, garlic salt and poultry seasoning. Brush on hens. Roast in 350-degree oven for 1 hour and 15 minutes, brushing with seasoned butter at least twice. Yield: 4 servings.

Mrs. Nancy Hunt
Delta Junior High School
Delta, Ohio

29

Duck

Of all the various game birds, ducks are the most popular, not only for eating, but also for hunting. They are said to be as crafty as they are delicious, and are, thus, a challenge to hunt.

Frozen duck is available all year round, but fresh duck is available only May through January. Most ducks come ready to cook. Shop for well-developed, broad-breasted birds. Make sure that frozen ducks are well-wrapped.

Duck is delicious served in a variety of ways, including grilled, broiled and roasted. In the following section, you'll find a wealth of recipes and serving suggestions.

SPIT-ROASTED DUCKLING WITH CHERRY-WINE SAUCE

1 4 to 5-lb. ready-to-cook domestic
   duckling
1 4-oz. jar red maraschino
   cherries
1 tbsp. lemon juice
5 1/2 tbsp. sugar
2 tbsp. dry sherry
1 1/2 tbsp. red wine vinegar
1 c. chicken bouillon
2 tbsp. cornstarch
Madeira

Rinse duckling; pat dry. Puncture skin across breast, back and thighs at 1-inch intervals with pointed edge of sharp knife. Place duckling in shallow pan; set aside. Drain syrup from cherries; reserve cherries. Add enough water to syrup to make 1/4 cup liquid; add lemon juice, 2 tablespoons sugar and sherry. Spoon about 1/3 of the marinade over duckling and into cavity. Cover; chill for 3 hours, basting twice more with remaining marinade. Drain; reserve marinade. Do not pat duckling dry; attach to rotisserie according to range directions. Roast for about 1 hour and 15 minutes for medium rare or 1 hour and 35 minutes for well done. Chop reserved cherries; add to reserved marinade. Set aside. Combine 1 1/2 tablespoons sugar and vinegar in small saucepan about 30 minutes before duckling is done; boil over medium heat until most of the vinegar has evaporated and mixture has caramel color. Add remaining sugar and bouillon; stir to dissolve. Combine cornstarch with 1 1/2 tablespoons Madeira; add to bouillon mixture. Stir over medium heat until mixture boils. Cover tightly; set aside. Remove duckling from rotisserie; keep warm. Remove fat from drippings. Add 1/2 cup Madeira to drippings; boil over high heat until reduced by about half. Strain drippings into sauce mixture. Add cherry marinade; heat through. Serve with duckling. Yield: 4 servings.

Photograph for this recipe on page 30.

DUCKLING AMANDINE

1 3 to 4-lb. duck
1 6-oz. can frozen orange juice
   concentrate
1/4 c. lemon juice
1/4 c. butter or margarine
1/2 tsp. salt
1/8 tsp. ginger
1/2 c. chopped celery
1/4 c. slivered blanched almonds

Clean duck; place in shallow baking dish. Combine orange juice concentrate, lemon juice, butter, salt and ginger; cook for 5 minutes. Brush duck with butter mixture. Roast in 325-degree oven for 25 minutes per pound or until done, brushing occasionally with orange juice mixture. Combine remaining orange juice mixture and celery; cook for 5 minutes. Add almonds; serve hot over carved duckling.

Mrs. Clara M. Charlesworth
Northeast Senior High School
Pasadena, Maryland

ALA-STUFFED DUCKLING WITH PLUM SAUCE

1 c. water
1/2 c. brown and wild rice mix
1 1/2 tbsp. seasoning from
   package mix
1/4 c. chopped onion
1/2 c. sliced mushrooms
2 tbsp. butter or margarine
1/2 c. Ala bulgar wheat
1 c. chicken broth or bouillon
1/4 tsp. salt
1/4 tsp. thyme
1/4 tsp. marjoram
2/3 c. cubed water chestnuts
2/3 c. chopped celery
1 4 to 5-lb. ready-to-cook
   duckling

Bring water to a boil; add rice. Stir in package seasoning. Bring to a boil; reduce heat. Cover; simmer for 15 minutes. Saute onion and mushrooms in butter in skillet. Add Ala; cook until golden. Stir in chicken broth, salt, thyme and marjoram; bring to a boil. Reduce heat; cover. Simmer for 15 minutes. Add rice, water chestnuts and celery; mix well. Place stuffing in duckling; truss. Place duckling on rack in roasting pan, breast side up. Roast in preheated oven at 325 degrees for 2 hours and 30 minutes.

Plum Sauce

2 tbsp. butter or margarine
Liver from duckling
1/4 tsp. garlic salt
1/3 c. Burgundy
1/2 c. chicken broth or bouillon
2 tbsp. flour
1 c. plum preserves
1 tbsp. grated lemon peel
1 tbsp. lemon juice

Melt butter in skillet. Brown liver in butter; add garlic salt. Remove liver from skillet; chop fine. Set aside in bowl. Heat Burgundy and chicken broth in same skillet. Stir in flour; cook until thickened. Remove from heat. Add preserves, grated peel, lemon juice and liver. Spread enough sauce over duckling to cover during last 10 minutes of roasting. Serve remaining sauce with duckling.

Mrs. Debi Jung
Weldon Valley School
Weldona, Colorado

DUCK BAKED IN BEER

1 duck, dressed
1 tsp. salt
1/4 tsp. pepper
1 apple, quartered
1 med. onion
1 stalk celery
1 carrot
1 med. potato
1 tbsp. flour
1/3 can beer

Clean duck well; soak in salted water for 30 minutes. Dry well. Sprinkle salt and pepper inside duck cavity; place apple, onion, celery, carrot and potato in cavity. Place flour in oven cooking bag; insert stuffed duck.

Pour beer into bag; seal. Punch 3 holes in top of bag. Bake at 325 degrees for 2 hours and 30 minutes. Remove from oven; let steam for 20 minutes in warm place. Remove from bag. Discard all vegetables and juices; slice duck. Serve warm or cold.

Mrs. Vanora A. Fry
Little River High School
Little River, Kansas

DUCK WITH STUFFING AND ORANGE SAUCE

1 duckling
Salt
Pepper
Paprika
1/4 lb. wild rice
2/3 c. brown rice
1 c. diced celery
1/3 c. sliced green onions
5 tbsp. butter
3 tbsp. parsley flakes
1 c. sugar
2 tbsp. cornstarch
1 tbsp. flour
1 1/4 c. orange juice
1/4 c. lemon juice
1 tsp. grated orange and lemon rind

Rinse duckling in water; rub inside and out with salt, pepper and paprika. Score skin at 1-inch intervals with sharp knife. Cook rices according to package directions; mix. Saute celery and onions in 4 tablespoons butter until tender; add to rice. Add parsley, 1/8 teaspoon paprika and 1/4 teaspoon salt; toss lightly. Place in cavity of duckling; place duckling in 9 x 13-inch shallow pan. Bake, uncovered, at 325 degrees for 3 hours to 3 hours and 30 minutes or until brown and crisp. Mix sugar, 1/4 teaspoon salt, cornstarch and flour in saucepan; stir in orange juice, lemon juice and 1/2 cup water. Boil for 3 minutes. Add remaining butter and grated rinds; mix well. Serve with duck. Duck may be quartered and stuffing placed under quarters, if desired; reduce baking time. Yield: 4 servings.

Mrs. Jean Mason
Hi-Plains School
Seibert, Colorado

BAKED DUCK A L'ORANGE

1   4 to 5-lb. duck
1 tbsp. salt
1 orange
2 med. carrots
2 med. onions
2 celery stalks, cut in half
1 tbsp. instant chicken bouillon
1/2 c. water
1 can frozen unsweetened orange
    juice
1 tbsp. flour
1 tsp. Kitchen Bouquet
1/2 tsp. sugar

Rub duck outside and inside with salt. Cut orange in half; remove seeds. Squeeze one of the halves into the cavity of duck; place carrots, onions and celery in cavity. Place squeezed orange half in cavity; close cavity with skewers or toothpicks. Pull neck skin over wings; secure as for cavity. Place on rack in roasting pan. Bake, uncóvered, at 325 degrees for 2 hours. Remove duck to shallow casserole. Increase oven temperature to 350 degrees; bake for 1 hour. Pour off excess fat from roasting pan, leaving brown drippings. Add chicken bouillon, water, orange juice, flour, Kitchen Bouquet and sugar to drippings; bring to a full boil, stirring constantly. Reduce heat; simmer to syrupy consistency. Pour off fat from casserole. Spread sauce over duck. Slice remaining orange; place on duck. Bake for 15-20 minutes longer. Remove from oven; let stand for 10 minutes before carving. Yield: 4-5 servings.

Mrs. Helen Stoffregen
Fairfield Junior High School
Fairfield, Ohio

DUCKLING IN RED WINE

1   5-lb. duck with giblets
Salt and pepper to taste
3/4 c. butter
1 lg. onion, sliced
1 carrot, chopped
2 slices bacon, diced
1 lg. peeled orange, quartered
1 tsp. garlic powder
1 bay leaf
1 c. red cooking wine
4 tbsp. flour

Cook giblets in 2 cups water until tender; remove giblets from stock. Cut duck into serving pieces; rub with salt and pepper. Brown each piece evenly in butter in skillet. Remove from skillet; place in casserole. Brown onion, carrot and bacon in butter remaining in skillet. Add orange, garlic powder, bay leaf, wine and 1 1/2 cup stock; bring to boiling point. Pour over duck; cover. Bake at 350 degrees for 2 hours and 30 minutes or until tender; remove duck to serving platter. Strain casserole juices; pour into saucepan. Stir in flour; cook, stirring, until slightly thickened. Spoon small amount of sauce over duck. Serve remaining sauce with duck. Garnish platter with parsley.

Charwynne Schultz
Rio Vista High School
Rio Vista, Texas

DUCKLING WITH ORANGE

2   4 to 5-lb. ducklings
1/3 c. butter
1 lg. carrot, coarsely chopped
1 med. onion, coarsely chopped
2 lg. sprigs of parsley
2 lg. sprigs of celery leaves
1 sm. bay leaf
1 tsp. savory
Salt and pepper to taste
2 c. red or white wine
2 c. beef broth
4 oranges
1 tbsp. cornstarch
Red currant or cranberry jelly
Sprigs of parsley or watercress

Preheat oven to 325 degrees. Dry ducklings well inside and out with paper toweling. Heat butter in small saucepan until foamy; skim off and discard foam. Pour clear yellow oil into large, heavy skillet; heat. Brown ducklings well on all sides in clarified butter. Place carrot, onion, parsley, celery leaves, bay leaf and savory in large Dutch oven or roaster. Sprinkle ducklings well inside and out with salt and pepper; place on vegetables in Dutch oven. Add wine and beef stock; cover tightly. Roast for about 2 hours or until ducklings are just tender. Uncover; roast for 15 minutes longer or until brown. Squeeze 2 oranges; strain juice. Set aside. Cut peel into large pieces. Cut away all white membrane; discard. Cut peel into short, thin slivers. Place in small saucepan; cover with boiling water. Cover; simmer for 10 to 15 minutes or until tender. Drain; set aside. Place ducklings on hot platter; cut into serving pieces. Keep warm. Strain drippings in Dutch oven; discard vegetables. Chill drippings by placing in ice water. Remove fat; discard. Pour remaining drippings into saucepan; boil, uncovered, until reduced by 1/4. Mix 3 tablespoons water and cornstarch; stir into boiling liquid slowly. Reduce heat. Add orange juice and orange rind; Simmer for 5 minutes. Cut remaining oranges into thick slices; center each slice with spoon of jelly. Garnish platter with orange slices and parsley. Spoon small amount of orange sauce over each serving of duckling. Recipe may be used for wild duck; serve with wild rice.

Mrs. Elsie Fahlgren
John Taylor Collegiate
Winnepeg, Manitoba, Canada

DUCKS WITH CROUTON DRESSING

1/2 c. chopped onion
1/2 c. chopped celery
3 tbsp. butter
1 pkg. seasoned croutons
Grated peel and juice of 2 oranges
3 or 4 ducks

Saute onion and celery in butter until tender. Place croutons and orange peel and juice in bowl. Add celery and onion mixture; mix well. Add water to dressing if too dry. Stuff ducks with dressing; place ducks in oven cooking bags. Place in baking pan. Bake at 350 degrees for 1 hour and 30 minutes.

Mrs. Doris Kirk
St. Croix Falls High School
St. Croix Falls, Wisconsin

GLAZED ROAST DUCK

2 or 3 oranges
2 or 3 onions
1 duck
Whole cloves
Juice of 1 orange
1 c. currant jelly

Quarter enough oranges and onions to fill cavity of duck. Place 1 clove in each quarter of duck; stuff cavity with oranges and onions. Pierce skin with fork. Mix orange juice and currant jelly; heat through. Place duck on rack in roasting pan. Roast, uncovered, at 375 degrees for 1 hour and 30 minutes to 2 hours, brushing with jelly mixture 4 times during last 45 minutes of baking. May be served cold.

Gaynelle C. James
Gardner Southwest High School
Gardner, Illinois

LONG ISLAND DUCK WITH CHERRIES

2 young Long Island ducks
Salt
1/4 c. kirsch
1 1/2 c. brown sauce
1 c. sour cherries
Pepper

Rub ducks inside and out with salt; place on rack in shallow pan. Roast at 350 degrees for 12 to 13 minutes per pound. Duck is done when leg joints move easily. Temperature may be increased to 500 degrees last 15 minutes of baking for crisper duck, if desired. Remove ducks to hot platter. Skim off all excess fat from pan. Add kirsch to pan; scrape up particles in bottom. Add to brown-sauce in small saucepan; bring to a boil. Reduce heat; simmer for 2 to 3 minutes. Add cherries; bring to boiling point. Add salt and pepper to taste, if needed; pour around duck. Canned brown gravy may be substituted for brown sauce. Yield: 4-6 servings.

Mrs. Mary V. Watson
Sullivan West School
Kingsport, Tennessee

FLAMING DUCK

1 wild duck, dressed
1/2 c. chopped celery
1/2 c. chopped carrots
2 tbsp. chopped onion
3 strips bacon
1 can cream of mushroom soup
1/2 c. water

Soak duck in salted water overnight; drain. Combine celery, carrots and onion; place in duck cavity. Place duck in Dutch oven; place bacon strips over duck. Combine soup and water; pour over duck. Cover. Roast at 350 degrees for 2 hours to 3 hours and 30 minutes, depending on size and age of duck, or until tender. Remove duck from soup; discard bacon, stuffing and skin from duck. Soup may be thickened for gravy.

Vesta M. Wicke
Augusta High School
Augusta, Kansas

JOHN'S DUCK

1 wild duck
Oil
Salt and pepper

Preheat oven at 350 degrees for 10 minutes. Rub duck with oil; season with generous amount of salt and pepper. Bake for 20 minutes. Turn control to broil if electric stove is used; place in broiler on lowest shelf if gas stove is used. Broil for 20 minutes. Turn duck; broil for 20 minutes longer. Serve immediately. Yield: 2-3 servings.

Mrs. Ethelyne Wooten
Ruleville Public Junior High School
Ruleville, Mississippi

GLORIFIED WILD DUCK

1/2 lb. thinly sliced bacon
Breasts of 3 or 4 wild ducks
Seasoned flour
1 med. onion, thinly sliced
1 can golden mushroom soup
1/2 soup can water
1 can mushrooms (opt.)

Fry bacon until light brown and nearly crisp. Remove from pan; drain. Slice duck breasts; coat with seasoned flour. Brown in bacon drippings. Place in shallow casserole; place bacon and onion slices over duck. Mix soup and water; pour over duck. Add mushrooms; cover. Bake at 325 degrees for 1 to 2 hours or until duck is tender; serve with rice. Duck breasts may be left whole, if desired. Wild taste is eliminated from ducks when using this recipe.

Romayne Albrecht
Rolla High School
Rolla, North Dakota

MARINATED DUCK

1 c. dry cooking sherry
1 c. sweet wine
2 tbsp. lemon juice
1 tbsp. salt
4 wild ducks
2 apples, chopped
1 stalk celery, chopped
1 sm. onion, chopped

Mix sherry, wine, lemon juice and salt. Pour over ducks; marinate in refrigerator for 24 hours. Drain ducks; stuff with apples, celery and onion. Place in roasting pan. Roast, uncovered, at 400 degrees for 30 minutes; cover. Reduce temperature to 350 degrees; roast for 1 hour and 30 minutes to 2 hours longer. Remove apples, celery and onions; discard. This mixture is used to take away wild taste of ducks.

Ruth Stoffel
Hazel Green High School
Hazel Green, Wisconsin

MONTANA DUCK

1 wild duck
1 tsp. dillseed
1 tbsp. sugar
1 No. 2 1/2 can sauerkraut
1 tsp. ginger
1/2 tsp. garlic powder

Wash duck thoroughly. Mix dillseed, sugar and sauerkraut; place in duck cavity. Mix ginger and garlic powder; rub on outside of duck. Place duck on rack in roasting pan; cover. Bake at 350 degrees for 2 hours or until brown. Serve with horseradish.

Verda Clawson
Junior High School
Deer Lodge, Montana

NORWEGIAN WILD DUCK

4 wild ducks
4 tsp. whole allspice
4 tsp. peppercorns

Place 1 teaspoon each allspice and peppercorns in cavity of each duck; place ducks in Dutch oven. Add enough water to Dutch oven to fill 1/4 inch deep. Place Dutch oven over medium heat; bring water to a simmer. Reduce heat to low; cover Dutch oven tightly. Cook for 3 to 5 hours or until ducks are tender, turning ducks every 30 minutes to brown evenly and adding water as needed.

Mrs. Margaret A. Campbell
Sierra Middle School
Roswell, New Mexico

SOUTHERN-STYLE BRAISED DUCK

1 4-lb. duck, quartered
2 tsp. salt
1/2 tsp. pepper
1/2 c. shortening
2 c. chicken broth
1/3 c. instant onion flakes
1/4 c. instant bell pepper flakes
1/4 tsp. instant minced garlic
1/4 c. water
1/2 lb. bulk pork sausage
1 c. rice
1 bay leaf
1/2 tsp. chili powder
1/2 tsp. thyme
1 tsp. parsley flakes
1/2 c. diced cooked ham
1 c. canned tomatoes

Rub duck with salt and pepper; brown in shortening over low heat. Pour off drippings; add broth. Cover; simmer for 1 hour and 30 minutes or until duck is tender. Add onion, bell pepper and garlic to water; let soak. Brown sausage; drain off excess fat. Add rice and rehydrated vegetables with water; cook until rice begins to stick, stirring constantly. Remove duck from pan. Add rice mixture to broth; add bay leaf, chili powder, thyme and parsley flakes. Toss lightly with fork to mix; cover. Cook for 10 minutes. Add ham and tomatoes; mix carefully so as not to mash rice. Place duck on top of ham mixture; cover. Cook for 10 minutes. Yield: 4 servings.

Mrs. Fay Taylor
Ingleside High School
Ingleside, Texas

WILD DUCK SUPREME

2 c. vinegar
10 whole cloves
4 bay leaves
3 tbsp. onion flakes
6 peppercorns
2 tbsp. lemon juice
2 tbsp. salt
2 tbsp. sugar
1/4 c. oil
3 sm. wild ducks
2 tbsp. prepared mustard
1 tbsp. catsup
1 tbsp. Worcestershire sauce
3 tbsp. margarine or butter

Mix 2 cups water, vinegar, cloves, bay leaves, onion flakes, peppercorns, lemon juice, salt, sugar and oil. Add ducks; marinate overnight or for 1 day in refrigerator. Drain ducks well; place in broiler pan. Mix 6 tablespoons water and remaining ingredients; heat until margarine melts. Baste ducks with sauce. Broil for 6 minutes on each side, basting with sauce after turning. Reduce temperature to 350 degrees; bake, turning and basting with sauce, until ducks are of desired doneness.

Mrs. Betty Peters
Cherry Hill High School
Inkster, Michigan

ROASTED MALLARDS

Mallards
Salt
Pepper
Onion
Apple
Carrot
Celery

Soak ducks in salted water for 30 minutes. Dry; rub inside and out with salt and pepper. Stuff with equal amounts of onion, apple, carrot and celery. Place in baking pan; cover with aluminum foil. Bake at 250 to 300 degrees until tender; may remove foil to brown, if desired. May baste with melted butter, if desired.

Sula Mae Majure
Cruger-Tchula Academy
Cruger, Mississippi

STUFFED DUCK A LA ORANGE

1 tsp. salt
1/4 tsp. pepper
1 3 to 4-lb. duckling
Orange juice
3/4 c. (packed) brown sugar
3 tsp. grated orange peel
1/2 tsp. dry mustard
1/4 tsp. allspice
1/8 tsp. ground ginger
2 tbsp. flour

Mix salt and pepper; rub duckling inside and out with salt mixture. Remove wing tips; fasten neck skin and wings to back of duckling with skewers. Stuff duckling with dressing, if desired; close cavity opening with skewers. Place on rack in roasting pan, breast side down. Roast in 450-degree oven for 30 minutes. Reduce temperature to 350 degrees; turn duckling breast side up. Continue roasting, allowing 30 minutes per pound. Mix 2 tablespoons orange juice, brown sugar, orange peel, mustard, allspice and ginger; spread on duckling 30 minutes before done. Continue basting duckling with drippings from pan until tender and skin is crisp and brown. Remove to platter; keep hot. Pour off grease from roasting pan, leaving only brown drippings. Stir flour into drippings; stir in 2 cups orange juice. Cook over low heat till thickened, stirring constantly. Strain into sauce dish; serve with hot duckling.

Jeanne Scheinoha
Valders High School
Valders, Wisoncsin

ALMOND DUCK

1 young duckling
1 tbsp. salt
5 tbsp. soy sauce
2 tbsp. sweet wine (opt.)
1/2 tsp. monosodium glutamate
1/4 tsp. cinnamon
1/4 tsp. cloves
1/4 tsp. ginger
1/4 tsp. nutmeg
Cornstarch
Oil
Shredded lettuce
Toasted almonds

Cover duckling with water; add salt. Bring to a boil; simmer for 1 hour or until tender. Drain duckling; reserve broth. Cool reserved broth; skim off fat. Cool duckling; place on cutting board. Cut slit down center of back, continuing all around, making 2 sections. Debone slowly, starting with drumsticks, then thighs, breast, and wings. Mix 2 tablespoons soy sauce, wine and monosodium glutamate; pat onto duck. Mix spices; sprinkle over duck. Cut two 12 x 18-inch pieces of aluminum foil; sprinkle 1/2 cup cornstarch on foil. Place duck on cornstarch; sprinkle with 1/2 cup cornstarch. Wrap carefully; freeze until firm. Remove from foil; fry in hot oil until brown. Bring 2 cups broth to a boil; add remaining soy sauce. Mix 2 tablespoons cornstarch and small amount of water until smooth; stir into broth mixture. Simmer for several minutes or until thickened. Cut duck into bite-sized pieces; place on lettuce. Pour sauce over duck; garnish with almonds.

Mrs. Helen Masumura
Wilson High School
Los Angeles, California

ROASTED STUFFED DUCK

1   5 to 6-lb. duckling with giblets
14 slices day-old bread
1/2 c. chopped celery
1/2 c. chopped onion
1/2 c. red wine
Oregano to taste
Poultry seasoning to taste
Salt and pepper to taste

Simmer giblets in 6 cups salted water until tender. Drain giblets; cool. Reserve broth. Chop giblets. Cut bread into cubes; place on cookie sheet. Bake at 200 degrees until dry. Place giblets, celery and onion in reserved broth; add wine. Simmer until celery is tender. Add bread and seasonings; mix well. Dressing should be moist. Place in cavity of duck; place on wire rack in roaster. Cover duck with tent of foil. Roast at 350 degrees for 2 hours. Remove foil; bake for 2 hours longer, adding enough water to roaster to keep duck from drying.

Sally S. Alex
Freeman High School
Spokane, Washington

STUFFED WILD MALLARD

2 fat mallards, cleaned
1/2 gal. buttermilk
Salt
3 slices dry bread
3 c. crumbled corn bread
3 eggs
3/4 c. chopped celery
1/2 c. chopped green onions and tops
1 sm. clove of garlic, finely chopped
1   4-oz. can mushrooms, drained
3/4 tsp. sage
1/2 tsp. pepper
3/4 c. slivered almonds

Soak ducks in buttermilk overnight to remove some of the wild taste. Corn bread may be prepared day before using. Rinse ducks in salted water to remove buttermilk; place in roaster with giblets, 5 cups water and 1 teaspoon salt. Bake at 350 degrees for 1 hour. Reduce temperature to 325 degrees.

Crumble bread; mix with corn bread crumbs. Add eggs, celery, green onions, garlic, mushrooms, sage, 1/2 teaspoon salt, pepper and almonds; mix. Add liquid from roaster; mix well. Dressing should be very moist. Stuff ducks with dressing; place remaining dressing around ducks. Cover roaster. Bake for 1 hour and 30 minutes. Uncover; bake until ducks are brown. Garnish with canned crab apples. Bouillon cubes dissolved in water or canned chicken broth may be added if not enough liquid is in roaster for dressing.

Sue Slusser
Agra High School
Agra, Oklahoma

WHACKY-DACKY DUCK

2 cans anchovy fillets, mashed
1/2 tsp. crumbled dried thyme
1/4 tsp. pepper
12 juniper berries, crushed
1 lg. duck, cleaned
2 c. dry red wine
1 c. water
1 med. red onion, sliced
2 lg. parsley sprigs
2 celery stalks with leaves,
   chopped
1 lg. carrot, chopped
2 tbsp. flour

Mix anchovies, thyme, pepper and juniper berries; rub cavity of duck with anchovy mixture. Place duck in large bowl. Combine remaining ingredients except flour; bring to a boil. Pour over duck. Cover; refrigerate for 1 to 2 days, turning duck 3 or 4 times. Place duck in roasting pan. Strain marinade; pour over duck. Cover. Bake in preheated 325-degree oven for 2 hours and 30 minutes. Remove cover; bake for 30 minutes longer. Place duck on hot serving platter. Strain liquid from pan; remove fat. Bring to a boil. Mix flour with 2 tablespoons water; stir into pan liquid. Cook until thickened. Serve with duck. Serve duck with potato dumplings and black currant jelly, if desired. Yield: 4 servings.

Mrs. Beverly Bourque
Williamsburg High School
Williamsburg, Kansas

Chicken

Chicken is, without question, the most popular poultry. It is delicious
served in such a variety of ways that we never seem to tire of it,
and we are constantly searching for new ways to prepare it.

Chicken is available all year round, fresh, frozen or canned, with
a peak season from May to October. There are even some freeze-dried
chicken products available. One of the main advantages in shopping
for chicken is that you are able to buy parts (breasts, thighs, legs,
wings or backs), or whole birds ready to cook.

On the following pages, you'll find some interesting and
delicious ways to prepare and serve chicken that are sure to delight
your family and friends.

GLAZED ROAST CHICKEN

1 3-lb. broiler-fryer
Salt
Melted margarine
1/2 c. sherry
1/3 c. dark corn syrup
2 tbsp. finely chopped onion
Dash of pepper
1 1/2 tbsp. cornstarch
3/4 c. water

Clean chicken; rub inside with salt. Truss; brush skin with melted margarine. Place, breast side up, on rack in shallow baking pan. Roast in 400-degree oven for 1 hour. Combine sherry, corn syrup, 2 tablespoons melted margarine, onion, 1/2 teaspoon salt and pepper. Baste chicken with some of the sherry mixture; roast, basting frequently and using all sherry mixture, for about 30 minutes longer or until chicken is tender. Remove chicken; place on warm platter. Blend cornstarch and water with spoon; stir into pan drippings. Boil over medium heat, stirring constantly, for 2 minutes or until thickened; serve with chicken. Yield: 4 servings.

Photograph for this recipe on page 40.

CHICKEN WITH MUSHROOMS

1 broiler-fryer
3 sprigs of parsley
1 sm. stalk celery
Few sprigs of basil
1 bay leaf
2 tbsp. margarine
1/2 lb. mushrooms, sliced
1 sm. onion, finely chopped
1 tsp. flour
1 tsp. salt
Dash of pepper
1/4 c. white wine
1/4 c. light cream
1 egg yolk

Cut chicken into serving pieces. Tie parsley, celery, basil and bay leaf together. Melt margarine in large skillet. Add chicken; cook over medium heat, turning as needed, until golden brown on all sides. Add mushrooms; cook, shaking skillet or stirring occasionally, for 5 minutes. Stir in onion, flour, salt and pepper, then add bouquet garni and wine. Cover; simmer for about 35 minutes or until chicken is tender. Remove chicken pieces; place in serving dish. Discard bouquet garni. Combine cream and egg yolk; stir in small amount of hot mixture. Stir into remaining hot mixture in skillet slowly; heat through, stirring constantly. Pour over chicken. One-fourth teaspoon dried basil may be substituted for basil sprigs. Yield: 4 servings.

Photograph for this recipe on page 40.

CHICKEN STEW IN A HURRY

2 2 1/2 to 3 1/2-lb. broiler-fryers,
    disjointed
1 chicken bouillon cube
2 tsp. salt
1 bay leaf
1/4 tsp. thyme leaves
2 c. celery, cut in 3-in. strips
2 c. carrots, cut in 3-in. strips
12 sm. white onions
1/3 c. cornstarch

Place chicken pieces, bouillon cube, salt, bay leaf, thyme and 5 cups water in large kettle; bring to a boil. Reduce heat; cover. Simmer for 30 minutes. Add celery, carrots and onions; cover. Simmer for about 10 minutes or until vegetables are tender. Mix cornstarch and 1 cup water; stir into chicken mixture. Bring to a boil; cook, stirring constantly, for 1 minute. Serve in soup plates. Yield: 8 servings.

Photograph for this recipe on page 40.

LEMON-FRIED CHICKEN

1 broiler-fryer
1/4 c. lemon juice
1/2 c. corn oil
1/4 tsp. garlic salt
3/4 tsp. salt
1/4 tsp. ground thyme
1/4 tsp. ground marjoram
1/8 tsp. pepper
1/2 tsp. grated lemon rind

1/2 c. flour
1/2 tsp. paprika

Cut chicken into serving pieces. Wash; dry well. Place in large, shallow pan. Mix lemon juice, 1/4 cup corn oil, garlic salt, salt, thyme, marjoram, pepper and lemon rind; pour over chicken. Marinate in refrigerator for at least 3 hours, turning occasionally. Drain chicken on absorbent paper. Mix flour and paprika. Coat chicken pieces with flour mixture; shake off excess. Heat remaining corn oil in heavy skillet over medium heat for about 3 minutes. Add chicken carefully; fry, turning once, for about 15 minutes or until golden brown. Cover; cook over low heat for 20 minutes longer. Remove cover; cook until tender. Yield: 4 servings.

Photograph for this recipe on page 40.

CAROL'S CHICKEN PUFFS

2 tbsp. butter
1/4 c. boiling water
1/4 c. sifted flour
Salt
1 egg
1/4 c. shredded Swiss process cheese
2 c. cooked minced chicken
1/4 c. minced celery
2 tbsp. minced canned pimento
2 tbsp. sauterne
1/4 c. mayonnaise
Dash of pepper

Preheat oven to 400 degrees. Melt butter in saucepan in boiling water. Add flour and dash of salt; stir vigorously. Cook, stirring until mixture forms a ball and leaves side of pan. Remove and cool. Add egg; beat vigorously until smooth. Stir in cheese. Drop dough by teaspoonfuls onto greased baking sheet. Bake for about 20 minutes. Remove puffs from oven; cool and split. Combine 1/2 teaspoon salt and remaining ingredients. Spoon about 2 teaspoons chicken mixture into each puff.

Carol J. Newfer
Clyde Senior High School
Freemont, Ohio

CURRIED CHICKEN BALLS

1/2 lb. cream cheese
1 c. chicken, finely cubed
2 tbsp. mayonnaise
1 c. almonds, chopped
1/2 c. coconut
1 tbsp. chutney, minced or
    Worcestershire sauce
1 tbsp. curry powder
1/2 tsp. salt

Soften cream cheese; add chicken, mayonnaise, almonds, coconut, chutney, curry and salt. Blend thoroughly; roll into 1-inch balls. Refrigerate until ready to serve.

Mrs. Ann Hohman
Juniata Valley High School
Alexandria, Pennsylvania

ELEGANT CHICKEN LIVER PATE

2 lb. chicken livers
2 c. butter
2 med. onions, quartered
1 tsp. (heaping) curry powder
1 tsp. paprika
1/4 tsp. salt
1/4 tsp. freshly ground pepper
1/4 c. cognac
1 jar pimento-stuffed olives
Top from fresh pineapple

Wash chicken livers; pat dry. Melt 1/2 cup butter in saucepan over medium heat; add livers, onions, curry powder, paprika, salt and pepper. Cook, covered, for 8 minutes. Melt remaining butter in small saucepan. Place liver mixture into blender container; add cognac and remaining melted butter. Blend until smooth; pour into bowl. Chill overnight. Unmold; shape into form of pineapple. Slice olives thinly. Decorate pate using olive slices to form pineapple eyes; top with fresh pineapple top. Serve with crackers or melba toast. Mixture may be frozen, if desired.

Mrs. John W. Detwiler
Upper Dublin Senior High School
Ft. Washington, Pennsylvania

CHICKEN PARTY PUFFS

1/2 c. margarine
1 c. flour
4 eggs
2 c. chopped chicken
1 c. chopped celery or apple
2 tsp. lemon juice
1/2 tsp. salt
1/8 tsp. pepper
1/2 c. mayonnaise
2 hard-cooked eggs, chopped
1 tbsp. minced onion

Preheat oven to 400 degrees. Bring margarine and 1 cup water to rolling boil in small saucepan; stir in flour all at once. Stir for 1 minute or until mixture forms ball and leaves side of pan; remove from heat. Beat in eggs, one at a time, beating until mixture is smooth. Drop dough by slightly rounded teaspoonfuls onto ungreased baking sheets. Bake for 25 minutes or until golden brown. Cool away from draft. Combine chicken, celery, lemon juice, salt, pepper, mayonnaise, eggs and onion; toss lightly. Slit puffs on 1 side; remove soft filling. Fill puffs with chicken mixture. Unfilled puffs may be frozen in airtight containers. Yield: 5 dozen puffs.

Mrs. Louise H. Griner
Baker High School
Columbus, Georgia

GOLDEN CHICKEN NUGGETS

4 chicken breasts, boned
1/4 c. grated Parmesan cheese
4 tbsp. grated Cheddar cheese
1/2 c. fine dried bread crumbs
2 tsp. monosodium glutamate
1 tsp. dried leaf thyme
1 tsp. salt
1 tsp. dried leaf basil
1/8 tsp. pepper
1/2 c. melted butter or margarine

Skin chicken breasts; cut into 1-inch squares. Combine Parmesan cheese, Cheddar cheese, crumbs, monosodium glutamate, thyme, salt, basil and pepper; blend well. Dip chicken pieces into butter; roll in crumb mixture. Arrange chicken in single layer on foil-lined baking sheets. Bake at 400 degrees for 10 minutes. May be served hot or cold. Garnish with parsley, if desired.

Mrs. Sandra Graman
Middletown High School
Middleton, Ohio

FONDUE ORIENTALE

1 12-oz. jar peach preserves
1 2-oz. jar pimentos, drained
    and chopped
1/4 c. white vinegar
1/3 to 1/2 lb. chicken breast per person
3 c. chicken broth

Combine preserves, pimentos and vinegar; blend well. Chill until ready to serve. Bone chicken; cut into paper-thin strips. Pour broth into fondue pot; heat to boiling. Reduce heat to medium setting; have broth at a rolling boil. Cook chicken strips in broth; serve with sauce. Barbecue sauce, sweet-sour sauce, hot mustard sauce or soy sauce may be served with chicken, if desired.

Mrs. Karen Williams
Elk River Junior High School
Elk River, Minnesota

JAPANESE CHICKEN AND BACON ROLLS

1 lb. chicken breasts
12 slices bacon
2 tbsp. oil
4 tbsp. soy sauce
1 tbsp. sugar
2 tbsp. mirin or dry sherry
2 tsp. saki (opt.)

Bone chicken breasts; remove skin. Cut chicken into 2 x 1-inch pieces; cut bacon slices in half. Wrap bacon around pieces of chicken, securing with wooden picks. Heat the oil in heavy skillet; add bacon and chicken rolls, frying until golden brown. Pour off excessive oil. Add soy sauce, sugar, mirin and saki to skillet; cook for 5 minutes, turning rolls occasionally. Remove rolls from skillet; remove wooden picks. Arrange on platter; garnish as desired. Yield: 20-24 appetizers.

Mrs. Sharon Wiedmeyer
Homestead High School
Meguon, Wisconsin

PICK-UP CHICKEN STICKS

3 lb. chicken wings
1 c. butter or margarine
1 1/2 c. sifted flour
1/3 c. sesame seed
1 tbsp. salt
1/2 tsp. ground ginger

Disjoint chicken wings; discard tips. Melt butter in shallow baking pan. Combine flour, sesame seed, salt and ginger; blend well. Roll chicken pieces in butter; drain any excess. Roll in flour mixture, coating generously. Arrange in single layer in pan in which butter was melted. Bake at 350 degrees for 1 hour. May be run under broiler until crisp and golden brown.

Mrs. Pauline D. Ralston
Millis Junior-Senior High School
Millis, Massachusetts

CHICKEN-CORN SOUP

1/3 c. chopped onion
3 tbsp. margarine
1 17-oz. can whole kernel corn
1 1/2 c. diced cooked chicken
1 to 2 c. water or chicken broth
Pepper to taste
Garlic powder to taste
1 tsp. dried parsley flakes (opt.)

Saute onion in margarine in saucepan till lightly browned. Add corn and chicken. Rinse corn can with water; add to chicken mixture. Season with pepper and garlic powder; cover. Simmer for 45 minutes, stirring occasionally. Add parsley flakes; serve hot. May be reheated. Yield: 4-6 servings.

R. Irene Stoltzfus
Northridge High School
Middlebury, Indiana

BRUNSWICK STEW

1 3-lb. chicken
6 c. water
1 tsp. rosemary
2 1/2 tsp. salt
1 bay leaf
2 potatoes, diced
1 can cream-style corn
1 can tomatoes
1 onion, finely chopped
1 pkg. frozen baby lima beans
1 c. sliced okra

Stew chicken in water with rosemary, salt and bay leaf for 1 hour. Remove chicken from water; cool. Bone chicken; cut into small pieces. Bring chicken broth to a boil. Add remaining ingredients; simmer until vegetables are done. Remove bay leaf; add chicken. Heat thoroughly.

Pat Bagley
Dimmitt High School
Dimmitt, Texas

CROWDED CHOWDER

1 2 1/2-lb. stewing chicken
1 c. chopped celery
1 6 1/2-oz. can crab meat
1 tsp. salt
1 tsp. pepper
1/4 tsp. nutmeg
1/4 tsp. garlic salt
1 c. milk
1 carton sour cream
Seasoned croutons

Place chicken in large saucepan; cover with boiling water. Simmer for 2 hours and 30 minutes. Strain broth; cool chicken. Remove chicken from bones; discard bones. Add celery to broth; simmer for 45 minutes. Add chicken, crab meat, salt, pepper, nutmeg, garlic salt, milk and sour cream; bring to boiling point over moderate heat. Ladle into serving bowls; sprinkle with croutons.

Mary M. DeLucia
West Haven High School
West Haven, Connecticut

PENNSYLVANIA DUTCH CHICKEN-CORN SOUP

1   5 to 6-lb. stewing chicken
1 or 2 med. onions, chopped
Salt
1/4 tsp. pepper
8 to 10 ears of corn, cut from cob
1 c. flour
1 egg, beaten
4 hard-cooked eggs, chopped
3 tbsp. chopped parsley
Celery salt to taste
Onion salt to taste

Cut chicken into serving pieces. Place in large stewing pan; add 3 to 4 quarts water. Add onions, 1 tablespoon salt and pepper. Cover; cook over low heat until chicken is tender. Remove chicken from broth; remove and discard skin and bones. Cut chicken in 1 to 1 1/2-inch pieces. Return chicken to broth; add corn. Cook over low heat for 15 to 20 minutes, stirring frequently. Combine flour, 1/8 teaspoon salt and beaten egg in a bowl; mix to form crumbs. Bring soup to a boil; add crumbs gradually. Cook for 15 minutes. Drop in hard-cooked eggs and parsley; simmer for several seconds. Add seasonings. Soup may be made ahead and frozen for future use.

I. Eugenia Spangler
Big Spring Junior High School
Newville, Pennsylvania

TEXAS CHICKEN STEW

1 lg. fryer
1/4 c. sugar
Salt and pepper to taste
1 tsp. chili powder
1/2 can tomatoes with green chilies
4 sm. potatoes, diced
1 lg. onion, chopped
1 No. 2 can mixed vegetables
2 No. 2 cans cream-style corn
1 No. 2 can whole kernel corn

Stew fryer in 2 to 3 quarts water until chicken is tender. Remove chicken from broth; cut in bite-sized pieces. Add chicken, sugar, salt, pepper, chili powder, tomatoes, potatoes and onion to broth; cook until potatoes are almost done. Add mixed vegetables and corn; cook until potatoes are soft and flavors are blended. The longer the stew is simmered, the better the flavor.

Judy Kay Lowe
Bellevue High School
Bellevue, Texas

BUFFET CHICKEN SALAD

3 c. cooked diced chicken breasts
3 tbsp. lemon juice
1 1/2 c. diced celery
1 c. drained pineapple tidbits
1 1/2 c. seedless grapes
1/2 c. broken pecans
1 c. mayonnaise
1/2 c. whipping cream, whipped
1 1/2 tsp. salt
1 tsp. dry mustard

Combine chicken with lemon juice; toss well. Chill in covered container for 1 hour. Add celery, pineapple, grapes and pecans. Combine mayonnaise, whipped cream, salt and mustard; stir into chicken mixture. Serve on lettuce leaves. Chicken may be stewed with carrots, celery and parsley for better flavor; prepared dessert topping may be substituted for whipped cream.

Mrs. Eva Mae Lloyd
Ballard High School
Louisville, Kentucky

CHARLESTON CHICKEN SALAD

1   6-oz. can orange juice
   concentrate
3/4 c. corn oil
1/4 c. vinegar
3 tbsp. sugar
1/2 tsp. dry mustard
1/4 tsp. salt
1/8 tsp. hot sauce
2 to 3 c. cooked diced chicken
1 c. chopped celery
1/2 c. sliced ripe olives
1 med. avocado, diced
1/4 c. slivered almonds

Place orange juice concentrate, corn oil, vinegar, sugar, dry mustard, salt and hot sauce in blender container; blend on high speed for 5 seconds or until smooth. Cover; refrigerate. Place chicken, celery, olives, avocado and almonds in salad bowl. Add 1/2 cup orange juice dressing; toss lightly. Cover; chill for at least 30 minutes before serving. Store remaining dressing in refrigerator for future use. Yield: 4-6 servings.

Mrs. Eleanor Holton Barfield
Summerville High School
Summerville, South Carolina

CHICKEN-APPLE SALAD

1 med. head lettuce
2 c. diced unpared apples
1 11-oz. can mandarin oranges,
    drained
2 c. cubed cooked chicken
1/3 c. coarsely chopped walnuts
1/2 c. mayonnaise or salad dressing
2 tsp. soy sauce
1 tsp. lemon juice
1/2 c. grated Cheddar cheese

Tear lettuce into bite-sized pieces. Combine lettuce, apples, oranges, chicken, and walnuts; toss together. Combine mayonnaise, soy sauce and lemon juice; mix well. Toss dressing gently with chicken mixture. Sprinkle with grated cheese. Yield: 4-6 servings.

Cynthia Atkins
Altoona-Midway Junior-Senior High School
Buffalo, Kansas

CHICKEN-GRAPE SALAD

3 c. diced cooked chicken
1 c. diced celery
1/2 lb. red grapes, cut into eighths
1 c. mayonnaise
Salt and pepper to taste

Combine chicken, celery and grapes; add mayonnaise. Toss to mix well. Add salt and pepper. Serve individual portions on lettuce leaves. Garnish with grape half.

Diane Spetman
Oelwein Community High School
Oelwein, Iowa

CHICKEN-FRUIT SALAD DELUXE

1 2 to 3-lb. broiler-fryer
    chicken
1/2 c. thinly sliced celery
1/2 c. drained mandarin orange
    sections
1 c. drained pineapple cubes
1/2 c. quartered maraschino cherries
2 bananas, sliced
1/4 c. mayonnaise
1/4 c. sour cream
1/2 tsp. lemon juice
1 tsp. sugar
Rum flavoring to taste
Hearts of lettuce

Cook chicken by roasting or stewing until tender. Debone; cut into cubes. Combine chicken, celery, orange sections, pineapple cubes, cherries and bananas in large bowl. Combine mayonnaise, sour cream, lemon juice and sugar. Pour over chicken mixture; toss gently. Chill thoroughly in refrigerator. Add rum flavoring, if desired. Line a bowl with hearts of lettuce. Fill bowl with salad. Garnish with additional fruit, if desired. Yield: 6-8 servings.

Sister Clotilda McCurdy, SND
Julienne High School
Dayton, Ohio

CHICKEN-EGG SALAD SUPREME

2 c. cooked diced chicken
2 tbsp. chopped green olives
3/4 c. chopped celery
1/2 c. toasted almonds
2 tbsp. chopped ripe olives
2 tbsp. sweet pickle relish,
    drained
2 hard-cooked eggs, chopped
3/4 c. mayonnaise

Combine all ingredients; serve on lettuce or watercress. Yield: 4 servings.

Mrs. Ann J. Hilliard
Plant City Senior High School
Plant City, Florida

CHICKEN-ALMOND SALAD

3 c. diced cooked chicken
1 1/2 c. diced celery
3 tbsp. lemon juice
1 c. mayonnaise
1/4 c. light cream
1 tsp. dry mustard
1 1/4 tsp. salt
1 c. seedless grapes
1 c. toasted almonds

Combine chicken, celery, lemon juice, mayonnaise, cream, mustard, salt, grapes and almonds in large bowl; toss lightly. Chill until serving time. Place on bed of lettuce on serving platter. Garnish with sliced hard-boiled eggs and tomato wedges.

Mrs. Evelyn Van Vleet
Garden City Senior High School
Garden City, Kansas

CHICKEN SALAD SUPREME

2 2 1/2-lb. chickens, cooked
1 c. diced celery
1 c. cooked peas
1 pkg. salted almonds
3 hard-cooked eggs, diced
5 sweet pickles, diced
10 stuffed olives, diced
1/2 tsp. salt
1 3-oz. package cream cheese
1 1/2 c. mayonnaise
2 apples, diced
1 tbsp. lemon juice

Remove chicken skin and bones; cut chicken into small pieces. Add celery, peas, almonds, eggs, pickles, olives and salt. Soften cream cheese; mix with mayonnaise. Add to chicken mixture; mix well. Mix apples and lemon juice; stir into salad just before serving. Garnish with asparagus and pimento strips, if desired. Yield: 12 servings.

Mrs. Florence Hopson
Dolgeville Central School
Dolgeville, New York

CHICKEN BUFFET ELEGANT

2 env. unflavored gelatin
1 c. milk
2 chicken bouillon cubes
2 eggs, separated
1 tsp. paprika
Dash of salt
1 1-lb. carton dry creamed
  cottage cheese
2 1/2 c. finely chopped cooked
  chicken
1/2 c. finely chopped almonds
2 tbsp. finely diced pimento
2 tbsp. lemon juice
1 c. whipping cream, whipped

Sprinkle gelatin over milk in saucepan. Add bouillon cubes and slightly beaten egg yolks; cook over medium-low heat until mixture thickens, stirring constantly with wooden spoon. Remove from heat. Add paprika, salt and cottage cheese. Stir in chicken, almonds, pimento and lemon juice. Set in refrigerator to chill until mixture drops in mounds from spoon. Beat egg whites with electric mixer until stiff; fold into gelatin mixture. Fold in whipped cream. Turn into gelatin mold with removable bottom or 8-inch springform pan. Chill until firm. Unmold on serving dish. Garnish with toasted almonds and dollops of whipped cream. Whipped cream may be tinted for holidays. Yield: 12-18 servings.

Mrs. Wilma Sauer
John Page Junior High School
Birmingham, Michigan

CHINESE CHICKEN SALAD

1/2 c. chopped canned water
  chestnuts
1 6 1/2-oz. jar boned chicken,
  drained and chopped
1 tsp. instant minced onion
1/2 tsp. salt
Dash of pepper
1/4 c. mayonnaise
1/4 c. minced parsley

Combine all ingredients in mixing bowl except parsley; chill for at least 1 hour. Serve on lettuce leaves; garnish with parsley. May be spread on tiny rounds of white bread.

Margery McCall
Wolcott Junior High School
Warren, Michigan

FLORIDA GRAPEFRUIT BASKETS

3 Florida grapefruit

Cut grapefruit in half. Insert 2 wooden picks 1/2 inch apart on each side of grapefruit. Cut through the peel 1/4 inch below the top of the half to make handle; do not cut between the picks. Cut around each section of fruit loosening from membrane. Cut around entire edge of grapefruit. Remove picks. Lift handles and tie together. Attach flower to handle. Yield: 6 servings.

Photograph for this recipe on page 49.

BAKED TANGERINES WITH ORANGE-CRANBERRY RELISH

6 Florida tangerines or Temple
  oranges
2 tbsp. sugar
2 tbsp. butter or margarine
2/3 c. Florida orange juice
Orange-Cranberry Relish

Make 8 vertical cuts in the tangerine skin from the blossom end to about 1 inch from the bottom. Pull peel down and turn pointed ends in. Remove white membrane. Loosen sections at the center and pull apart slightly. Fill each center with 1 teaspoon sugar and dot with 1 teaspoon butter. Pour orange juice over tangerines. Bake in preheated 325-degree oven for 30 minutes. Garnish center with a small amount of Orange-Cranberry Relish. Serve with turkey.

Orange-Cranberry Relish

2 Florida oranges, quartered and
  seeded
4 c. fresh cranberries
2 c. sugar

Force orange quarters with peel and cranberries through food chopper. Add sugar and mix well. Chill in refrigerator for several hours before serving. This relish will keep well in refrigerator for several weeks.

Photograph for this recipe on page 49.

ORANGE CREPES WITH ORANGE SAUCE

3 eggs
2 egg yolks
1/2 c. milk
1/2 c. Florida orange juice
2 tbsp. salad oil
1 c. all-purpose flour
3/4 teaspoon salt
1 tbsp. sugar
1 tsp. grated orange rind

Beat eggs and egg yolks together. Add remaining ingredients and beat until smooth. Let stand at room temperature for at least 1 hour. Brush hot 7 or 8-inch skillet lightly with additional salad oil. Add 2 tablespoons batter to skillet; turn and tip skillet so mixture covers bottom evenly. Batter will set immediately into thin lacey pancake. Loosen with spatula and flip over in about 15 to 20 seconds or when browned. Brown other side and turn crepe out onto foil or waxed paper. Repeat with remaining batter.

Orange Sauce

1/2 c. soft butter
1/2 c. confectioners' sugar
1 tbsp. grated orange rind
3 tbsp. orange liqueur
1/3 c. Florida orange juice
1 c. Florida orange sections

Cream butter with confectioners' sugar and orange rind. Blend in orange liqueur gradually. Spread about 1/2 teaspoon of mixture over side of crepe that was browned second. Roll up crepes. Place remaining mixture with orange juice in large skillet or chafing dish; heat until bubbly. Add rolled crepes and heat, spooning sauce over tops. Add orange sections; heat for just 2 to 3 minutes longer. Yield: 6 servings.

Photograph for this recipe on page 49.

ROAST TURKEY WITH ORANGE-RICE STUFFING

1   12 to 14-lb. turkey
Salt and pepper to taste
Orange-Rice Stuffing

Wash turkey in cold running water. Pat inside dry with paper toweling, leaving outside moist. Sprinkle turkey cavities with salt and pepper. Stuff turkey with Orange Rice Stuffing. Fasten neck skin to body with skewer. Push legs under band of skin at tail or tie to tail. Place turkey, breast side up, on rack in shallow open roasting pan. Cover with a loose covering or tent of aluminum foil, if desired. Bake in a preheated 325-degree oven for 4 hours and 30 minutes to 5 hours or until tender.

Orange-Rice Stuffing

1 c. butter or margarine
1 c. chopped onion
4 c. water
2 c. Florida orange juice
3 tbsp. grated orange rind
4 c. chopped celery
2 tbsp. salt
1 tsp. poultry seasoning
5 1/3 c. packaged precooked rice
1/2 c. chopped parsley

Melt butter in a large saucepan; add onion and cook until tender but not brown. Add water, orange juice, orange rind, celery, salt and poultry seasoning. Bring to a boil; stir in rice. Cover; remove from heat and let stand for 5 minutes. Add parsley and fluff with fork. Any leftover stuffing may be wrapped in foil and placed in oven last 30 minutes of baking time.

Photograph for this recipe on page 49.

LAMB CHOP AND TOMATO BROIL WITH HORSERADISH SAUCE

6   1-in. thick loin lamb chops
3 med. tomatoes, halved
1/4 c. butter, melted
1/2 tsp. salt

1/8 tsp. pepper
12 sm. boiled potatoes
Chopped parsley
3 tbsp. drained horseradish
1 c. sour cream

Place lamb chops and tomato halves on rack in shallow pan. Broil 4 to 6 inches from source of heat for 8 to 12 minutes or to desired degree of doneness, turning once. Combine butter, salt and pepper; brush chops and tomatoes frequently with butter mixture. Peel potatoes; brown lightly in additional butter in skillet. Arrange chops, tomatoes and potatoes on heated platter; sprinkle tomatoes with parsley. Blend horseradish with sour cream. Season to taste with additional salt. Serve sauce with lamb chop dish. Yield: 6 servings.

Photograph for this recipe on page 50.

CHICKEN SUMMER SALAD

1   4-lb. chicken
Celery leaves
2 1/2 tsp. salt
1 1/2 c. diced celery
1 c. orange slices
1 c. pineapple tidbits
1/2 c. salted almonds, slivered
2 tbsp. salad oil
2 tbsp. orange juice
2 tbsp. vinegar
1 egg, well beaten
1/4 c. lemon juice
1/4 c. pineapple juice
1/2 c. sugar

Place chicken in stewing pot; cover with water. Add celery leaves and 2 teaspoons salt. Cook until meat falls from bones. Cool in broth. Debone; dice chicken coarsely. Combine chicken, celery, oranges, pineapple and almonds in large bowl. Combine oil, orange juice, vinegar and remaining salt; pour over chicken mixture, tossing to mix well. Refrigerate for 1 hour and 30 minutes before serving. Combine egg, juices and sugar in top of double boiler. Place over boiling water on medium heat. Cook, stirring occasionally,for 15 to 20 minutes or until thickened. Chill. Drain chicken mixture in colander; combine with pineapple dressing. Serve in a lettuce cup. Yield: 4 servings.

Carol Johnson
Forest City Community Schools
Forest City, Iowa

CHICKEN MOUSSE DELICIOUS

1 pkg. unflavored gelatin
1 c. mayonnaise
1 c. heavy cream, whipped
3/4 c. finely chopped celery
1/2 c. pecans
3/4 c. pineapple tidbits
2 c. diced cooked chicken
1/4 c. chopped pimento

Soak gelatin in 2 tablespoons cold water. Add 2 tablespoons boiling water to gelatin. Set over boiling water in double boiler; stir mixture until dissolved. Combine gelatin and mayonnaise in bowl. Fold in whipped cream. Add celery, pecans, pineapple, chicken and pimento; mix gently. Pour into 1 large mold or 8 to 10 individual molds. Chill until set. Unmold; garnish with strips of pimento and nuts.

Mary A. Filko
North High School
Akron, Ohio

CHICKEN SALAD WITH YOGURT

1 env. unflavored gelatin
1 1/4 c. pineapple juice
1/2 tsp. salt
1 8-oz. carton lemon yogurt
1/4 c. mayonnaise
1 1/3 c. diced cooked chicken
1/4 c. chopped celery
2 tbsp. slivered toasted almonds

Soften gelatin in pineapple juice in small saucepan; add salt. Heat, stirring, until gelatin dissolves. Combine yogurt and mayonnaise; stir in gelatin. Chill until partially set. Fold in chicken, celery and almonds. Pour

into 6 individual molds; chill until firm. Unmold onto lettuce cups; garnish with cherry tomatoes or clusters of green grapes. Yield: 6 servings.

Ruth Nolte
Waco High School
Waco, Texas

CONGEALED CHICKEN SALAD DELUXE

1 3 to 4-lb. cooked hen
1 env. unflavored gelatin
1 c. chicken broth
1 1/2 c. salad dressing
2 c. chopped celery
3 hard-cooked eggs, chopped
1 c. chopped almonds
3 c. seedless grape halves
1 tbsp. Worcestershire sauce
1 tbsp. chowchow

Remove chicken from bones; chop. Soften gelatin in 1/2 cup cold water. Bring chicken broth to boiling point; stir in gelatin until dissolved. Chill until thickened. Stir in chicken. Stir in remaining ingredients; place in mold. Chill until firm.

Mrs. Mildred Sanders
Clint High School
Clint, Texas

CREAM-CHICKEN SALAD

1 can chicken soup
1 box lemon gelatin
1 c. diced chicken
1 c. chopped celery
1 c. whipped cream
1/2 c. chopped nuts
1/2 c. salad dressing

Pour chicken soup in saucepan; bring to a boil. Pour over gelatin in large bowl, stirring until dissolved. Chill until thickened; whip until frothy. Fold in chicken, celery, whipped cream, nuts and salad dressing. Pour into desired mold; chill until firm. Unmold; serve on lettuce. Yield: 4-6 servings.

Mrs. Beverly Haas
Elgin High School
Elgin, North Dakota

CRANBERRY TOP CHICKEN LOAF

2 env. unflavored gelatin
1/2 c. cold water
1 1-lb. can jellied cranberry sauce
1/2 c. orange juice
1/2 c. diced celery
1/4 c. chopped pecans
1 c. hot chicken broth or bouillon
2/3 c. mayonnaise
1/2 c. evaporated milk
1/2 tsp. salt
2 c. diced canned or cooked chicken

Soften 1 envelope gelatin in 1/4 cup cold water. Mash cranberry sauce; add orange juice. Heat, stirring, until cranberry sauce melts. Stir in gelatin; chill until slightly thickened. Add celery and pecans; pour into 9 1/2 x 5 x 3-inch loaf pan. Chill until firm. Soften remaining gelatin in remaining cold water; stir into broth until dissolved. Chill until partially set. Blend mayonnaise with milk, salt and gelatin mixture. Add chicken; spoon over cranberry layer. Chill until firm.

Myra Willms
Runge High School
Runge, Texas

CHICKEN-PINEAPPLE BUFFET SALAD

1 pkg. unflavored gelatin
1/2 c. water
2 c. chicken broth
2 1/2 tbsp. lemon juice
6 c. chopped cooked chicken
1 c. crushed pineapple
3 hard-cooked eggs, chopped
8 oz. cubed Cheddar cheese
3/4 c. chopped celery
1 c. mayonnaise
2 tsp. salt

Sprinkle gelatin on water in saucepan; place over low heat, stirring until gelatin is dissolved. Combine gelatin mixture, chicken broth and lemon juice in large bowl. Add remaining ingredients; stir gently until well combined. Pour into 3-quart mold; chill

overnight or until firm. Serve on crisp lettuce leaf and garnish with tomato slices.

Mrs. Larry Reece
Carroll High School
Ft. Wayne, Indiana

CRUNCHY CHICKEN SALAD

5 c. diced cooked chicken breasts
1 c. sliced water chestnuts
2 c. pineapple tidbits
1/2 c. diced celery
1 tbsp. sliced green onion
4 tbsp. chutney
1 c. mayonnaise
1 tsp. curry powder
1 c. sour cream
1 lg. can Chinese noodles

Combine chicken, water chestnuts, pineapple, celery and green onion in large bowl. Combine chutney, mayonnaise, curry powder and sour cream; mix well. Add dressing to chicken mixture about 1 hour before serving time; toss to mix well. Chill. Add noodles at serving time. Yield: 8-10 servings.

Mrs. Helen M. Hall
Imperial Junior High School
Ontario, California

FESTIVE CHICKEN SALAD

3 chicken breasts
2 unjointed chicken legs
1 slice onion
1 slice green pepper
1 lg. slice celery
Salt
1/2 c. diced celery
1/3 c. diced green pepper
1 tbsp. diced onion
1/3 c. pickle relish
4 hard-cooked eggs, chopped
1/2 c. Thousand Island dressing
1/4 c. French dressing
3/4 c. mayonnaise
1 tbsp. mustard
1 tbsp. catsup
Dash of garlic powder
1 c. seedless grapes, halved

1/2 c. drained crushed pineapple
Pepper

Cook chicken pieces in water with onion, green pepper and celery slices and salt to taste until chicken is tender. Cool chicken to room temperature; remove from broth. Bone and cube chicken. Combine chicken, diced celery, green pepper and onion, pickle relish and eggs in large mixing bowl. Cover; chill. Combine dressings, mayonnaise, mustard, catsup and garlic powder in small mixing bowl; pour over chicken mixture. Add grapes and pineapple; toss until all ingredients are mixed. Season with salt and pepper to taste; chill until serving time. Serve on crisp lettuce beds; garnish with Spanish olives or strips of pimento and paprika. Yield: 12 servings.

Mrs. Maxine Thompson
East Chicago Washington High School
East Chicago, Indiana

BAKED CHICKEN SALAD

1 c. cooked diced chicken
1 can cream of chicken soup
1 c. diced celery
2 tsp. diced onion
1/2 c. pecans
1 1/2 tsp. salt
2 tsp. lemon juice
1/4 tsp. pepper
1/4 c. mayonnaise
3 hard-cooked eggs, sliced
2 c. crumbled potato chips
2 tbsp. flour
1 c. milk

Place chicken in casserole; add soup. Add celery, then onion; sprinkle with pecans. Sprinkle 1/2 teaspoon salt, lemon juice and pepper over pecans; add mayonnaise. Place eggs on mayonnaise; cover with potato chips. Mix flour and remaining salt. Add 2 tablespoons milk; stir until smooth. Stir in remaining milk; pour into saucepan. Heat, stirring, until thickened; pour over potato chips. Bake at 350 degrees for 15 minutes.

Mrs. Mavis Holley
Palatka Central High School
Palatka, Florida

HAPPY FACE CHICKEN SALAD

1 lg. chicken
1/4 c. chopped celery
1/3 c. minced onion
1/4 c. chopped green pepper
1/2 c. pickle relish
1 tsp. salt
1/4 tsp. pepper
1/2 c. salad dressing
Black olives
Apple wedges

Combine chicken, celery, onion, green pepper, relish, salt and pepper in large bowl; add salad dressing. Toss with fork until well mixed. Use ice cream scoop to place serving on lettuce. Make eyes with black olives. Use apple wedges for mouth. Yield: 4-8 servings.

Mrs. Lubertha Alford
West District Junior High School
Sumner, Mississippi

OVEN CHICKEN SALAD

1 8-oz. can water chestnuts
2 c. diced cooked chicken
3/4 c. diced celery
1 tbsp. chopped pimento
1 3 1/2-oz. can French-fried onions
2 tbsp. mayonnaise
1 1 1/4-oz. package chicken gravy mix
1 c. milk
1 tsp. salad seasoning

Preheat oven to 400 degrees. Drain water chestnuts; slice. Combine chicken, celery, pimento, water chestnuts, half the onions and mayonnaise in large bowl. Prepare chicken gravy according to package directions, using 1 cup milk in place of water and adding salad seasoning. Pour hot gravy over chicken mixture; mix until blended. Pour into 1-quart baking dish; top with remaining onions. Bake for 10 to 15 minutes or until heated through.

Mildred Arndt
Winona Senior High School
Winona, Minnesota

GINGER-CHICKEN SALAD

3 c. cooked cubed chicken
1/2 c. halved green grapes
1 c. diced celery
1/2 c. slivered almonds
1/4 c. shredded coconut
1/2 c. fresh or canned pineapple
   chunks
1/4 c. whipping cream
3/4 c. mayonnaise
1/4 tsp. ginger

Combine chicken, grapes, celery, almonds, coconut and pineapple chunks in large bowl. Whip cream until stiff peaks form. Fold mayonnaise into cream; stir in ground ginger. Pour over chicken mixture; mix lightly. Chill. May be served in scooped-out pineapple half.

Mrs. Linda K. McGregor
Twin Bridges High School
Twin Bridges, Montana

HAWAIIAN CHICKEN SALAD

1 pineapple
1 1/2 c. cubed cooked chicken
1 c. chopped celery
1 c. halved green grapes
1/2 c. chopped walnuts
3/4 c. mayonnaise
3/4 tsp. salt

Quarter pineapple lengthwise; remove and discard core. Remove pulp, leaving 1 inch on shells; cut pineapple pulp into cubes. Combine pineapple cubes with chicken, celery, grapes, walnuts, mayonnaise and salt; toss lightly. Place on pineapple quarters; garnish with maraschino cherries. Yield: 4-8 servings.

Maxine Loran
Struggs Junior High School
Lubbock, Texas

CHICKEN EVERY SUNDAY

1 1/2 c. diced cooked chicken breast
1/2 c. mayonnaise
2 hard-cooked eggs, diced
1 c. finely chopped celery
1/2 c. slivered almonds
1 tsp. grated onion
1/2 c. cracker crumbs
2 tsp. Worcestershire sauce
1/4 tsp. curry powder
1 c. crushed potato chips

Mix all ingredients in bowl except potato chips; pour into greased 2-quart baking dish. Sprinkle with potato chips. Bake at 350 degrees for 30 minutes. May be frozen. Yield: 4-6 servings.

Elizabeth P. Carlton
Huntsville Junior High School
Huntsville, Alabama

CALIFORNIA CHICKEN SALAD

4 c. diced chicken
2 c. diced celery
1 c. finely chopped pecans or
   walnuts
1 can cream of chicken soup
1 c. mayonnaise
2 c. cooked rice
2 green onions, chopped
6 hard-boiled eggs, chopped
1/2 c. buttered bread crumbs

Combine all ingredients except bread crumbs; place in buttered 3-quart casserole. Top with bread crumbs. Bake at 350 degrees for about 20 minutes.

Hazel C. Tassis
Imperial High School
El Centro, California

HOT CHICKEN-ALMOND SALAD

2 c. cubed cooked chicken
2 c. sliced celery
1/2 c. slivered almonds
2 tbsp. minced onion
2 tbsp. lemon juice
1 green pepper, chopped
1 tsp. salt
1 c. mayonnaise
1/2 c. light cream
3/4 c. crushed potato chips

2 tbsp. grated cheese
Paprika to taste

Mix chicken, celery, almonds, onion, lemon juice, green pepper, salt, mayonnaise and cream. Place in greased 1 1/2-quart casserole; cover with potato chips. Sprinkle with cheese, then with paprika. Bake in 350-degree oven for 30 minutes or until brown. Yield: 6 servings.

Mrs. Edna Earle Skinner
Wingo School
Wingo, Kentucky

HOT CHICKEN-CHEESE SALAD

3 c. cooked diced chicken
2 c. thinly sliced celery
1/2 c. slivered almonds
1/4 c. chopped olives
1 c. grated American cheese
1 1/4 c. mayonnaise
3 tbsp. lemon juice
2 tbsp. grated onion
1 tsp. salt
1/4 tsp. pepper
1 c. crushed potato chips

Combine chicken, celery, almonds, olives and 1/2 cup cheese. Blend mayonnaise with lemon juice, onion and seasonings; mix with chicken mixture. Place in greased casserole or individual ramekins. Mix potato chips and remaining cheese; sprinkle over chicken mixture. Bake at 375 degrees for 30 minutes or until heated through and lightly browned.

Mrs. James Gundersen
Mason County School
Scottville, Michigan

SEASONED CHICKEN SALAD

1 c. mayonnaise
2 tbsp. lemon juice
1/2 tsp. salt
1/2 tsp. Beau Monde seasoning
2 c. cooked diced chicken
2 c. diced celery
1/2 c. slivered toasted almonds
1/4 c. sliced green onions
1 c. crushed potato chips

Mix mayonnaise, lemon juice, salt and Beau Monde seasoning in large bowl. Add chicken, celery, almonds and green onions; stir until well mixed. Pour into ungreased 9 x 13 x 2-inch baking dish or 2-quart casserole. Bake, uncovered, in 450-degree oven for 10 to 15 minutes. Remove from oven; sprinkle potato chips on top. Bake for 5 minutes longer or until potato chips are golden brown; serve immediately. Yield: 6-8 servings.

Mrs. Virginia Richards
Dunbar High School
Lubbock, Texas

HOT CHICKEN SALAD
Third Place

4 whole chicken breasts
1/8 tsp. ginger
1/2 tsp. nutmeg
1/4 tsp. garlic powder
Pepper to taste
1/3 c. white cooking wine
3 tbsp. lemon juice
9 hard-cooked eggs, chopped
1/2 c. chopped onion
1/4 tsp. basil
1/4 tsp. rosemary
3/4 c. slivered almonds
2 cans cream of celery soup
1 can cream of chicken soup
1 1/2 c. mayonnaise
1 1/3 c. finely crushed potato
    chips

Place chicken breasts in baking pan; add ginger, 1/4 teaspoon nutmeg, garlic powder, pepper, wine and lemon juice. Bake at 325 degrees until tender; let chicken cool in pan juices. Remove chicken from bones; chop. Add eggs, onion, remaining nutmeg, basil, rosemary, almonds, soups, mayonnaise and 2/3 cup potato chips; place in baking dish. Sprinkle remaining potato chips on top. Bake at 350 degrees for 30 to 35 minutes. May be served as hot dip by heating after mixing and omitting 2/3 cup potato chip crumbs.

Mrs. Linda Bailey
Powhatan High School
Powhatan, Virginia

KASPER'S HOT CHICKEN SALAD

4 c. cooked chicken breasts,
    cut in chunks
2 c. chopped celery
3/4 c. mayonnaise
3/4 c. undiluted chicken soup
4 c. hard-cooked eggs, chopped
1 tsp. minced onion
1 tsp. salt
2 tbsp. lemon juice
2 pimentos, chopped
1 tsp. monosodium glutamate (opt.)
1 1/2 c. crushed potato chips
1 c. grated Velveeta cheese
2/3 c. finely chopped almonds

Mix chicken, celery, mayonnaise, soup, eggs, onion, salt, lemon juice, pimentos and monosodium glutamate; place in greased 12 x 14 x 2-inch baking dish. Add potato chips; sprinkle with cheese. Add almonds. Bake at 400 degrees for 20 to 25 minutes. Gravy made from melted cheese and mushroom soup may be served with salad, if desired. Yield: 6-8 servings.

Mrs. Willodean M. Hopkins
Central High School
North Little Rock, Arkansas

PARTY SALAD

2 c. cooked rice
2 c. cubed cooked chicken
2 c. chopped celery
2 tsp. minced onion
2 tbsp. lemon juice
1/2 tsp. salt
1/2 c. toasted almond slivers
1 c. salad dressing
1/2 c. grated American cheese
1 c. crushed potato chips

Combine all ingredients except cheese and potato chips; press into 9 x 13-inch pan. Sprinkle with cheese, then potato chips. Bake at 450 degrees for 10 minutes; serve hot. Garnish with parsley sprigs.

Mrs. Eleanor Ford
South Junior High School
Grand Forks, North Dakota

MANDARIN CHICKEN SALAD

1 c. macaroni rings
2 c. chopped cooked chicken
1 tbsp. minced onion
1 tsp. salt
1 c. green grapes
1 c. chopped celery
1 c. mandarin oranges
1/2 c. slivered almonds
1 c. salad dressing
1 c. cream, whipped

Cook macaroni according to package directions; drain. Allow to cool. Combine chicken, onion and salt. Chill for several hours. Combine grapes, celery, oranges, almonds, macaroni and salad dressing; toss to mix well. Combine chicken and macaroni mixtures; fold in whipped cream. Yield: 12 servings.

Mrs. Liz Nelson
Grandin School
Grandin, North Dakota

POLKA DOT CHICKEN SALAD

1 tbsp. lemon juice
2 c. diced Winesap apples
4 c. finely chopped cooked chicken
1 1/2 c. finely chopped celery
1 c. green grapes, cut in quarters
Salad dressing
3/4 tsp. salt
1/2 tsp. pepper
1 8-oz. package cream cheese,
    softened

Sprinkle lemon juice over apples. Add chicken, celery, grapes, 2/3 cup salad dressing and seasonings; mix lightly. Press into 1 1/2-quart bowl; chill for several hours. Unmold on serving platter. Combine cream cheese and 1/4 cup salad dressing, mixing until well blended; frost chicken salad. Garnish with grapes and lemon leaves. Yield: 8 servings.

Mrs. Barbara Doland Coatney
Alexandria Junior High School
Alexandria, Louisiana

OLIVE'S CHICKEN SALAD SUPREME

3 tbsp. salad oil
6 tbsp. lemon juice
1 tsp. salt
3 c. cooked cubed chicken
2 c. diced celery
5 hard-cooked eggs, sliced
1/2 c. chopped sweet pickles
1/4 c. mayonnaise
1/4 c. whipped cream

Mix oil, lemon juice and salt. Add chicken; marinate for at least 2 hours. Add celery, eggs and pickles. Mix mayonnaise and whipped cream. Add chicken mixture; toss well. Serve in lettuce cups or on shredded lettuce. Garnish with tomato wedges, olives and green peppers. May be used to stuff tomatoes.

Mrs. Olive Espe
Nesco Community School
Zearing, Iowa

FLYING FARMER CHICKEN SALAD

5 c. cooked chicken, cut in chunks
2 tbsp. salad oil
2 tbsp. orange juice
2 tbsp. vinegar
1 tsp. salt
3 c. cooked rice
1 1/2 c. small green grapes
1 1/2 c. sliced celery
1   13 1/2-oz. can pineapple tidbits,
*   drained*
1   11-oz. can mandarin oranges,
*   drained*
1 c. toasted slivered almonds
1 1/2 c. mayonnaise

Combine chicken, oil, orange juice, vinegar and salt; let stand while preparing remaining ingredients. May be refrigerated overnight. Add remaining ingredients; toss gently. Yield: 12 servings.

Ruth Baumback
North Douglas High School
Drain, Oregon

RICE-CHICKEN SALAD SUPREME

1 c. cooked instant rice
1/4 c. chopped green onion
1/2 c. finely chopped celery
1/2 tsp. salt
1/4 tsp. white pepper
3 c. cooked cubed chicken
1 sm. jar pimentos, finely chopped
1 1/2 c. salad dressing
1 c. cooked diced carrots
1 c. cooked string beans, cut into
*   1/2-in. lengths*

Combine all ingredients except carrots and green beans; mix in carrots and green beans carefully. Cover; chill. Serve in lettuce cups. May be spread lightly on bread for open-faced sandwiches. Each sandwich may be topped with slice of process cheese and broiled just until cheese melts.

Mrs. Barbara J. Suttner
Ridgway Community High School
Ridgway, Illinois

CHICKEN MAYONNAISE

1   4-lb. hen
1 c. tiny green peas
2 c. chopped celery
1/2 c. chopped pickles
1 c. chopped pecans
6 hard-boiled eggs, chopped
1 tbsp. unflavored gelatin
1 1/4 c. chicken broth
1 1/4 c. mayonnaise

Cook hen by roasting or stewing until tender; debone and chop. Combine chopped chicken, peas, celery, pickles, pecans and eggs in large bowl. Soften gelatin in 1/4 cup chicken broth. Bring remaining broth to a boil; pour over softened gelatin, stirring until dissolved. Combine gelatin and chicken mixture; stir in mayonnaise. Pour into glass baking dish; chill until firm. Cut in squares to serve.

Mrs. L. S. Burton
RSM Middle School
Ridge Spring, South Carolina

BROILED CHICKEN SANDWICHES

2 c. chopped cooked chicken
1/2 c. chopped celery
1/3 c. mayonnaise or salad
    dressing
1/4 c. chopped green pepper
1 tbsp. chopped onion
1 tbsp. lemon juice
Salt and pepper to taste
6 slices bread
Butter or margarine
Grated American cheese

Combine all ingredients except bread, butter and cheese in a bowl; mix well. Toast bread slices on one side; butter untoasted side. Spread chicken mixture on buttered side, covering all edges. Broil for about 3 minutes or till chicken mixture is thoroughly heated. Sprinkle with cheese; broil for one minute or till cheese is bubbly. Serve while warm. Yield: 6 servings.

Mrs. Eileen Lindley
Detroit High School
Detroit, Texas

CHICKEN SALAD FILLING

1/4 lb. American cheese, shredded
3 hard-cooked eggs, chopped
2 5-oz. cans boned chicken
2 tbsp. chopped green pepper
2 tbsp. chopped onion
2 tbsp. chopped stuffed olives
2 tbsp. chopped sweet pickles
1/2 c. salad dressing
Buns

Combine all ingredients except buns in large bowl; mix lightly. Fill buns. Bake in 350-degree oven for 25 to 30 minutes before serving. May be used cold with lettuce in sandwich. Store filling in refrigerator until ready to use.

Mrs. Clarence Anderson
Kingsley-Pierson Community School
Pierson, Iowa

CHICKEN SALAD BUNWICHES

2 c. cut-up chicken or turkey
1/2 c. diced celery
1/2 c. diced cheese
1/4 c. minced onion
1/2 tsp. salt
1/8 tsp. pepper
1/4 c. salad dressing or
    mayonnaise
1/4 tsp. celery salt
1 tbsp. lemon juice
8 hamburger buns, sliced and
    buttered

Preheat oven to 350 degrees. Place chicken, celery and cheese in a bowl. Combine onion, salt, pepper, salad dressing, celery salt and lemon juice; mix well. Combine dressing mixture with chicken mixture. Spread on buns. Wrap each bun in aluminum foil; place on an ungreased baking sheet. Bake for 20 to 30 minutes or until heated through.

Mrs. Ken G. Peterson
Lancaster High School
Lancaster, Minnesota

HOT CHICKEN SANDWICHES

1/4 lb. American cheese, cubed
3 hard-cooked eggs, cut up
1 c. chopped cooked chicken
1 tbsp. chopped green pepper
2 tbsp. chopped onion
3 stuffed olives, chopped
2 tbsp. pickle relish
1/2 c. mayonnaise or salad dressing
6 lg. buns

Combine all ingredients except buns in a bowl; mix thoroughly. Spread one side of each bun with chicken mixture; top with remaining side. Wrap buns individually in aluminum foil. Bake at 300 degrees for 15 minutes. May be made day ahead, stored in refrigerator and heated just before serving. Twelve small buns may be used, if desired.

Merilyn Ann Wey
LeRoy High School
LeRoy, Illinois

CHICKEN SWISS-WICHES

1 1/2 c. diced cooked chicken
1/3 c. mayonnaise
1/4 c. diced celery
1/4 c. diced process Swiss cheese
8 slices bread
1   14 1/2-oz. can asparagus spears
1/2 c. melted butter
1   2 3/8-oz. package seasoned
    coating mix for chicken

Combine chicken, mayonnaise, celery and cheese; mix well. Spread on 4 slices bread. Drain asparagus; place spears over filling on each bread slice. Top asparagus with remaining bread slices. Brush outside of sandwich with butter; coat with seasoned mix. Brown sandwiches on both sides in remaining butter on griddle or in skillet. Yield: 4 servings.

Elsie Klassen
George P. Vanier School
Donnelly, Alberta, Canada

CHICKEN SALAD SANDWICHES

2 c. chopped cooked chicken
1 c. chopped celery
2 tsp. salt
2 tsp. lemon juice
1 1/2 tbsp. ground chowchow
1/2 tsp. Worcestershire sauce
1/2 c. mayonnaise

Combine chicken, celery, salt, lemon juice, chowchow and Worcestershire sauce in a bowl. Add mayonnaise; mix to spreading consistency. Spread on favorite bread slices for sandwiches. Chopped chicken may be stored in freezer and used when needed. Yield: 13 sandwiches.

Mrs. Claudette N. Simoneaux
Plaquemine High School
Plaquemine, Louisiana

CHICKEN LIVERS CHASSEUR WITH RICE

1/2 lb. chicken livers
1/4 lb. onions, sliced
1 med. tomato, diced
1/4 c. sliced mushrooms
1/2 c. chicken bouillon
1/2 c. tomato juice
Dash of garlic powder
Salt and pepper to taste
1/2 c. cooked rice
1/2 tsp. chopped parsley

Cook livers and onions in nonstick skillet for about 5 minutes or until lightly browned. Add tomato, mushrooms, bouillon, tomato juice and garlic powder; cook over low heat for 10 minutes or until mixture thickens. Season with salt and pepper; serve over rice. Sprinkle with parsley. Yield: 2 servings.

Joan McCready
Missouri Valley High School
Missouri Valley, Iowa

CHICKEN LIVERS IN WINE

1 med. onion
2 tbsp. butter
1   4-oz. can mushrooms
1 lb. chicken livers
1/2 c. flour
1 tsp. salt
1/4 tsp. pepper
1/8 tsp. paprika
1/8 tsp. garlic powder
3 tbsp. vegetable oil
3/4 c. red wine

Slice onion; separate into rings. Melt butter in saucepan. Add onion and mushrooms; saute over low heat until onion is tender and transparent. Remove from heat; set aside. Rinse chicken livers in water; drain on paper toweling. Combine flour, salt, pepper, paprika and garlic powder in plastic bag. Heat oil in skillet, being careful not to let oil smoke. Place livers in plastic bag with flour mixture; shake until each is coated. Remove livers, shaking off excess flour; place in oil. Fry until lightly browned and crisp. Reduce heat; add onions and wine. Cover; simmer for 20 to 30 minutes.

Edie Hambright
Pocahontas Community School
Pocahontas, Iowa

CHICKEN LIVER CASSEROLE

1/2 lb. chicken livers
1 med. onion, chopped
3 stalks celery with leaves, chopped
1 tsp. chopped parsley
2 tbsp. margarine
1/2 tsp. basil
1/2 tsp. thyme
1/2 tsp. salt
Pepper to taste
1 can cream of chicken soup
2 c. cooked rice

Clean, wash and drain livers. Cook onion, celery and parsley in margarine until soft. Add livers; cook until brown. Add remaining ingredients; stir well. Place in greased casserole. Bake at 350 degrees for 30 minutes.

Mary Anne Guender
Garnet Valley High School
Concordville, Pennsylvania

CREAMED CHICKEN LIVERS

4 slices bacon
2 tbsp. all-purpose flour
Dash of pepper
1/2 lb. chicken livers
1 tbsp. chopped onion
1 can cream of mushroom soup
1/4 c. water
1 c. hot cooked rice

Fry bacon in skillet till crisp. Remove from skillet; drain, reserving drippings. Combine flour and pepper. Coat livers with flour mixture; brown livers and onion in 2 tablespoons reserved bacon drippings. Cover; cook over low heat for 8 to 10 minutes. Blend soup with water; stir into liver mixture. Heat through. Spoon over rice; top with bacon strips. Yield: 2 servings.

Kathryn G. Motsinger
Central High School
Winston-Salem, North Carolina

CHEESY CHICKEN BAKE

6 oz. sharp Cheddar cheese
1 8-oz. package cream cheese
1 tbsp. butter or margarine
1 tbsp. flour
1 1/3 c. milk
1 4-oz. jar whole pimentos
1 lg. onion, sliced
1 med. green pepper, diced
1 tbsp. parsley flakes
1 tsp. salt
1/2 tsp. pepper
3 c. cooked chopped chicken
3/4 c. crushed potato chips
Parmesan cheese
Paprika

Cut Cheddar cheese in small chunks. Allow cream cheese to soften at room temperature. Melt butter in saucepan; stir in flour to make a paste. Add 1 cup milk slowly. Add Cheddar cheese, stirring occasionally until cheese is melted. Combine remaining milk and cream cheese in deep bowl; cream with electric mixer. Add to cheese sauce. Cut pimentos in long thin strips. Add onion, green pepper, pimentos, parsley, salt, pepper and chicken to cheese sauce; mix well. Pour mixture into casserole. Sprinkle potato chips over top; shake Parmesan cheese and paprika lightly over chips. Dot with additional butter; cover. Bake at 350 degrees for 1 hour.

Shirley A. Osborne
Groveton High School
Groveton, New Hampshire

BONELESS CHICKEN CACCIATORE SUPREME

3 tbsp. cooking oil
2 sm. onions, chopped fine
1 med. green pepper, chopped fine
1/8 tsp. garlic salt
1 2 1/2 to 3-lb. cooked chicken, cut up
1 1/4 tsp. salt
1/8 tsp. pepper
1/4 tsp. oregano
1/4 tsp. celery flakes
2 tbsp. chopped parsley
2 bay leaves
1 16-oz. can tomatoes, chopped
1 8-oz. can tomato sauce
1 10-oz. can tomato soup

Preheat oil in frying pan to 340 degrees. Add onions, green pepper and garlic salt; cook for 5 minutes. Add chicken, seasonings, tomatoes, tomato sauce and tomato soup; mix well. Reduce heat to about 240 degrees; let simmer for about 1 hour, stirring occasionally. Serve plain or with spaghetti or elbow or shell macaroni.

Sandra Lord
Old Orchard Beach High School
Old Orchard Beach, Maine

CHICKARONI A LA ORANGE

1 pkg. chicken Rice-A-Roni
2 tbsp. margarine
1 c. orange juice
1 orange
3 c. cooked shredded chicken
2 cans cream of mushroom soup
Salt and pepper to taste

Brown Rice-A-Roni in margarine according to package directions. Substitute 1 cup orange juice for 1 cup water; follow remaining directions on package. Grate 1 orange with peeling in blender; add to rice. Combine rice, chicken, soup, salt and pepper; mix well. Place in greased casserole. Bake at 350 degrees for 35 to 45 minutes or until mixture begins to bubble. Remove from oven; serve. May be placed in chafing dish and garnished with twisted slices of orange and parsley sprigs.

Mrs. Linda K. Turner
Hibberd Junior High School
Richmond, Indiana

CHICKEN BALLS

6 to 8 slices day-old bread
4 tbsp. butter
3 tbsp. flour
1 1/3 c. milk or chicken broth
2 c. cooked chopped chicken
1 tbsp. chopped parsley
Salt and pepper to taste
1 egg, beaten
1 3-lb. can shortening
1 can mushroom soup
1/2 c. mushrooms

Remove crusts from bread; pull bread into 1/2-inch cubes with fingers. Melt 2 tablespoons butter in saucepan. Add flour; stir until well blended. Add 1 cup milk slowly; cook over medium heat until thickened, stirring frequently. Cool. Add chicken and seasonings; mix well. Chill for 2 to 3 hours. Shape into 4 or 5 balls. Roll in egg, then in bread. Return balls to refrigerator; let stand for 2 to 3 hours or until coating has dried. Heat shortening in deep fat fryer to 375 degrees. Fry Chicken Balls in shortening until brown. Drain on absorbent paper. Place mushroom soup, remaining butter, mushrooms and remaining milk in saucepan; bring to boiling point. Serve with Chicken Balls. Chicken Balls may be frozen; remove from freezer about 1 hour before frying. Tuna may be substituted for chicken.

Charlotte Chafin
Nolan Junior High School
Killeen, Texas

CHICKEN-BROCCOLI DELIGHT

1 chicken
2 pkg. chopped broccoli
2 sticks margarine
2 cans cream of chicken soup
1/2 c. mayonnaise
1 1/2 tsp. lemon juice
1 c. bread crumbs
1/2 pkg. stuffing mix

Simmer chicken in water until tender; drain. Bone chicken; cut into bite-sized pieces. Cook broccoli according to package directions; drain off liquid. Melt 1 1/2 sticks margarine. Add soup, mayonnaise and lemon juice; mix thoroughly. Melt remaining margarine; mix with bread crumbs. Place alternate layers of chicken, broccoli, stuffing mix and soup mixture in 13 x 9 x 2-inch pan or large casserole, ending with soup mixture. Top with buttered crumbs. Bake at 350 degrees for 20 to 30 minutes or until bubbly and golden brown. Yield: 10-12 servings.

Mrs. Anita Himbury
Shidler High School
Shidler, Oklahoma

CHICKEN-BRAZIL NUT CASSEROLE

1 c. chopped celery
1 c. chopped Brazil nuts
1/4 c. chopped onions
1 c. Chinese noodles
1 can cream of chicken soup
1 c. milk
2 c. chopped cooked chicken
1 can mushrooms
2 tbsp. chopped pimento

Combine celery, Brazil nuts, onions, 3/4 cup Chinese noodles, soup, milk, chicken, mushrooms and pimento; spoon into 2-quart casserole. Bake at 300 degrees for 45 minutes. Sprinkle remaining Chinese noodles on top; bake for 15 minutes longer.

Mrs. Betty G. Brant
Shanksville Stonycreek High School
Shanksville, Pennsylvania

CHICKEN CASHEW

1 whole chicken breast
Powdered ginger to taste
1/2 tsp. salt
1/4 tsp. monosodium glutamate
3 tbsp. salad oil
1 clove of garlic, thinly sliced
1/2 c. diagonally sliced celery
1/2 c. green onions, cut in 1-in.
  pieces
1/2 tsp. sugar
1 sm. can water chestnuts, sliced
2 tsp. cornstarch
1/2 c. water or chicken broth
1 tbsp. soy sauce
1 tsp. bottled browning sauce
1/2 c. salted cashew nuts

Remove chicken from bone; cut into bite-sized pieces. Sprinkle chicken with ginger, salt and monosodium glutamate. Heat oil in heavy skillet; add chicken. Cook until chicken loses pink color; do not brown. Add garlic, celery and onions; sprinkle with sugar. Cook for 5 minutes; vegetables should retain crispness. Add chestnuts; continue to stir. Combine cornstarch, water, soy sauce, browning sauce and cashew nuts; pour over chicken mixture. Serve with hot rice and seasoned snow peas.

Mrs. Rowena Hardinger
Lincoln Middle School
Albia, Iowa

CHICKEN-CHEESE SCALLOP

1 hen
1 c. grated American cheese
1 can mushroom soup
1 onion, minced
3 eggs, beaten
1 c. chopped celery
4 round buttery crackers, crumbled
Salt and pepper to taste

Cook hen in boiling salted water until tender. Remove from broth, reserving broth. Remove and discard skin and bones; cut up chicken. Combine chicken, cheese, soup, onion, eggs, celery, cracker crumbs, salt and pepper and enough chicken broth to moisten thoroughly. Pour into lightly greased 9 by 13-inch baking dish. Bake at 350 degrees for 20 to 30 minutes or until thick and light brown.

Irene M. Storrer
Linn High School
Linn, Kansas

CHICKEN-CHESTNUT CASSEROLE

2 cans whole green beans, drained
3 cooked chicken breasts, shredded
3/4 c. mayonnaise
2 tsp. lemon juice
1/2 tsp. curry powder
1 sm. can sliced water chestnuts
2 cans cream of chicken soup
1/2 c. shredded sharp Cheddar cheese

Arrange beans in greased shallow baking dish. Mix chicken with remaining ingredients except cheese; place over beans. Sprinkle cheese over top. Bake at 350 degrees for 30 minutes or until bubbly. Yield: 6 servings.

Mrs. Betty J. Roose
Carmel High School
Carmel, Indiana

CHICKEN AND CHIP CASSEROLE

2 c. frozen peas
2 cans cream of mushroom soup
1 c. milk
2 c. cooked diced chicken
2 1/2 c. crushed potato chips

Cook peas according to package directions; drain. Mix soup and milk. Add chicken, 2 cups potato chips and peas; mix lightly. Pour into buttered 2-quart baking dish; sprinkle remaining potato chips over top. Bake at 350 degrees for 30 minutes or until golden brown. Yield: 8 servings.

Carolyn Reif
Western Dubuque High School
Epworth, Iowa

CHICKEN MAME

1 tsp. lemon juice
1/2 c. mayonnaise
1 can cream of chicken soup
1 c. yogurt
2 pkg. chopped broccoli, cooked
4 c. cooked chopped chicken
1/2 c. bread crumbs
1/2 c. grated Parmesan cheese

Combine lemon juice, mayonnaise, soup and yogurt. Spread broccoli in bottom of buttered 6 x 12-inch baking dish; pour yogurt mixture over broccoli. Place chicken on broccoli; sprinkle bread crumbs and cheese over chicken. Bake at 350 degrees for 25 minutes. Yield: 8 servings.

Mary Ann Mabry
Fernandina Beach Junior High School
Fernandina Beach, Florida

CHICKEN ENCHILADA PIE

1 3-lb. chicken
1 can cream of mushroom soup
1 can cream of chicken soup
1 4-oz. can chopped green chilies
1 tsp. chili powder
4 tsp. minced onion
1/8 tsp. garlic powder
1/4 tsp. pepper
1/4 tsp. hot sauce
4 c. corn chips
2 c. grated sharp Cheddar cheese

Cook chicken in boiling, salted water until tender. Drain chicken; reserve 1 cup broth. Cool chicken; remove chicken from bones. Combine soups, green chilies, chili powder, onion, garlic powder, pepper, hot sauce and reserved chicken broth; blend well. Cover bottom of 2 1/2 or 3-quart casserole with 2 cups corn chips; spread half the chicken over corn chips. Add half the soup mixture; add half the cheese. Repeat layers, ending with cheese. Bake at 350 degrees for 25 to 30 minutes.

Mary S. Bonner
University Junior High School
Waco, Texas

CHICKEN CUSTARD

1 5-lb. hen
6 c. bread crumbs
3 1/2 c. milk
6 eggs
1 1/2 c. flour

Cook hen in 3 to 4 cups boiling water until tender. Remove skin; grind with bread crumbs. Bone hen; cut into bite-sized pieces. Combine 3 1/2 cups broth and milk in saucepan; heat. Separate 2 eggs; beat 4 eggs and 2 egg whites until light. Combine eggs and flour in bowl; add small amount of hot liquid, stirring constantly. Add remaining liquid, stirring until smooth. Cool. Combine remaining egg yolks and ground bread crumb mixture. Place half the crumb mixture in baking dish; cover with half the custard mixture. Add hen in layer; cover with remaining custard mixture. Top with remaining crumb mixture. Bake at 350 degrees for 1 hour or until brown and bubbly.

Mrs. Donna Walter
Central Heights School
Richmond, Kansas

CHICKEN GALA

1   4-lb. stewing hen
1 tbsp. salt
1/2 tsp. pepper
1/2 c. flour
6 tbsp. chopped pimento
2 tbsp. lemon juice
1/2 tsp. celery seed
1/2 c. chopped water chestnuts
1 c. canned bean sprouts, drained
1 c. crushed sesame seed crackers
2 tbsp. melted butter

Cook hen in boiling water with salt and pepper until tender. Drain chicken; reserve 3 cups broth. Cool, bone and dice chicken in 2-inch pieces; set aside. Bring reserved broth to a boil. Mix flour with 1/2 cup water until smooth; stir into broth. Cook until thick, stirring constantly; set aside to cool slightly. Place half the chicken in 9 x 12-inch casserole. Mix pimento, lemon juice, celery seed, water chestnuts and bean sprouts; place half the pimento mixture over chicken. Add 1 1/2 cups thickened broth. Repeat layers. Mix sesame seed cracker crumbs with melted butter; sprinkle over casserole. Bake at 350 degrees for 30 minutes. Let stand for 15 minutes; cut in squares to serve.

Mrs. Armetta Watson
Mayberry Junior High School
Wichita, Kansas

CHICKEN TOWERS

2 c. diced cooked chicken
1/2 c. diced celery
1/2 c. minced onions
1 can mushroom pieces and stems
1 can cream of celery soup
1/2 c. milk
1/2 c. sliced almonds
1 recipe biscuit dough
Melted butter
Fine bread crumbs

Combine chicken, celery, onions, mushrooms, soup, milk and almonds; place in greased 9 x 13-inch casserole or baking pan.

Bake at 400 degrees for 20 to 25 minutes or until bubbly. Knead dough 8 to 10 times, then roll 1/2 inch thick. Cut equal amounts of biscuits with 2 1/2 to 3-inch cutter and a smaller cutter such as doughnut hole cutter or juice glass. Dip each biscuit in butter and roll in crumbs. Put two sizes together and place each set on hot, bubbly casserole. There should be about 12 towers. Bake for 10 to 15 minutes or until biscuits are golden brown. One can sliced olives, 2 hard-cooked eggs, chopped, and 1/2 cup grated sharp Cheddar cheese may be added to chicken mixture, if desired.

Joan Hoech
Curtis High School
Tacoma, Washington

CHICKEN SUPREME

5 chicken breasts
3 tbsp. butter
1/2 green pepper, sliced
1 stalk celery, sliced
1 sm. onion, sliced
4 tbsp. flour
1/2 c. chopped ripe olives
2 pimentos, sliced
1   4-oz. can sliced mushrooms
1 c. light cream
1 tsp. salt
1/2 c. grated Swiss cheese
1/2 c. slivered almonds

Cook chicken breasts in enough water to cover until tender; drain, reserving broth. Bone and skin chicken, leaving chicken in large chunks. Melt butter in saucepan. Add green pepper, celery and onion; cook for several minutes or until vegetables are limp. Stir in flour until smooth. Add 2 cups reserved chicken broth; cook until bubbly. Add olives, pimentos, mushrooms, cream, salt and cheese. Cook, stirring constantly, until heated through. Arrange chicken in greased casserole. Pour sauce over chicken; sprinkle with almonds. Bake at 350 degrees for 30 minutes. Yield: 6-8 servings.

Mrs. A. David Buehler
Mainland Senior High School
Daytona Beach, Florida

ROAST PORK WITH SAUERKRAUT AND APPLE

1   3 1/2-lb. pork loin roast
Onion salt to taste
Marjoram to taste
Pepper to taste
1 qt. drained sauerkraut
2 red apples, thinly sliced
1/2 c. apple brandy
1 tbsp. light brown sugar
2 tbsp. butter

Sprinkle pork with onion salt, marjoram and pepper; score fatty side. Secure on spit. Insert meat thermometer. Adjust spit about 8 inches from prepared coals, placing foil pan under pork to catch drippings. Roast for 15 to 20 minutes per pound or until meat thermometer registers 185 degrees. Place on heated serving platter; keep warm. Combine sauerkraut, apple slices, brandy, brown sugar and butter in skillet. Simmer, covered, for 5 minutes or until apples are tender. Spoon into serving dish. Garnish with additional apple slices and parsley. Serve with pork.

Photograph for this recipe on page 67.

FILBERT TORTE WITH STRAWBERRY WHIPPED CREAM

Graham cracker crumbs
2 c. sugar
1/2 tsp. ground allspice
1 lb. filberts, ground
1 tsp. grated lemon peel
6 eggs, separated
1/4 tsp. salt
1 tbsp. light corn syrup
1 tsp. water
1 egg white, slightly beaten

Grease 9-inch 6 1/2-cup ring pan; sprinkle with graham cracker crumbs. Set aside. Mix sugar and allspice together; mix in filberts and lemon peel with tossing motion. Beat egg yolks until thick and lemon colored; blend into filbert mixture, working in well with hands. Beat egg whites until frothy; add salt. Beat until stiff but not dry; fold into filbert mixture. Turn into prepared ring pan. Bake at 350 degrees for 35 to 40 minutes or until cake tests done. Cool for 5 minutes. Loosen cake with spatula; turn out onto ungreased baking sheet. Blend corn syrup and water; brush over top of torte. Brush entire torte with egg white. Bake for 5 minutes longer. Cool; place torte on serving plate.

Strawberry Whipped Cream

2 pt. fresh strawberries
1 1/2 c. heavy cream
3 tbsp. kirsch

Slice strawberries, reserving 1 cup for garnish. Whip cream until stiff, adding kirsch gradually. Fold in sliced strawberries. Mound in center of torte; garnish with reserved strawberries.

Photograph for this recipe on page 67.

HOT POTATO SALAD WITH BACON

4 lb. pared potatoes, sliced
1/2 c. chopped onion
2/3 c. bacon drippings
1/2 c. vinegar
2 tbsp. chopped parsley
2 tsp. sugar
1 tsp. paprika
1/2 tsp. salt
1/4 tsp. pepper
12 slices fried bacon, crumbled

Cook potatoes in saucepan in 2 inches salted water until tender; drain. Saute onion in bacon drippings until tender; stir in vinegar, parsley, sugar, paprika, salt and pepper. Combine potatoes, bacon, and onion mixture. Toss gently. Serve warm with pork roast and sauerkraut.

Photograph for this recipe on page 67.

GRILLED CHICKEN WITH KRAUT RELISH

6 c. sauerkraut
1 4-oz. jar pimento
2 med. green peppers, chopped
2 med. onions, chopped
1/4 tsp. paprika
Freshly ground pepper to taste
1 clove of garlic, minced
1/2 c. melted butter
1/4 c. wine vinegar
1/2 c. (firmly packed) dark brown
  sugar
2 tbsp. Worcestershire sauce
2 tbsp. cornstarch
1/4 c. water
12 chicken legs with thighs

Drain the sauerkraut and reserve liquid. Drain the pimento and chop. Toss sauerkraut with green peppers, pimento, half the onions, paprika and pepper in a bowl and chill. Saute remaining onion and the garlic in butter in a saucepan until golden. Add the vinegar, sugar, Worcestershire sauce, pepper and reserved sauerkraut liquid and stir until sugar is melted. Bring to a boil over medium heat. Blend the cornstarch with water and stir into onion mixture. Boil for 30 seconds, stirring constantly, then remove from heat. Place chicken on grill 7 to 8 inches from source of heat; cook for 10 minutes. Brush with sauce and continue grilling for 10 minutes. Turn chicken and grill an additional 10 minutes or until done, brushing frequently with sauce to glaze. Serve kraut relish with grilled chicken.

Photograph for this recipe on page 68.

OLD-FASHIONED STRAWBERRY SHORTCAKE

2 c. sifted all-purpose flour
4 tsp. baking powder
1/2 tsp. salt
1/2 tsp. cream of tartar
1/4 c. sugar
1/2 c. vegetable shortening
1/3 c. milk
1 egg
Butter
3 pt. fresh California strawberries,
  sliced and sweetened
Whipped cream

Sift flour, baking powder, salt, cream of tartar and sugar together. Cut in shortening until mixture resembles coarse meal. Combine milk with egg; stir into flour mixture with a fork until soft dough is formed. Turn out onto lightly floured board and pat or roll into 8-inch circle 1/2 inch thick. Place on ungreased baking sheet. Bake in preheated 425-degree oven for 10 to 12 minutes or until golden brown. Split and spread butter on both halves. Pile strawberries and whipped cream between layers and on top. Yield: 8 servings.

Photograph for this recipe on page 68.

CHINESE CHICKEN DELIGHT

4 chicken breasts
2 egg whites
1/2 tsp. salt
1/2 tsp. monosodium glutamate
Dash of pepper
Cooking oil
1/2 tsp. ground ginger
1/2 c. carrot sticks
1/2 c. celery sticks
1/2 c. sliced green onions
1/2 c. cashew nuts

Remove bones from chicken. Cut chicken into bite-sized pieces; place on board. Pound lightly. Beat egg whites until frothy; add salt, monosodium glutamate and pepper. Beat for several seconds. Add chicken pieces; mix until all pieces are coated with egg white mixture. Heat 5 tablespoons oil in 10-inch skillet; add ginger. Add chicken when oil is hot but not smoking. Chicken should turn white immediately if oil is hot enough. Stir gently. Cook for about 4 minutes. Remove the chicken from skillet. Maintain high heat, adding 2 tablespoons oil, if needed; add carrots. Saute for about 2 minutes. Add celery and green onions; cook for 3 to 5 minutes.

Vegetables should remain crisp. Return chicken to skillet; mix lightly until chicken is hot. Add cashews; serve over warm Chinese noodles. May be served over steamed rice. White pepper may be added to egg whites.

Mrs. Sue Stilley
Forestburg High School
Forestburg, Texas

CHINESE-FRIED CHICKEN IN SWEET-SOUR SAUCE

4 chicken breasts
2 cloves of garlic, minced
1/2 tsp. powdered ginger
1/2 tsp. salt
3/4 tsp. pepper
1 egg, beaten
3/4 c. flour
1 c. salad oil
Sweet-Sour Sauce

Remove bones from chicken breasts. Pound and slice into thin strips about 1 by 1 1/2 inches. Combine garlic, ginger, salt, pepper, egg and flour in a bowl. Add sliced chicken; stir until chicken slices are thoroughly coated. Heat oil in electric frypan at 350 degrees or heat oil in frypan on top of stove to 350 degrees. Drop chicken slices in hot oil; fry for about 10 minutes or until golden brown on both sides. Drain on paper towels, then stir into Sweet-Sour Sauce. Heat sauce and chicken slices for 15 minutes on medium heat or until sauce is heated through. Serve over hot rice.

Sweet-Sour Sauce

2 stalks celery
2 lg. carrots
1 green pepper
1 c. (firmly packed) brown sugar
1 c. vinegar
1 1-lb. can stewed tomatoes
1/2 c. cornstarch
1/8 tsp. salt

Slice celery and carrots crosswise into sections about 1/4 inch wide. Cut green pepper into long thin strips. Place in 1 quart boiling water; boil, uncovered, for 10 minutes or until carrots are tender. Drain and set vegetables aside. Bring 1 1/2 cups water to a boil in large saucepan. Add brown sugar; cook for 1 minute. Add vinegar and stewed tomatoes with juice; cook for 1 minute. Place cornstarch in small bowl; stir in 1 cup water gradually. Bring tomato mixture to a boil; add cornstarch mixture slowly. Boil and stir for 3 minutes. Stir in salt, carrots, celery and green pepper.

Mrs. Janet Trigg
Hawthorne Junior High School
Wauwatosa, Wisconsin

COMPANY CREAMED CHICKEN

4 tbsp. butter
1/2 c. flour
1 1/2 tsp. salt
1/4 tsp. pepper
2 c. half and half
1 c. cream
1 c. chicken broth
2 1/2 c. cooked diced chicken breasts
1/4 c. chopped pimento
1/2 c. diced green pepper
1/4 lb. mushrooms, chopped
1/4 c. cream sherry

Melt butter in saucepan; blend in flour, salt and pepper. Add half and half, cream and broth. Cook, stirring constantly, until sauce is of medium consistency. Add chicken, pimento, green pepper and mushrooms. Stir until thoroughly blended and heated through. Add sherry just before serving. Serve in patty shells or tart shells. Garnish with pimento bits and sprig of parsley. The green pepper may be cooked in the chicken broth until tender and removed for broth to be used in white sauce. This dish may be prepared ahead, placed in the freezer, and kept for 2 to 3 months. A small amount of sherry may be added before reheating.

Mrs. Idelle P. Tucker
Herbert Spaugh Junior High School
Charlotte, North Carolina

CHINESE CHICKEN WITH PEANUTS

2 lb. chicken breasts
4 tsp. cornstarch
1 egg white
3 tbsp. soy sauce
2 green peppers
2 lg. onions
1 garlic clove
1 tsp. sesame oil (opt.)
1 tsp. sugar
1/2 tsp. salt
1 tbsp. wine (opt.)
1/4 c. salad oil
1/2 to 2 red peppers (opt.)
1 c. roasted peanuts

Remove bone from chicken; cut chicken into 1-inch cubes. Mix 3 teaspoons cornstarch, egg white and 1 tablespoon soy sauce. Add chicken; marinate for at least 1 hour. Remove seeds from green peppers; cut green pepper into 1-inch cubes. Blanch. Cut onions into quarters; separate layers. Slice garlic clove. Mix remaining soy sauce, remaining cornstarch, sesame oil, sugar, salt and wine; set aside. Heat salad oil in wok or electric frypan until very hot. Fry garlic in oil until golden; remove and discard. Fry chicken in oil for 4 minutes, stirring constantly; add onions, green peppers, red peppers and peanuts. Add salt mixture; cook, stirring, until thick. Serve with rice.

Marion Croizier
Rochester School Number 22
Rochester, New York

CHICKEN AND CREPES

1 c. pancake mix
2 eggs
1 c. milk
2 tbsp. oil
6 tbsp. butter
1 c. chopped celery
1 c. chopped onion
1 clove of garlic, crushed
1/4 c. chopped green pepper
1 c. sliced water chestnuts
1/2 tsp. monosodium glutamate
1/2 tsp. salt
Dash of pepper
1/4 c. flour
1 tbsp. soy sauce
2 c. chicken broth
3 c. shredded cooked chicken
2 c. bean sprouts
1/2 c. toasted slivered almonds

Combine pancake mix, eggs, milk and oil in blender container; blend until smooth. Grease 5 or 6-inch frypan lightly; heat until hot. Pour about 3 tablespoons batter into frypan; tip until bottom is entirely coated. Fry until golden brown on both sides. Store between layers of waxed paper. Crepes may be made ahead of time; store between layers of waxed paper. Wrap in foil; store in freezer or refrigerator. Melt butter in large frypan. Saute celery, onion, garlic, green pepper and water chestnuts in butter until onion is tender-crisp. Add monosodium glutamate, salt and pepper. Add flour; mix well. Add soy sauce and chicken broth; cook stirring, until thick. Add chicken, bean sprouts and almonds; simmer for 5 minutes. Spoon 1/2 cup chicken mixture into center of each crepe; fold over. Place in baking dish, seam side down. Bake at 325 degrees for 30 minutes. Bake for 15 minutes if crepes are warm. Yield: 18 crepes.

Cheryl Drewel
Roosevelt High School
Seattle, Washington

CHICKEN CREPES AU GRATIN

3 tbsp. butter
3 tbsp. flour
1/2 tsp. salt
1 1/4 c. milk

Melt butter in saucepan; blend in flour and salt. Stir in milk gradually. Cook over medium heat, stirring constantly, until thickened. Remove from heat; cover. Set aside.

Filling

2 tbsp. chopped green onion
1   4 1/2-oz. can sliced mushrooms, drained

2 tbsp. butter
2 c. finely diced cooked chicken
2 tbsp. chopped pimento
Salt and pepper to taste

Saute onion and mushrooms in butter in saucepan until onion is tender. Add chicken and pimento; cook for 1 minute longer. Add 1/2 cup white sauce, stirring just until blended. Remove from heat; add salt and pepper. Refrigerate until ready to use.

Crepes

3/4 c. flour
1/4 tsp. salt
1 1/4 c. milk
Salad oil
1 egg
1 egg yolk

Combine flour, salt and 1/2 cup milk in a bowl. Beat mixture, adding 1 tablespoon salad oil, egg and egg yolk. Beat until well blended. Refrigerate for 2 to 24 hours. Stir in remaining milk gradually when ready to cook crepes. Batter is consistency of cream. Brush pan lightly all over with oil; set over high heat until oil almost smokes. Remove from heat; pour 1/3 cup batter in middle of pan. Tilt pan all around to cover bottom with thin film of batter. Pour out any excess. Return pan to heat; cook for about 1 minute or until batter forms tiny bubbles and begins to leave side of pan. Turn with spatula when golden brown underneath; cook remaining side for about 30 seconds. The first side is the outside. Slide onto plate. Arrange crepes with first side down. Spoon 1 heaping tablespoon Filling down center of each crepe; fold sides over Filling. Arrange in buttered 9 by 13-inch baking dish; cover with foil. Bake at 350 degrees for 20 to 25 minutes or until heated through.

Topping

1/2 c. mayonnaise
1/4 c. whipping cream, whipped
Parmesan cheese

Combine remaining white sauce and mayonnaise; mix well. Fold in whipped cream. Uncover hot crepes. Spoon Topping over crepes; sprinkle with Parmesan cheese. Broil 4 to 6 inches from heat until brown. Crepes may be prepared and filled ahead, covered with foil and refrigerated. White sauce and mayonnaise may be combined and refrigerated. Whipped cream may be folded into topping just before serving and broiled.

Mrs. Jane K. Marsh
Delta Senior Secondary School
Delta British Columbia, Canada

CREPES FLORENTINE

1 3/4 c. flour
1 1/2 tsp. salt
3 eggs, beaten
3 1/2 c. milk
1/4 c. butter
1 tsp. dry mustard
1 tsp. Worcestershire sauce
1 10-oz. package frozen spinach
2 c. cooked diced chicken
1 c. sharp American cheese,
   shredded

Sift 1 1/2 cups flour and 1/2 teaspoon salt together. Combine eggs and 1 1/2 cups milk. Add to flour mixture; beat until smooth. Pour enough into hot, lightly buttered 6 or 7-inch skillet to cover bottom of skillet; cook until browned on both sides. Remove from skillet. Cook remaining batter; separate each crepe with sheet of waxed paper. Keep warm. Melt butter in saucepan; blend in remaining flour, mustard, remaining salt and Worcestershire sauce. Add remaining milk; cook, stirring constantly, until thick. Cook spinach according to package directions; drain. Blend 3/4 cup sauce with chicken and spinach. Fill each crepe with 1 heaping tablespoon filling; roll up. Place crepes in shallow 13 x 9-inch baking dish, seam side down. Pour remaining sauce over crepes; top with cheese. Bake at 350 degrees for 20 minutes or until heated thoroughly.

Mrs. Mary Jane Kline
Thomas S. Wootton High School
Rockville, Maryland

CHICKEN-COCONUT CURRY

2 1/2 c. milk
6 c. grated coconut
1 tsp. sugar
10 tbsp. flour
2 tbsp. curry powder
1 sm. clove of garlic, chopped
1 3/4-in. piece of gingerroot,
    chopped
2 lg. onions, chopped
2 c. chicken stock
2 c. cooked chopped chicken
Salt to taste
8 c. cooked rice
2 c. mango chutney
1/2 lb. cooked bacon, chopped
9 green onions, chopped
1 c. chopped peanuts
1 c. raisins

Bring milk to a boil; remove from heat. Add 2 cups coconut; let stand for 1 hour to 1 hour and 30 minutes. Drain milk; discard coconut. Mix sugar, flour, curry powder, garlic, gingerroot, onions and chicken stock; simmer for 1 hour. Add chicken; bring to a boil. Add salt and additional curry powder, if needed. Mixture will be thick; mixture will separate if salt is added too soon. Add 2 cups coconut milk; heat through. Serve with rice and condiments of chutney, remaining coconut, bacon, green onions, peanuts and raisins. Yield: 8 servings.

Mrs. Diane Manono May
Gove Junior High School
Denver, Colorado

MAINE CURRY-CHICKEN

1 4 to 5-lb. chicken
Garlic salt to taste
Celery salt to taste
Bay leaves to taste
Salt and pepper to taste
3 or 4 med. onions, peeled
2 pkg. frozen broccoli spears
2 cans cream of celery soup
1 c. mayonnaise
1/4 c. lemon juice
5 tsp. curry powder

Boil chicken in water with garlic salt, celery salt, bay leaves, salt, pepper and whole onions until done. Remove chicken from bone; cut into large pieces. Cook broccoli according to package directions until half done; place in bottom of buttered 9 x 13-inch pan. Place chicken over broccoli. Mix soup, mayonnaise, lemon juice and curry powder; pour over chicken. Bake at 350 degrees for 30 minutes; serve hot. Garnish with pimento strips, if desired.

Mrs. Pauline Webster
Mattanawcook Academy
Lincoln, Maine

QUICK CHICKEN CURRY

2 chicken bouillon cubes
1 5-oz. can boned chicken
1 tbsp. instant minced onion
1 4-oz. can sliced mushrooms
1/2 tsp. salt
1/2 tsp. pepper
1 tsp. (about) curry powder
4 tsp. cornstarch

Dissolve bouillon cubes in 2 cups water in a saucepan; bring to a boil. Cut chicken into small pieces; add to bouillon. Add onion, mushrooms, salt, pepper and curry powder; cover. Simmer for 5 minutes. Mix cornstarch and 1/4 cup water; stir into onion mixture. Cook, stirring, until clear and thickened. More cornstarch mixed with water may be added if thicker sauce is desired. Serve over hot rice with condiments of coconut, chopped peanuts, chutney and raisins. Yield: 4-6 servings.

Marilyn Davis
Redmond High School
Richmond, Oregon

SPICY CHICKEN CURRY

1 med. chicken
1/2 tsp. chili powder
1/2 tsp. curry powder
1/4 tsp. turmeric
1/4 tsp. cinnamon
1/8 tsp. salt

3 tbsp. cooking oil
1 c. diced or sliced onions
1/2 tsp. dry mustard
1 c. cream
1 tbsp. lemon juice
Cooked wild rice
1 c. chopped walnuts

Cook chicken in boiling water until tender; drain and cool. Remove chicken skin; remove chicken from bone. Cut up enough chicken to measure 2 to 3 cups; place in 1-quart bowl. Add chili powder, curry powder, turmeric, cinnamon, and salt; mix well. Heat oil in large, deep frypan; add onions. Cook over low heat, stirring, until onions are light brown; drain off most of the excess fat. Add mustard and chicken mixture to onions, stirring constantly over low heat. Add 1/2 of the cream; cook until thickened. Check seasonings; milk may be added if mixture is too hot or spicy. Add lemon juice and remaining cream; cover. Cook over low heat for 5 to 10 minutes longer. Place in serving dish; garnish with parsley. Mix rice and walnuts; serve chicken curry with rice mixture. May be prepared day or 2 ahead of serving, refrigerated, then reheated. Yield: 4-6 servings.

Judith A. McKinley
Rupert A. Nock Middle School
Newburyport, Massachusetts

CHICKEN AND DRESSING DELUXE

1 8-oz. package herb-seasoned
    stuffing mix
3 c. cooked or canned chicken
1/2 c. margarine
1/2 c. flour
3 tsp. salt
1/4 tsp. pepper
4 c. chicken broth, heated
6 eggs, beaten
1 can mushroom soup
1/4 c. milk
1 8-oz. carton sour cream
1/4 c. chopped pimentos

Prepare stuffing mix according to package directions; spread in bottom of 9 x 12-inch baking dish. Add chicken. Melt margarine; blend in flour, salt and pepper. Stir into hot chicken broth. Mix small amount of the broth with eggs; stir back into broth. Pour over chicken. Bake at 350 degrees for 45 minutes. Mix remaining ingredients; heat through. Do not boil. Serve with chicken mixture.

Phyllis Drummond
Phillips High School
Birmingham, Alabama

CHICKEN WITH DRESSING

1 3 to 4-lb. chicken, disjointed
1 stalk celery
1 onion, sliced
Salt
3 or 4 peppercorns
1 1/2 qt. dry bread crumbs or cubes
1/2 tsp. sage
1/4 tsp. pepper
1/4 c. minced onion
1/3 c. butter or drippings
3/4 c. flour
4 egg yolks, beaten

Simmer chicken, celery, sliced onion, 1 tablespoon salt and peppercorns in water to almost cover for about 2 hours or until chicken is tender. Remove chicken from broth; cool. Remove chicken from bones in large pieces; arrange in 2-quart casserole. Strain broth; cool. Remove fat. Combine bread crumbs, sage, half the pepper and 1/2 teaspoon salt. Brown minced onion in butter; add to bread mixture. Spread over chicken. Melt 1/2 cup chicken fat in heavy skillet. Add flour, 1 1/2 teaspoons salt and remaining pepper; cook, stirring constantly, until smooth. Blend in 4 cups chicken broth; cook until smooth, stirring constantly. Mix some of the hot gravy with egg yolks; stir back into remaining gravy. Cook over medium heat for 3 minutes, stirring frequently; pour over dressing. Bake in 375-degree oven for 35 minutes or until gravy is set and top is golden brown.

Mrs. Candice Gehlhar Dempsey
Newport Public School
Towner, North Dakota

CHICKEN CASSEROLE WITH SAUCE

1 8-oz. package herb-seasoned
    stuffing mix
3 c. cooked sliced chicken
1/2 c. margarine
1/2 c. flour
1/4 tsp. salt
1/4 tsp. pepper
4 c. chicken broth
6 eggs, slightly beaten
1 can mushroom soup
1/4 c. milk
1 c. sour cream
1/4 c. chopped pimento

Place stuffing mix in 13 x 9 x 2-inch pan; place chicken on stuffing mix. Melt margarine in large saucepan. Add flour and seasonings; mix. Add broth; cook over medium heat until thick, stirring frequently. Stir in eggs slowly; pour over chicken. Bake in 325-degree oven for 45 minutes. Cut into squares. Mix remaining ingredients; heat thoroughly. Do not boil. Serve over each square. Turkey may be substituted for chicken.

Mrs. Vergie Hill
Owensboro High School
Owensboro, Kentucky

CHICKEN AND DRESSING CASSEROLE

1 onion, diced
1 c. diced celery
1 stick butter
1 loaf dry bread, crumbled
Sage, salt and pepper to taste
2 cans cream of chicken soup
1 soup can water
4 eggs, beaten
1 canned chicken, boned and diced

Saute onion and celery in butter until tender. Add bread crumbs, sage, salt and pepper; mix well. Mix soup and water in saucepan; bring to a boil. Stir some of the soup mixture into eggs, then stir back into soup mixture. Place 1/3 of the chicken in casserole; add 1/3 of the dressing. Add 1/3 of the soup mixture; repeat layers twice. Bake at 325 degrees for 1 hour.

Jeraldine Sanders
Dixie High School
St. George, Utah

QUICK AND EASY CHICKEN CASSEROLE

1/4 lb. mushrooms, sliced
1 tbsp. butter
3 c. cooked chopped chicken
3 c. soft bread crumbs
1 c. milk
1/4 c. finely chopped pimento
2 eggs, beaten
2 tsp. minced onion
Salt and pepper to taste
Celery salt and paprika to taste

Preheat oven to 350 degrees. Saute mushrooms in butter until tender. Add remaining ingredients; mix well. Place in greased 2-quart baking dish; set in pan containing 1 inch water. Bake for about 1 hour and 30 minutes; serve with cooked noodles. One 4-ounce can sliced mushrooms may be substituted for fresh mushrooms.

Jane Angel
Wagon Mound School
Wagon Mound, New Mexico

SCALLOPED CHICKEN CASSEROLE

1 egg, lightly beaten
1/2 tsp. salt
1/4 tsp. pepper
1 8-oz. can cream-style corn
1 10-oz. package frozen chopped
    broccoli, partially thawed
3 1/2 c. cooked diced chicken
1/4 c. melted butter
2 c. herb-seasoned stuffing mix
2 c. chicken broth
1/4 c. flour
1/4 tsp. sage

Preheat oven to 325 degrees. Combine egg, 1/4 teaspoon salt, pepper, corn and broccoli in medium mixing bowl; spread in greased 9 x 14-inch baking dish. Top with chicken. Combine butter and stuffing mix; spread over chicken. Mix broth, flour, sage and remaining salt in saucepan; cook until thick. Pour over stuffing mixture. Bake for 25 to 30 minutes. Yield: 6-8 servings.

Mrs. Alma Lee Hicks
Murphysboro Township High School
Murphysboro, Illinois

SCALLOPED CHICKEN AND DRESSING

1   5 to 6-lb. stewing hen
1 1/8 c. flour
Salt
1/4 tsp. white pepper
2 c. half and half
1/4 c. chopped onion
1 c. chopped celery
1/2 to 1 tsp. sage
1/3 c. melted butter
4 c. cubed day-old bread, toasted

Simmer hen in boiling, salted water until tender. Remove chicken from broth; cool. Remove chicken from bones. Skim fat from broth. Heat 1 cup chicken fat in large skillet. Blend in flour, 1 tablespoon salt and pepper; cook over low heat until bubbly, stirring constantly. Stir in 4 1/2 cups chicken broth and half and half slowly. Boil for 3 minutes, stirring constantly; remove from heat. Combine remaining ingredients in bowl; toss lightly to mix. Place in two 2-quart baking dishes; place chicken on bread mixture. Cover with sauce. Mix with fork to moisten dressing. Bake at 350 degrees for 1 hour. Yield: 16 servings.

Mrs. Eleanor Weatherhead
Northridge Middle School
Dayton, Ohio

EASY CHICKEN AND DUMPLINGS

1 fryer
8 1/2 c. water
Salt

Pepper
1 can cream of chicken soup
1 egg
1 1/2 c. flour

Cut chicken into serving pieces. Pour 8 cups water into large saucepan; add 1 teaspoon salt and 1/2 teaspoon pepper. Bring to a boil. Add chicken; bring to a boil. Cover; simmer until tender. Add soup; bring to a boil. Beat egg; add remaining water and salt and pepper to taste. Mix well. Add flour; stir well. Dough should be stiff enough to handle. Roll out on floured board to 1/4-inch thickness. Cut with knife into strips 1/2 inch wide and 3 inches long. Drop strips into boiling chicken mixture, one at a time, submerging each strip as added. Cook until dumplings are done.

Mrs. Dorothy Sue T. Hill
East Beauregard High School
DeRidder, Louisiana

THRIFTY CHICKEN AND DUMPLINGS

Back, wings, neck, gizzard, liver
    and any excess fat from 1 fryer
Salt
1 1/4 c. milk
2 c. flour
1 tbsp. butter or margarine

Cover chicken parts with water; add salt to taste. Cook until chicken is tender. Remove chicken from bones; return to broth. Chicken may be left on bones. Reserve 3/4 cup broth; cool. Bring chicken mixture to a boil. Mix reserved broth, 1/4 cup milk and 1/2 teaspoon salt. Add flour; mix well. Add more flour, if needed, to make stiff dough. Roll out on floured surface to 1/8-inch thickness; cut into narrow strips. Drop strips into boiling broth, one at a time, until all strips have been added; add remaining milk and butter. Cook until dumplings are tender. Add more milk, if desired. Heat through; serve hot.

Mrs. Jane S. Funderburk
Loyd Star High School
Brookhaven, Mississippi

BEST-EVER CHICKEN

1 chicken
1 loaf stale bread
1 med. onion, chopped
4 hard-cooked eggs, chopped
Salt and pepper to taste
Sage to taste
3 tbsp. flour
4 eggs, well beaten
Milk
Buttered bread crumbs

Cook chicken in enough water to cover until tender. Remove chicken from broth; cool. Remove chicken from bones; cut into small pieces. Chill chicken broth; skim fat from top. Cut bread into small pieces. Cook onion in 2 tablespoons chicken fat until tender; add to bread. Add hard-cooked eggs and seasonings; moisten with some of the chicken broth. Place in 1 large or 2 small baking pans; add chicken. Melt remaining chicken fat; stir in flour. Mix beaten eggs, remaining chicken broth and enough milk to make 1 quart liquid. Add to flour mixture; boil for 3 minutes, stirring constantly. Pour over chicken; cover top with buttered bread crumbs. Bake at 350 degrees for 30 minutes.

Ruth Aylor
Monroney Junior High School
Midwest City, Oklahoma

SOUTHERN CHICKEN AND DUMPLINGS

1 stewing hen
4 tsp. salt
Pepper to taste
3 c. all-purpose flour
3 tbsp. butter

Place hen in deep kettle; cover with water. Add 3 teaspoons salt and pepper; bring to a boil. Reduce heat; cover tightly. Simmer for at least 2 hours or until hen is very tender. Hen may be cooked in pressure cooker. Remove chicken from broth; cool. Remove chicken from bones; chop. Mix flour and remaining salt; stir in just enough water to make stiff dough. Place on floured board;

knead until very stiff. Roll out dough, 1/4 at a time, until paper-thin. Cut into 2-inch strips. Bring chicken broth to a boil. Add 1/4 of the strips; cook for about 5 minutes. Add remaining dough, 1/4 at a time, bringing to a boil after each addition and stirring frequently. Cook until dumplings are tender, adding boiling water to keep liquid soupy. Add chicken and butter; heat through.

Mrs. Mildred March
Jones High School
Orlando, Florida

VIRGINIA CHICKEN AND DUMPLINGS

1 can cream of mushroom soup
1 can cream of chicken soup
1 green pepper, chopped
1 onion, chopped
1 c. cooked chopped chicken
Salt and pepper to taste
Chopped celery to taste
1 can refrigerator biscuits

Combine soups, half the green pepper, half the onion and 1/4 cup water; bring to boiling point. Reduce heat to medium. Season chicken with salt and pepper. Add remaining green pepper, remaining onion and celery; mix well. Separate biscuits; roll each out on lightly floured surface. Place chicken mixture in center of each biscuit. Fold over; seal edges. Drop into soup mixture; cook for about 15 minutes or until done. Yield: 10 dumplings.

Joann Gardner
Pembroke High School
Poquoson, Virginia

EASY SCALLOPED CHICKEN

1 5-lb. chicken
14 slices bread
1/2 green pepper, chopped
1 pimento, chopped
5 eggs, beaten

Cook chicken in boiling, salted water until tender. Drain chicken; reserve 4 cups broth.

Cool chicken; remove from bones. Cut bread in cubes. Place alternate layers of bread cubes, chicken, green pepper and pimento in greased baking dish; pour reserved broth over all. Pour eggs over top. Bake at 350 degrees for 1 hour. Yield: 12 servings.

Mrs. Bette Sandrock
Shaler Junior High School
Etna, Pennsylvania

GOURMET CHICKEN CASSEROLE

2 c. diced chicken
1 c. diced celery
1/2 c. salted cashews
3 tbsp. lemon juice
1/2 c. chopped green pepper
1/4 tsp. salt
1 c. mayonnaise
1/2 c. milk or broth
1/4 c. chopped pimento
3 1/2 c. French-fried onions
Paprika

Combine chicken, celery, cashews, lemon juice, pepper, salt, mayonnaise, milk, pimento and 3 cups onions. Place in greased 1 1/2-quart casserole. Bake, covered, at 350 degrees for 30 minutes. Top with remaining onions; sprinkle with paprika. Bake, uncovered, for 5 minutes.

Mrs. Evangeline Maxwell
Spencer Junior High School
Spencer, Iowa

CHICKEN-MACARONI CASSEROLE

1 5-lb. hen, disjointed
1 bay leaf
1 onion
1 bunch celery tops
1 c. flour
1/2 c. milk
Salt and pepper to taste
1 4-oz. can pimentos
1 c. chopped celery, cooked
1 8-oz. can mushrooms
1 8-oz. can tomato puree
Dash of garlic salt

2/3 lb. macaroni
1/2 c. grated sharp Cheddar cheese

Place chicken in kettle; cover with water. Add bay leaf, onion and celery tops; bring to a boil. Simmer until chicken is tender. Drain chicken; reserve broth. Discard bay leaf, onion and celery tops. Cool chicken; remove from bones. Cut chicken into 1-inch cubes. Cool reserved broth; remove fat from top. Melt 1 cup chicken fat in large saucepan; stir in flour. Stir in 4 cups broth slowly; stir in milk. Add salt and pepper; cook, stirring constantly, until thick. Drain and chop pimentos. Add pimentos, celery, mushrooms, tomato puree and garlic salt to broth mixture; heat through. Stir in chicken; let stand for 1 hour. Cook macaroni according to package directions; drain well. Add to chicken mixture; mix well. Place in large casserole; sprinkle cheese over top. Bake at 350 degrees for 45 minutes. Casserole may be covered well and frozen. Yield: 10 servings.

Mrs. Dorothy Walker
Bowling Green High School
Bowling Green, Kentucky

LAYERED CHICKEN DISH

1/2 c. milk
2 c. chicken broth
1/4 c. soft butter
6 tbsp. flour
Dash of nutmeg
Dash of celery salt
2 1/2 c. cooked chopped chicken
1 c. zwieback crumbs
Slivered almonds

Combine milk and broth in saucepan; heat. Blend butter, flour and seasonings together; stir into hot mixture. Cook for about 15 minutes or until smooth and creamy, stirring occasionally. Place alternating layers of chicken, gravy and crumbs in 8-inch square baking dish. Repeat until all ingredients are used. Dot with additional butter. Sprinkle almonds over top. Bake at 350 degrees for 20 to 30 minutes.

Mrs. Alice Applegate
Knoxville Senior High School
Knoxville, Iowa

CHILI-MAC CHICKEN

1 lg. fryer
1 stick margarine
1 med. onion, chopped
1/2 bell pepper, chopped
1 sm. jar stuffed olives
2 tsp. chili powder
1 can tomato soup
1 can mushroom soup
2 lb. elbow macaroni
Sliced Velveeta cheese

Cook chicken in boiling, salted water until tender. Drain and cool. Remove chicken from bones and cut into bite-sized pieces. Melt margarine. Add onion and bell pepper and cook, stirring, until tender. Drain and slice olives. Add olives and chili powder to onion mixture; cook for 3 minutes, stirring constantly. Add tomato soup and mushroom soup, stirring until smooth. Add chicken; remove from heat. Cook macaroni in boiling salted water until tender; drain. Place alternate layers of macaroni and chicken mixture in large casserole; cover top with slices of Velveeta cheese. Bake at 350 degrees until cheese melts. May be prepared in 2 small casseroles, using 1 package of macaroni. One casserole may be frozen for later use.

Mrs. Jean Benson
South Panola High School
Batesville, Mississippi

MEXICAN CASSEROLE

2 med. onions
1 sm. green pepper
4 tbsp. cooking oil
1 1/2 c. cooked diced chicken
1 1/2 c. cut corn
1/2 c. mushrooms
1/2 c. tomato juice
1 1/2 c. elbow macaroni
1/4 c. grated Cheddar cheese

Peel and dice onions; dice green pepper. Saute onions and green pepper lightly in oil. Add remaining ingredients except macaroni and cheese; simmer for 5 minutes. Cook macaroni in boiling, salted water until tender; drain. Add to chicken mixture. Pour into greased 2-quart casserole; sprinkle with cheese. Bake, uncovered, at 350 degrees for 25 to 30 minutes; garnish with chopped parsley.

Mrs. Daphne Moser
Chamdler Park Junior Secondary School
Smithers, British Columbia, Canada

MADAME WU'S SWEET-SOUR CHICKEN

1/2 c. flour
Cornstarch
1/2 tsp. baking powder
1/4 tsp. salt
1 c. cubed cooked chicken
Cooking oil
1   13 1/2-oz. can pineapple
    chunks
3/4 c. catsup
1/4 c. white vinegar
3 tbsp. sugar
1/2 c. chopped white onion
1/2 c. chopped green pepper

Blend flour, 1/4 cup cornstarch, baking powder and salt. Stir in 3/4 cup water until batter is smooth and runs in a thin stream. Dip chicken cubes in batter, shaking to remove excess batter. Drop into hot oil; cook until golden. Drain on paper towel; keep warm. Drain pineapple, reserving syrup. Combine catsup, vinegar, sugar and reserved syrup in a large saucepan or skillet; bring to a boil over high heat. Add onion and pepper. Blend 1 tablespoon cornstarch with a small amount of water to form a paste; stir into catsup mixture. Cook and stir until glossy and translucent. Add pineapple chunks. Bring again to a boil; add chicken cubes. Serve over rice, if desired. Yield: 4 servings.

Mrs. Marguerite S. Darnall
Corona Senior High School
Corona, California

CHICKEN BREAST STROGANOFF

1/2 c. chopped onion
2 tbsp. oil
2 c. diced uncooked chicken breast
1 c. cooked or canned mushrooms

1 c. sour cream
1 tsp. salt
1 lb. noodles, cooked

Saute onion in oil until clear but not brown. Add chicken; cook until the pink color turns white. Stir in mushrooms; bring to boiling point. Blend in sour cream and salt; serve over hot noodles.

Pauline Benson
Ida M. Fisher Junior High School
Miami Beach, Florida

HUNTINGTON CHICKEN

1 3 to 4-lb. hen
1 1/2 c. small shell macaroni
1 8-oz. package cream cheese
1/2 c. flour
4 c. bread crumbs
2 tbsp. butter
1/2 c. cream

Cook chicken in boiling, salted water until tender. Remove chicken from broth; cool. Reserve broth. Remove chicken from bones; cut into cubes. Cook macaroni in boiling, salted water until tender; drain. Dice cream cheese into small cubes. Bring 4 cups reserved broth to a boil. Mix flour with 1/2 cup water until smooth; stir into broth. Mix chicken, macaroni, cheese and broth; place in greased 8 x 12-inch baking dish. Brown bread crumbs in butter. Add cream; mix well. Spread over top of chicken mixture. Bake in 325-degree oven for 30 minutes. Yield: 6 servings.

Cheryl Wooton
Biggers-Reyno High School
Biggers, Arkansas

PUFFY CHICKEN DELIGHT

1 3-lb. canned whole chicken
4 stalks celery and leaves, chopped
1/2 c. chopped onion
3/4 c. butter
3 1/2 c. bread crumbs
3 c. grated carrots
1 tbsp. dried parsley
1 tsp. sage
1/2 tsp. poultry seasoning
Salt

Pepper
1/2 c. flour
1 c. milk
4 eggs, slightly beaten

Drain broth from chicken; measure. Add water to make 3 cups liquid. Remove chicken from bones; cut chicken into small pieces. Set aside. Saute celery and onion in 2 tablespoons butter in small skillet; add 2 1/2 cups bread crumbs, carrots, parsley, sage, poultry seasoning, 1 teaspoon salt and 1/4 teaspoon pepper. Use only enough broth to moisten. Set aside. Melt 1/2 cup butter; remove from heat. Add flour and salt and pepper to taste; stir until smooth. Add 2 cups broth and milk; cook, stirring, until thick. Remove from heat; add eggs, stirring thoroughly. Do not cook after adding eggs. Grease 1 large or 2 medium-sized casseroles; place alternate layers of dressing, chicken and gravy in casserole until all are used. Melt remaining butter; add remaining bread crumbs. Sprinkle over gravy. Bake at 325 degrees for 50 minutes for large and 30 minutes for medium casserole. Yield: 10-12 servings.

Marilyn Jepsen
North Cache Junior High School
Richmond, Utah

QUICK CHICKEN CASSEROLE

2 c. chicken stock
2 eggs, slightly beaten
3 c. cooked diced chicken
1 c. bread crumbs
1/2 tsp. salt
1/8 tsp. paprika
1/2 c. diced celery
1 tsp. Worcestershire sauce
1/2 tsp. lemon juice
Olives to taste

Combine chicken stock and eggs; add remaining ingredients. Pour into buttered baking dish; sprinkle with additional bread crumbs. Bake at 300 degrees for 1 hour. Yield: 8 servings.

Mrs. Nina Groce
Forbush High School
East Bend, North Carolina

ALMOND-CHICKEN AND RICE

1 lb. chicken breasts
2 tbsp. vegetable oil
1 tsp. garlic salt
1   1-lb. can fancy Chinese
   vegetables
1 c. thinly sliced celery
1 tbsp. cornstarch
1 tsp. sugar
2 tbsp. soy sauce
1/3 c. chicken broth
1/2 c. blanched almonds
1 c. well-drained pineapple tidbits
3 c. hot cooked rice
1/3 c. thinly sliced green onions

Bone and skin chicken; cut in small, thin strips. Saute in oil with garlic salt until browned. Drain Chinese vegetables; reserve liquid. Add Chinese vegetables, celery and 1/3 cup reserved liquid to chicken; cover pan. Steam for about 3 minutes or until celery is just tender. Blend cornstarch, sugar, soy sauce and chicken broth. Stir into chicken mixture with half the almonds. Cook until thickened and clear, stirring constantly. Add pineapple. Serve over rice; sprinkle with onions and remaining almonds. Yield: 6 servings.

Beverlee Brown Williams
Campbell High School
Campbell, California

CHICKEN CASSEROLE

1 c. packaged precooked rice
1 can water chestnuts
1/2 c. salad dressing
1 can cream of chicken soup
1 onion, grated
1 pkg. frozen green beans
2 c. cooked diced chicken or
   turkey
Buttered crumbs
Parmesan cheese (opt.)

Prepare rice according to package directions. Drain and slice water chestnuts. Mix all ingredients except crumbs and cheese; place in casserole. Cover with crumbs and cheese.

Bake at 350 degrees for 30 minutes or until bubbly and brown. May be kept warm in oven before serving. Yield: 4-6 servings.

Mrs. Sue Stephens
Wheatland High School
Wheatland, Wyoming

CHICKEN CHOW MEIN

1   5-lb. hen
Salt and pepper to taste
1 bunch celery
3 green bell peppers
3 lg. onions
1   16-oz. can Chinese vegetables
2   8 1/2-oz. cans bamboo sprouts
2   8 1/2-oz. cans water chestnuts
1 lg. can pimentos, chopped
1 bottle soy sauce
Cooked rice
1 can Chinese noodles

Cook hen in boiling water until tender. Remove hen from stock. Remove chicken from bones. Make thick gravy of stock; season with salt and pepper. Cut celery, bell peppers and onions in large pieces. Cook in 1/2 cup water till tender-crisp. Do not drain. Drain Chinese vegetables, bamboo sprouts and water chestnuts; slice water chestnuts. Add chicken, Chinese vegetables, bamboo sprouts, water chestnuts, celery mixture and pimentos to gravy; add soy sauce. Serve over rice; sprinkle Chinese noodles on top. Better made day before served; freezes well. Yield: 16 servings.

Mrs. H. Thomas Ward
G. P. Babb Junior High School
Forest Park, Georgia

CHICKEN-HAM-SHRIMP DISH

6 tbsp. butter
1/4 c. chopped onion
6 tbsp. flour
1 tsp. salt
1 1/2 c. milk
1 1/2 c. chicken broth
1 c. shredded cheese
1 green pepper, diced

3 c. cooked diced chicken
1 lb. cooked ham, diced
1 1/2 lb. cleaned shrimp, cooked
1 4-oz. can mushroom slices,
    drained
2 tbsp. pimento, cut in strips
Cooked rice

Melt butter in saucepan. Saute onion in butter until tender; do not brown. Stir in flour and salt until smooth. Add milk and chicken broth gradually, stirring until smooth; cook until mixture comes to a boil and is of medium thickness, stirring constantly. Add cheese; heat, stirring, until cheese is melted and sauce is smooth. Stir in remaining ingredients except rice; heat through. Serve over rice. May be frozen. Yield: 12 servings.

Elizabeth Ann Seefeldt
Dakota Community High School
Dakota, Illinois

CHICKEN-WILD RICE QUICKIE

1 pkg. long grain and wild rice
1 can water chestnuts
1 can cream of celery soup
1/2 c. mayonnaise
1 can French-cut green beans,
    drained
1 c. slivered almonds
1/4 c. chopped pimento
2 c. cooked diced chicken
Salt and pepper to taste

Prepare rice according to package directions. Drain water chestnuts; cut in thin slices. Add water chestnuts, undiluted soup and remaining ingredients to rice; mix well. Heat through, then serve.

Mrs. H. A. Hollman
Kenedy High School
Kenedy, Texas

CHICKEN PAPRIKA

1 hen
1 tsp. salt
4 tbsp. margarine
3/4 c. chopped green onions and tops
1/2 c. chopped celery and leaves

1 tbsp. (heaping) flour
1 tbsp. (heaping) paprika
1/2 pt. light cream
Juice of 1 lemon
1 c. toasted slivered almonds
Cooked rice

Boil hen in salted water until tender. Remove from broth, reserving broth. Remove skin and bones from chicken. Chop chicken; set aside. Melt margarine in saucepan; add onions and celery. Saute until limp, stir in flour and paprika. Add cream and enough chicken broth to cook to thickness desired. Add chicken; cook for several minutes. Add lemon juice and almonds. Serve on rice.

Martha Lou Long
McCamey High School
McCamey, Texas

CHICKEN AND WILD RICE CASSEROLE

1/2 c. chopped green pepper
1 1/2 c. chopped onions
1 1/2 c. chopped celery
1 4-oz. can mushrooms
2 cans cream of mushroom soup
1 tsp. pepper
1 tsp. salt
1/4 tsp. curry powder
1/4 tsp. sage
1 12-oz. package wild rice
2 eggs, beaten
4 c. cooked diced chicken
1 c. slivered almonds

Saute green pepper, onions and celery in small amount of fat until tender. Add mushrooms and liquid, 1 can mushroom soup and seasonings. Cook wild rice according to package directions. Combine rice and eggs. Add onion mixture; mix well. Add chicken; stir in almonds. Spoon into greased 3-quart casserole. Bake at 350 degrees for 1 hour. Mix remaining mushroom soup and 1/2 cup water in saucepan; heat, stirring, until smooth. Serve with chicken casserole. Yield: 12 servings.

Marilyn Reneau
Wilkinson Junior High School
Mesquite, Texas

SCALLOPED CHICKEN SUPREME

2 c. cooked rice
3 c. chicken broth
6 tbsp. butter or chicken fat
6 tbsp. flour
1 tsp. salt
1/8 tsp. pepper
1 c. cream
3 c. cooked diced chicken
1/2 c. toasted slivered almonds
2 tbsp. minced pimento
1/2 c. sauteed sliced mushrooms
Buttered crumbs or potato chips

Combine rice and 1 cup chicken broth; set aside. Melt butter in saucepan over low heat; stir in flour, salt and pepper until bubbling. Remove from heat; stir in remaining chicken broth and cream. Add chicken; mix well. Place layer of rice mixture in 12 by 7 1/2 by 2-inch baking dish; top with layer of chicken mixture. Sprinkle almonds, pimento and mushrooms over chicken mixture. Repeat layers. Top with crumbs. Bake at 350 degrees for 45 minutes.

Lorene L. Arent
Wausa Public Schools
Wausa, Nebraska

JAVANESE RICE TAFEL

2 3-lb. stewing chickens
8 c. milk
3 c. canned coconut
4 tbsp. butter
1 onion, chopped
2 cloves of garlic, minced
1 3-in. piece of gingerroot, diced fine
3 tbsp. curry powder
4 tbsp. flour
4 tbsp. cornstarch
Salt and pepper to taste
Paprika to taste
4 c. rice
1 lg. can fried noodles
1 bunch green onions, minced
5 hard-cooked eggs, sieved
1 sm. can peanuts, grated
1 lb. bacon, fried and crumbled

1 10 1/2-oz. jar chutney
1 lg. jar candied ginger, diced
Grated fresh coconut (opt.)

Cook chickens in boiling water for 1 hour; drain and cool. Reserve 2 cups broth. Dice chicken; set aside. Scald milk; add canned coconut. Let stand in cool place for 2 hours. Melt 2 tablespoons butter; saute chopped onion and garlic in butter until light brown. Add gingerroot, curry powder and reserved chicken stock. Add to coconut mixture; stir. Combine 6 tablespoons of the liquid with flour and cornstarch; stir in more liquid until consistency of thin paste. Heat coconut sauce; stir in flour paste. Cook, stirring until thickened. Season with salt, pepper and paprika. Strain sauce. Mix half the sauce with chicken; reserve remaining sauce. Cook rice in 8 cups boiling water with remaining butter and salt for 20 minutes; rice should be dry and flaky. Heat chicken mixture and reserved sauce in separate pans. Place rice on individual plates; add chicken. Add desired condiments; serve with remaining sauce. Yield: 10-12 servings.

Mrs. Jean D. Lang
Bonita High School
La Verne, California

SCRUMPTIOUS BAKED CHICKEN

1 4 to 5-lb. stewing chicken
2 c. fresh bread crumbs
1 1/2 tsp. salt
1 c. packaged precooked rice
2 tbsp. diced pimento
4 eggs, well beaten
1/2 c. butter or margarine
1/4 c. flour
1/8 tsp. paprika
1/4 c. cream
1/2 tsp. minced parsley
1 8-oz. can mushrooms
1/2 tsp. lemon juice

Simmer chicken in enough water to cover until tender. Remove chicken from broth; cool. Remove chicken from bones; cut into small pieces. Combine chicken with 3 cups chicken broth, bread crumbs, salt, rice, pimento and eggs; place in 9 x 13-inch baking dish. Bake at 325 degrees for 1 hour and 30 minutes. Melt butter in saucepan; stir in flour and paprika. Add cream, parsley, mushrooms, 2 cups chicken broth and lemon juice; cook, stirring, until thickened. Cut chicken mixture into squares; serve with mushroom sauce.

Mrs. Marian Rich
WACO Community School
Wayland, Iowa

TAVERN-STYLE CHICKEN

1   3 1/2 to 5-lb. chicken
1 onion, peeled
Celery to taste
1/2 c. butter
1/2 c. flour
1 c. evaporated milk
2   3-oz. cans mushrooms
1 tsp. salt
1/2 tsp. turmeric
1/4 tsp. oregano
1/2 c. grated Cheddar cheese
3 c. cooked rice

Place chicken, onion and celery in Dutch oven; add about 1 quart water. Cook, covered, until chicken is tender. Remove skin; dice chicken. Reserve broth. Melt butter in saucepan; blend in flour. Combine milk, liquid from mushrooms and enough chicken broth to make 4 cups liquid. Add salt, turmeric and oregano. Stir liquid into flour mixture. Cook, stirring, until thickened. Add cheese, stirring until melted. Place rice in a shallow baking dish. Add chicken and mushrooms; pour sauce over all. Bake at 350 degrees for 30 minutes.

Mrs. Cheryl Assenheimer
Troy Junior High School
Avon Lake, Ohio

SAVORY CHICKEN DIVAN

1/2 c. margarine
1/2 c. flour
1/2 tsp. salt
Dash of pepper

2 c. water
2 chicken bouillon cubes
2 c. croutons
1   10-oz. package frozen broccoli
8 lg. slices cooked chicken or
    turkey breasts
1/4 c. grated Parmesan cheese

Melt margarine in saucepan; stir in flour, salt and pepper. Add water gradually, stirring constantly; add bouillon cubes. Cook until thickened, stirring occasionally. Spread croutons in bottom of greased 1 1/2-quart baking dish. Pour 1/2 of the sauce over croutons. Arrange broccoli over croutons and sauce; top with chicken slices. Cover with remaining sauce; sprinkle with cheese. Bake in 350-degree oven for about 20 minutes or until thoroughly heated. Two cups chicken broth may be substituted for water and bouillon cubes. Yield: 4-6 servings.

Mrs. Marie Heltzel
Lake Butler Middle School
Lake Butler, Florida

CELERY-SCALLOPED CHICKEN

4 c. cooked diced chicken
1/4 lb. saltine crackers, crushed
1 can mushroom soup
1 sm. can mushrooms, drained
1 sm. jar pimento strips, drained
1/2 c. chopped green pepper
1/2 c. chopped celery
1/2 tsp. celery salt
1/2 tsp. onion salt
Crushed potato chips

Combine chicken, cracker crumbs and soup. Stir in mushrooms, pimento, green pepper and celery; season with celery salt and onion salt. Place in greased casserole; cover with potato chips. Bake at 350 degrees for 45 minutes. Celery or chicken soup may be substituted for mushroom soup; 1 can fried onion rings may be used instead of potato chips. Yield: 8 servings.

Mrs. Ross McNaught
Virden High School
Virden, Illinois

DELICIOUS CHICKEN-SPAGHETTI

1 3 to 4-lb. hen
1 pkg. long spaghetti
2 No. 2 cans tomatoes
2 med. onions, chopped
2 garlic cloves, chopped fine
4 bay leaves
6 whole cloves
Juice and rind of 2 lemons
2 tbsp. chili powder
1 tsp. cayenne pepper
1 tsp. salt
2 cans tomato soup
1 tbsp. sugar
1 tsp. pepper
Parmesan cheese to taste

Cook hen in enough water to cover for about 3 hours or until tender. Remove hen from broth; cool. Remove chicken from bones; cut into small pieces with kitchen shears. Cook spaghetti according to package directions. Rinse with cool water and set aside. Place remaining ingredients in chicken broth; cook over medium heat for 45 minutes. Add chicken and spaghetti and cook over low heat 1 hour, stirring occasionally. Remove lemon rind and bay leaves. Place chicken mixture on serving platter; sprinkle with Parmesan cheese.

Mrs. Dorothy R. Baylor
Gainesville High School
Gainesville, Georgia

LAYERED CHICKEN-SPAGHETTI

1 hen
2 c. chopped onions
2 c. chopped celery
2 cloves of garlic, chopped
2 c. chopped green peppers
1 lg. can tomato sauce
1 can mushroom soup
1 4-oz. can pimentos
1 sm. can chopped ripe olives, drained
1 sm. can chopped mushrooms
Seasoned salt to taste
Pepper to taste

1 16-oz. package spaghetti
2 c. grated cheese

Cook chicken in boiling water until tender. Drain chicken; cool. Cool broth. Remove fat from top; set aside. Remove chicken from bones; dice. Saute onions, celery, garlic and green peppers in chicken fat until tender. Add tomato sauce, mushroom soup and chicken. Drain pimentos; chop. Add pimentos, olives, mushrooms, seasoned salt and pepper to chicken mixture; mix well. Cook spaghetti in boiling, salted water until tender; drain. Combine spaghetti with chicken mixture. Place alternate layers of chicken mixture and cheese in baking dish. Bake in 350-degree oven until cheese melts. Add chicken broth if mixture becomes too dry.

Mrs. Lynn Chambers
Silsbee High School
Silsbee, Texas

CHICKEN-CHILI ENCHILADAS

3 tbsp. flour
4 tsp. chili powder
3 tbsp. salad oil
2 1/2 c. water
12 tortillas
2 c. cooked chicken, heated
1 tsp. salt
1/4 tsp. pepper
4 c. grated American or Monterey Jack cheese
1/2 c. chopped onion

Preheat oven to 350 degrees. Brown flour and chili powder in oil; stir in water slowly. Simmer for 30 minutes. Wrap tortillas in foil; heat in oven while chili mixture is simmering. Season chicken with salt and pepper. Place some of the chicken on each tortilla; add small amount of cheese and onion. Roll each tortilla; place in baking dish, seam side down. Sprinkle remaining cheese over top. Pour chili powder mixture over enchiladas. Bake until cheese is melted.

Twanda Page
Hydro High School
Hydro, Oklahoma

SPANISH CHICKEN

1 stewing chicken
Salt
1 tsp. poultry seasoning
1   4-oz. can sliced mushrooms,
    drained
3 tbsp. butter or margarine
8 hard-cooked eggs, diced
2 c. soft bread crumbs or cooked
    noodles
1/2 tsp. paprika
Pepper
1/2 c. crushed corn flakes

Cut chicken into serving pieces; place in large saucepan. Cover with water, add 1 1/2 teaspoons salt and poultry seasoning. Simmer until chicken is tender. Drain chicken; cool. Remove broth. Bone and cut chicken into bite-sized pieces. Thicken 4 cups reserved broth. Brown mushrooms in 2 tablespoons butter. Mix chicken, eggs, mushrooms, bread crumbs and thickened broth; add paprika and salt and pepper to taste. Turn into 2-quart casserole. Melt remaining butter; toss with corn flake crumbs until mixed. Sprinkle on top of chicken mixture. Bake at 325 degrees for 1 hour and 30 minutes. Yield: 6-8 servings.

Mrs. Dorothy J. Watson
O'Fallon Township High School
O'Fallon, Illinois

CHOPANDANGOS

1 doz. corn tortillas
1 c. hot fat
1 cooked chicken, boned
1   4-oz. can green chilies, chopped
2 lg. fresh tomatoes, chopped
1/8 tsp. garlic powder
2 tbsp. chopped onion
1 c. chicken broth
1 c. evaporated milk
Salt and pepper to taste
1 lb. Monterey Jack cheese, grated

Dip tortillas in hot fat; blot excess fat with paper towels. Arrange 6 tortillas in 2-quart casserole. Mix remaining ingredients, except cheese, in bowl. Pour half the chicken mixture over tortillas; sprinkle with half the cheese. Repeat layers. Bake at 350 degrees for 30 minutes.

Mrs. Mary Hale
Hallsville Junior High School
Hallsville, Texas

KING RANCH CASSEROLE DELIGHT

1 can tortillas
1 c. cooked diced chicken
1 can tomatoes with green chilies
1 med. onion, chopped
1 c. chicken broth
1 can cream of mushroom soup
1 can cream of chicken soup
1 c. shredded Cheddar cheese

Cut tortillas into small pieces. Add remaining ingredients except cheese; mix well. Place in casserole; cover with cheese. Refrigerate for 8 hours. Bake at 350 degrees for 45 minutes. May be frozen. Yield: 6-8 servings.

Jane Wheeler
Waco High School
Waco, Texas

SHREDDED CHICKEN TACOS

2 lg. tomatoes
Lettuce
2 cooked chicken breasts
Oil or shortening
Minced garlic to taste
Salt to taste
2 green chili peppers, chopped
1 doz. corn tortillas or taco shells
Shredded sharp Cheddar cheese

Chop tomatoes and lettuce; set aside. Remove chicken from bones; shred. Cook chicken in small amount of oil until light brown; season with garlic and salt. Add chili peppers; cook until almost dry. Fry corn tortillas in small amount of oil; drain. Fill tortillas with chicken mixture, cheese, tomatoes and lettuce. Serve with refried beans and Spanish rice, if desired.

Mrs. Noemi M. Jimenez
McFarland High School
McFarland, California

MEXICAN CHICKEN

12 tortillas
Chicken broth
1 cooked chicken, deboned
2/3 c. chopped onion
2/3 c. chopped bell pepper
2 c. grated cheese
1 can cream of chicken soup
1 can cream of mushroom soup
1 tsp. chili powder
1 can tomatoes with green chilies

Soak tortillas in chicken broth. Line 13 x 9 x 2-inch baking pan with tortillas; place chicken on tortillas. Sprinkle onion and bell pepper over chicken; sprinkle cheese over onion mixture. Mix soups and chili powder in bowl; pour over cheese. Pour tomatoes over top. Bake at 350 degrees for 30 minutes. Turn oven off; let set for 15 minutes longer.

Paula Duvall
Boswell Public School
Boswell, Oklahoma

CHICKEN-DRESSING LOAF

1 stewing hen
1 recipe dressing
1/2 c. flour
1/2 c. butter
2 c. milk
1 c. chicken broth
4 eggs, beaten
Salt and pepper to taste
Crushed potato chips

Cook hen in boiling water until tender. Remove meat from bones; reserve broth. Line a large pan with dressing 1 inch thick. Cream flour and butter together until smooth; add milk, broth, eggs, salt and pepper. Pour half the sauce on the dressing; place chicken pieces over the sauce. Pour on remaining sauce. Bake at 350 degrees for 30 minutes. Remove from oven; top with potato chips. Return to oven; bake for 15 to 30 minutes longer. Yield: 6-8 servings.

Mrs. Robert Wassell
Weatherwax High School
Alberdeen, Washington

CHICKEN LOAF WITH MUSHROOM SAUCE

1   3 1/2 to 4-lb. chicken
3 eggs
1 1/2 c. soft bread crumbs
1 c. cooked rice
1/2 c. light cream
1 1/2 c. milk and chicken stock
1 sm. can pimentos, chopped
Salt to taste
Hot sauce to taste
Grated cheese
Crumbled saltines
Paprika to taste
Butter

Cook chicken in boiling salted water in large pot until tender. Debone chicken and dice. Reserve stock. Place eggs in large bowl; beat well. Add bread crumbs, rice, chicken, cream, milk and chicken stock, pimentos, salt and hot sauce; mix thoroughly. Pour into buttered loaf pan; sprinkle with cheese, crackers and paprika. Dot with butter. Bake at 350 degrees for about 1 hour.

Mushroom Sauce

1/4 c. butter
1/4 c. flour
1 c. chicken stock
1 c. milk
1 c. light cream
1/2 lb. fresh or canned mushrooms
1/2 tsp. chopped parsley
1/4 tsp. paprika
Salt and pepper to taste
Onion salt to taste

Melt butter in saucepan; blend in flour. Combine stock and milk; add to flour mixture gradually, stirring constantly. Cook and stir until thickened. Add cream; bring to a boil. Chop mushrooms; add with parsley, paprika, salt, pepper and onion salt to white sauce. Serve as accompaniment to chicken loaf. Small amount of grated cheese may be added, if desired.

Mrs. Virginia O. Savedge
Northampton Senior High School
Eastville, Virginia

CHICKEN AND SOUTHERN DRESSING

1 4-lb. dressed hen and giblets
Salt
4 c. corn bread crumbs
1 c. finely chopped celery
3 hard-boiled eggs, chopped
1 tsp. sage
5 biscuits, crumbled
4 tbsp. minced onion
1/2 tsp. freshly ground pepper
2 eggs, beaten
1/4 c. butter
1/4 c. flour

Cover hen and giblets with water; add 1 1/2 tablespoons salt. Bring to a boil; simmer until almost tender. Remove hen and giblets from broth; chop giblets. Place hen in baking pan. Bake at 375 degrees for 40 minutes or until well browned and tender. Bring chicken broth to a boil. Place corn bread crumbs in mixing bowl; add 3 cups chicken broth. Cover; let stand for 5 minutes. Add celery, 2 hard-boiled eggs, sage, biscuits, onion, pepper and beaten eggs; mix well. Add more broth, if needed. Pour into' greased baking dish. Bake at 375 degrees for 1 hour. Melt butter. Add flour and 1/2 teaspoon salt; blend well. Add 2 cups chicken broth, giblets and remaining hard-boiled egg; cook until thick, stirring constantly. Serve with chicken and dressing.

Hilda Harman
Smithville High School
Smithville, Mississippi

PEAR-STUFFED CHICKEN

2 3-lb. roasting chickens
2 fresh pears
1/3 c. chopped onion
3/4 c. chopped celery
1/2 c. butter
1 8-oz. package corn bread
    stuffing mix
3 tbsp. chopped parsley
1/4 tsp. salt
1/8 tsp. pepper
1/4 tsp. savory

1/4 c. hot water
Vegetable shortening

Wash chickens; clean thoroughly. Core and dice pears. Saute onion and celery in butter until tender; place in large mixing bowl. Add pears, stuffing mix, parsley, salt, pepper, savory and hot water; mix lightly, but thoroughly. Stuff chickens. Rub shortening over outside of chickens; wrap in roasting wrap or aluminum foil. Roast at 375 degrees for 1 hour and 30 minutes to 2 hours or until chicken is done.

Shirley Marie Spurgeon
Flathead High School
Kalispell, Montana

POLLO ASADO

1 4 to 5-lb. roasting chicken
1 1/2 tsp. salt
2 cloves of garlic, chopped
1 1/2 tbsp. chopped parsley
Juice of 1 lemon
4 strips bacon
1 lg. onion
1 c. water
1 c. white wine or dry sherry

Clean chicken; remove giblets. Sprinkle chicken with salt, garlic and parsley. Sprinkle with lemon juice; rub well. Place bacon lengthwise over breast and thighs of chicken to cover exposed skin; tie bacon on carefully with thread or light string. Place, breast side up, in 9 x 11-inch baking dish. Peel onion; cut into quarters. Place onion in bottom of baking dish; pour water and wine over chicken and onion. Roast at 325 degrees for 1 hour. Turn chicken; bake for 1 hour longer, basting occasionally. Remove thread. Cut chicken into serving pieces; arrange on platter. Place pan liquids, bacon and onion in blender container; blend for several seconds. Pour 1/2 of the mixture over chicken; serve remaining mixture as gravy. Serve with rice, if desired.

Nancy K. Cochran
Narraguagus High School
Harrington, Maine

SMOTHERED CHICKEN

1   3 to 3 1/2-lb. roasting chicken
Salt and pepper to taste
1 c. vinegar
1 sm. onion, chopped
Flour

Rub cavity of chicken with salt and pepper. Place chicken on rack in 3-quart roasting pan, breast side up; sprinkle with salt and pepper. Add vinegar, 2 cups water and onion. Roast, covered, at 325 degrees for 2 hours or until thermometer registers 180 degrees. Stick fork or skewer into thick part of thigh; chicken is done if fork turns easily. Remove chicken from pan. Dilute juices in pan with 1 cup boiling water. Skim off fat; reserve. Measure stock. Use 1 1/2 tablespoons reserved fat and 1 1/2 tablespoons flour for each cup of stock. Mix flour and fat; cook over low heat until smooth. Add stock; bring to a boil, stirring constantly. Boil for 1 minute; add salt and pepper. Serve with rice or noodles.

Sister Augustine
Seton High School
Baltimore, Maryland

POLYNESIAN CHICKEN PLATTER

2   4-lb. roasting chickens
Hilo Stuffing
3 tbsp. melted butter
Curry-Fruit Glaze

Rinse chickens inside and out with cold water. Drain; pat dry. Stuff neck and body cavities lightly with Hilo Stuffing. Smooth neck skin over stuffing; skewer to back. Tie legs to tails with string. Place chickens on rack in roasting pan; brush with butter. Roast in 350-degree oven for 1 hour. Spoon part of the Curry-Fruit Glaze over each chicken to make thick coating. Continue roasting, basting 2 or 3 times with remaining glaze, for 1 hour or until tender.

Hilo Stuffing

1 c. white rice
4 tbsp. butter
1/2 c. chopped onion
2 chicken bouillon cubes
2 1/2 c. water
1/2 c. chopped macadamia nuts
1/2 c. flaked coconut

Saute rice in butter, stirring frequently, until golden. Stir in onion, bouillon cubes and water; bring to boiling point. Cover; simmer for 20 minutes or until water is absorbed. Sprinkle with nuts and coconut; toss lightly to mix.

Curry-Fruit Glaze

4 slices bacon, diced
1/2 c. chopped onion
2 tbsp. flour
1 tbsp. sugar
2 tsp. curry powder
1/2 tsp. salt
1 tbsp. bottled steak sauce
1 c. water
1   4-oz. jar baby-pack strained
    apples and apricots

Saute bacon in medium saucepan until almost crisp; remove bacon. Stir onion into drippings; saute just until soft. Stir in flour, sugar, curry powder and salt; heat until bubbly. Stir in remaining ingredients and bacon. Simmer, stirring several times, for 15 minutes or until thick.

Marilyn L. Staton
Roosevelt Junior High School
Coffeyville, Kansas

APPLE CIDER CHICKEN

1   3-lb. broiler-fryer
6 tbsp. flour
1/4 c. salad oil
1 sm. onion, sliced
1/2 clove of garlic, minced
1 env. chicken broth mix
1/2 tsp. salt
1/8 tsp. pepper
1/2 c. apple cider
2 tbsp. catsup
1 tsp. grated lemon rind

Cut chicken into serving pieces; coat well with 4 tablespoons flour. Brown chicken in oil in large skillet over medium heat; remove from skillet. Stir onion and garlic into pan drippings; saute until tender. Blend in remaining flour, broth mix, salt and pepper; cook, stirring constantly, until bubbly. Stir in cider, 1/2 cup water, catsup and lemon rind. Cook, stirring constantly, over medium heat until sauce thickens and comes to a boil; boil for 1 minute. Return chicken to skillet. Simmer, covered, for 45 minutes or until tender. Serve with noodles. Yield: 4 servings.

Darla Jo Black
Forbes Road Junior-Senior High School
Harrisonville, Pennsylvania

BAKED CHICKEN IMPERIAL

2 sm. fryer chickens, quartered
1 tsp. monosodium glutamate
1/8 tsp. pepper
1/4 c. oil
1 can cream of chicken soup
3/4 c. sauterne
1 5-oz. can water chestnuts,
    drained and sliced
1/2 lb. fresh mushrooms, sliced
1/4 c. chopped green pepper
1/4 tsp. thyme
1/2 c. sliced almonds or chopped
    cashew nuts

Season chickens with monosodium glutamate and pepper; brown over low heat in skillet in oil. Place chickens, skin side up, in 9 x 12 x 2-inch baking dish. Add soup to pan drippings in skillet; stir in sauterne gradually. Add water chestnuts, mushrooms, green pepper and thyme. Heat to boiling point. Pour sauce over chickens; cover with aluminum foil. Bake at 350 degrees for 15 minutes. Remove foil; add almonds. Bake for 25 to 35 minutes longer or until chickens are tender. May be served over hot rice, noodles or potatoes. Yield: 6-8 servings.

Mrs. Doris Burr
Sunset High School
Hayward, California

BAKED COCONUT-CURRY CHICKEN

1/3 c. frozen orange juice
    concentrate, thawed
1 tsp. salt
1 egg, slightly beaten
1 2 1/2-lb. frying chicken,
    disjointed
1 c. crushed corn flakes
1/2 c. shredded coconut
1 tsp. curry powder
1/4 c. melted butter or margarine
Orange slices

Mix orange juice concentrate, salt, and egg together; add chicken. Marinate for 15 minutes. Remove chicken; reserve marinade. Combine corn flakes, coconut and curry powder; coat chicken with coconut mixture, pressing to make coating stick. Place on lightly oiled foil-lined pan. Combine reserved marinade and melted butter; drizzle over chicken. Cover pan with aluminum foil. Bake at 350 degrees for 30 minutes. Uncover. Bake for 30 to 40 minutes longer or until well browned. Serve on platter with garnish of orange slices. Yield: 4 servings.

Mrs. Margaret Perry
Damascus Area School
Damascus, Pennsylvania

SWEET AND SOUR BAKED CHICKEN

1 3-lb. chicken
1 tsp. salt
2 tbsp. vinegar
2 tbsp. prepared mustard
2 tbsp. brown sugar

Season chicken with salt. Combine vinegar, mustard and brown sugar; mix thoroughly. Place long sheet of foil in baking dish. Place chicken on foil; brush with vinegar mixture. Cover chicken with foil; seal securely. Bake at 350 degrees for 1 hour and 30 minutes.

Mrs. Pat Duncan
Haltom Junior High School
Fort Worth, Texas

BAKED CURRIED CHICKEN

handwritten: 11/5 go it

1/4 c. flour *(handwritten: use thighs & breasts)*
1 tsp. paprika
1 2-lb. chicken, disjointed
Oil
2 tsp. curry powder
1 tsp. salt
1 can cream of chicken soup
1 16-oz. can cling peach slices, drained

Combine flour and paprika; coat chicken well. Brown chicken on all sides in hot oil in skillet. Sprinkle with curry powder and salt. Blend soup with 1 cup of water; pour over chicken. Bring to a boil. Place chicken mixture in casserole; cover. Bake at 325 degrees for 1 hour or until chicken is tender. Add peach slices; heat through. Garnish with celery leaves. Yield: 4 servings.

handwritten: Serve w/ rice.

Mrs. Mary Irish
Shawano High School
Shawano, Wisconsin

BRASSIE BIRD

1 3-lb. chicken, disjointed
2 c. seasoned flour
1/2 c. shortening
1 c. halved seedless grapes
2 c. sour cream

Dust chicken with flour. Brown chicken in shortening in large skillet over medium heat; remove to casserole. Place grapes and sour cream over chicken. Bake at 350 degrees for 20 minutes or until chicken is tender.

Madeline W. Martin
South Broward High School
Hollywood, Florida

BUTTER-CHICKEN POLONAISE

2 med. onions, sliced
2 carrots, sliced
1/4 c. chopped parsley
2 stalks celery, chopped
2 frying chickens, disjointed
Salt and pepper to taste
3/4 c. butter

Combine onions, carrots, parsley and celery in medium roasting pan. Sprinkle chicken with salt and pepper; arrange skin side down over vegetables. Dot with butter. Bake at 350 degrees for 45 minutes; baste occasionally. Bake, covered, for 10 minutes longer. Arrange chicken on heated platter; pour pan drippings over chicken.

Genevieve B. Grenzicki
Ottawa Junior High School
St. Clair Shores, Michigan

BUTTERMILK-PECAN CHICKEN

1/2 c. margarine
1 c. buttermilk
1 slightly beaten egg
1 c. flour
1 c. ground pecans
1 tbsp. paprika
1 tbsp. salt
Pepper to taste
1/4 c. sesame seed
2 broiler-fryer chickens, disjointed
1/4 c. pecan halves

Melt margarine in 13 x 9 x 2-inch baking dish. Blend buttermilk and egg in shallow dish. Combine flour, ground pecans, paprika, salt, pepper and sesame seed in separate dish. Dip chicken in buttermilk; roll in flour mixture. Place chicken, skin side down, in melted margarine in baking dish, turning each piece to coat well. Place several pecan halves on each piece. Bake at 350 degrees for 1 hour and 15 minutes or until tender. Yield: 8 servings.

Mrs. Patsy Lenz
Windsor High School
Windsor, Illinois

CALIFORNIA CHICKEN CACCIATORE

1 12-oz. can tomato sauce
2 cloves of garlic, minced
1/2 tsp. sweet basil
1/2 tsp. oregano
Salt

Pepper
Oil
1 2 to 2 1/2-lb. chicken, disjointed
1 bay leaf
2 med. onions, chopped
1 tsp. chopped parsley
1 lb. fresh mushrooms, sliced
3 oz. sauterne

Combine tomato sauce, 1 clove of garlic, sweet basil, oregano, 1/8 teaspoon salt and 1/8 teaspoon pepper in saucepan. Bring to a boil; reduce heat. Simmer for 10 minutes. Remove from heat; let stand. Heat oil in skillet to medium; add chicken pieces, bay leaf and remaining garlic. Brown chicken on all sides; season with salt and pepper to taste. Remove chicken from skillet; add onions and parsley. Saute until onions are tender. Add mushrooms to skillet; saute for about 1 minute. Stir in sauterne, chicken and tomato sauce; cover tightly. Simmer for 30 to 40 minutes or until chicken is tender.

Alice Mary Phillips
Roosevelt High School
Fresno, California

CHAMPAGNE CHICKEN

1/4 c. flour
Salt and pepper to taste
1/4 tsp. ground ginger
1 broiling chicken, disjointed
1/4 c. butter
1 med. onion, quartered
1 carrot, cut into 4 pieces
1 bay leaf
1 c. champagne or dry white wine
1 6-oz. package long grain and
   wild rice
1 c. heavy cream
1 8-oz. can white seedless grapes

Combine flour, salt, pepper and ginger in paper bag; add chicken pieces. Shake bag until chicken is coated with seasoned flour. Melt butter in skillet; add chicken pieces. Cook over low heat until chicken is lightly browned. Add onion, carrot, bay leaf and champagne. Cover skillet; simmer for about 30 minutes or until chicken is tender. Prepare rice according to package directions; arrange on heated serving platter. Place chicken over rice. Remove onion, carrot and bay leaf from skillet; add cream and grapes to gravy. Heat through; spoon over chicken. Yield: 4-6 servings.

Marie Denny
Putnam County Senior High School
Cookeville, Tennessee

CHICKEN ASADO

2 tbsp. sherry
2 tbsp. vinegar
2 tbsp. Worcestershire sauce
1/2 tsp. paprika
1 bay leaf
1/4 tsp. pepper
1/4 c. soy sauce
5 cloves of garlic
2 chicken breasts, halved
4 chicken thighs
4 chicken legs
4 chicken wings
Oil
6 sm. onions
1 8-oz. can tomato sauce
1 1/2 tsp. salt
4 med. potatoes
3 lg. green peppers

Combine sherry, vinegar, Worcestershire sauce, paprika, bay leaf, pepper and soy sauce. Crush 3 cloves of garlic; add to sherry mixture. Place chicken pieces in marinade; marinate for about 6 hours or longer. Reserve marinade. Heat 3 tablespoons oil in skillet; brown chicken pieces until golden. Remove chicken from skillet. Fry remaining garlic in pan drippings. Add onions, tomato sauce, salt and 1 cup of water; stir in reserved marinade. Bring to a boil; stir. Add chicken pieces; simmer for 1 hour or longer. Peel potatoes; cut into eighths. Fry potatoes in hot oil in skillet until golden brown; set aside. Cut green peppers into strips; add potatoes and green peppers to chicken mixture. Simmer for 15 minutes longer; serve. May thicken gravy if desired.

Mrs. Edith Baldwin
Base Line Junior High School
Boulder, Colorado

93

CHICK-A-DILLY

8 fryer legs or thighs
Salt and pepper to taste
Oil
2 c. water or chicken broth
1 c. apricot preserves
1/2 c. dill pickle juice
1/2 tsp. dillseed
2 tbsp. cornstarch
2 tsp. cold water
1   13 1/2-oz. can pineapple chunks,
*   drained*
1 c. Polish dill pickle chunks
1/2 c. maraschino cherries
3 c. hot rice

Season fryer legs with salt and pepper; brown in small amount of oil in 11-inch frypan over medium heat. Add water, apricot preserves, dill pickle juice and dillseed. Simmer for about 45 minutes, covered, or until chicken is tender. Blend cornstarch and cold water until smooth; add to chicken mixture. Cook over low heat until thickened, stirring constantly. Add pineapple chunks, dill pickle chunks and cherries. Heat for about 3 to 4 minutes or until warmed through. Serve over rice. Yield: 4 servings.

Val Slaid
Terrell Junior High School
Houston, Texas

CHICKEN ACAPULCO

1 frying chicken, disjointed
1/2 c. olive oil
6 lg. shrimp in shells
4 slices Canadian bacon
1 1/4 tsp. salt
1/8 tsp. pepper
1/8 tsp. red pepper
1 green pepper, cut in strips
1 med. onion, chopped
2 cloves of garlic, minced
2 tomatoes, chopped
2 c. uncooked rice
1/4 tsp. saffron
2 c. chicken broth
1/2 c. green peas
1/2 c. pimentos, cut in strips
1 1/2 c. black olives

Brown chicken in oil in large deep skillet over medium heat. Add shrimp, bacon, salt, pepper and red pepper; blend well. Stir in green pepper, onion and garlic. Simmer, covered, for 3 minutes. Stir in tomatoes. Simmer, covered, for 3 minutes longer. Add rice gradually, stirring constantly; stir in saffron and broth. Simmer, covered, for 10 minutes longer; add peas. Simmer, covered,for 5 minutes longer. Place chicken mixture in large serving dish; garnish with pimentos and olives.

Mrs. Anona Moore
Alvin Junior High School
Alvin, Texas

CHICKEN A L'ORANGE

1 frying chicken, disjointed
3 tbsp. flour
3 tbsp. cooking oil
2 tbsp. cornstarch
1 c. frozen orange juice concentrate
6 tbsp. (packed) brown sugar
1/4 c. vinegar
1 tsp. nutmeg

Coat chicken with flour. Brown in hot oil in skillet. Place chicken in baking dish. Combine cornstarch and small amount of orange juice in small saucepan, blending well. Cook, stirring, over low heat while adding remaining orange juice. Stir in brown sugar, vinegar and nutmeg. Cook, stirring constantly, until thickened. Pour sauce over chicken. Bake at 350 degrees for 40 to 50 minutes or until chicken is tender. Yield: 4 servings.

Mrs. Margery Creek
Francis Scott Key Junior High School
Silver Spring, Maryland

CHICKEN BAKE WITH MUSHROOMS AND SOUR CREAM

1   3-lb. fryer, cut up
Salt and pepper to taste
1/2 c. flour
1 tsp. paprika
1 tsp. baking powder
1 tsp. poultry seasoning
Oil or margarine

1 6-oz. can sliced mushrooms
1 can golden mushroom soup
1 c. sour cream
1 c. Cheddar cheese, shredded

Season chicken with salt and pepper. Combine flour, paprika, baking powder and poultry seasoning; roll chicken in mixture. Brown chicken lightly in small amount of oil; arrange in 13 x 9-inch baking dish. Drain mushrooms, reserving liquid; add water to measure 1/2 cup liquid. Combine soup, mushrooms, liquid and sour cream, blending thoroughly; pour over chicken. Bake at 350 degrees for 1 hour or until chicken is tender. Sprinkle with cheese. Bake for three minutes longer or until cheese is melted. Yield: 6 servings.

Mrs. D. J. Dear
Stringer High School
Stringer, Mississippi

CHICKEN CHIPS

1 frying chicken
Salt and pepper to taste
1 can evaporated milk
1 c. corn flake crumbs
1 1/2 tsp. parsley flakes
1 1/2 tsp. dried chives
2 tsp. grated Parmesan cheese

Bone chicken, removing skin; cut into 2-inch squares. Season chicken with salt and pepper; dip into milk. Combine crumbs, parsley, chives and cheese in shallow pan; blend well. Roll chicken in crumbs; arrange on greased baking sheet. Bake at 350 degrees for 25 minutes or until tender. Chicken may be fried in margarine in skillet, if desired.

Mrs. Margaret Amoroso
Turkey Valley School
Jackson Junction, Iowa

CHICKEN BOMBAY

1/3 c. flour
1 tsp. paprika
1 tsp. salt
8 chicken pieces
4 tbsp. butter
1 med. onion, sliced

4 chicken bouillon cubes
1 1/2 c. packaged precooked rice
1/2 c. white raisins
1/2 c. flaked coconut
1 sm. can mandarin oranges
1 tsp. curry powder
1/2 c. sliced almonds

Combine flour, paprika and 1/2 teaspoon salt; coat chicken well with flour mixture. Brown chicken in butter in large skillet over medium heat; remove chicken. Saute onion in remaining butter in skillet. Dissolve bouillon cubes in 1 1/2 cups boiling water. Stir rice, bouillon, raisins, coconut, oranges and curry powder into onion; blend well. Spoon mixture into 13 x 9 x 2-inch baking dish; arrange chicken over top. Bake at 350 degrees for 1 hour; sprinkle with almonds. Bake for 15 minutes longer.

Barsha Elzey
Terra Linda High School
San Rafael, California

CHICKEN AND BISCUIT CASSEROLE

1/2 c. flour
2 tsp. salt
1/4 tsp. pepper
1 tsp. paprika
1/4 c. margarine
1 3-lb. frying chicken, cut up
1 can cream of mushroom soup
1/2 c. milk
1/2 tsp. dillseed
1/2 c. sliced stuffed olives
1 can refrigerator biscuits

Combine flour, salt, pepper and paprika in shallow bowl; mix well. Melt margarine in 13 x 9-inch pan. Roll chicken in flour mixture; arrange in margarine, skin side down. Bake at 400 degrees for 40 minutes; turn chicken. Combine soup, milk, dillseed and olives; blend well. Pour soup mixture over chicken; arrange biscuits over top. Bake for 10 minutes longer or until biscuits are golden. Serve hot.

Gertrude Chambers
Westmont Junior High School
Westmont, Illinois

CHICKEN CERISE

2 broiler chickens with giblets
1 tsp. monosodium glutamate
1 chicken bouillon cube
Seasoned flour
Butter
Parsley
1 c. pearl onions
1 sm. clove of garlic, minced
1 lg. can Bing cherries
3 tbsp. cornstarch

Simmer chicken necks and giblets in 2 cups water; strain, reserving stock. Add monosodium glutamate and bouillon cube to reserved liquid. Quarter chicken; coat with flour. Brown chicken in small amount of butter in large skillet over medium heat; transfer to large casserole. Dot generously with additional butter; add 1 cup boiling water, several sprigs of parsley and onions. Bake, covered, at 375 degrees for 35 minutes. Remove cover. Increase temperature to 500 degrees; bake until brown. Strain skillet drippings; add melted butter to measure 4 tablespoons. Combine butter mixture, chopped pearl onions and garlic in saucepan; saute until onion is golden. Drain cherries, reserving juice; blend cornstarch with reserved juice, reserved stock, onion mixture and cherries. Simmer, stirring constantly, until smooth and thickened. Serve sauce with chicken. Yield: 4 servings.

Mrs. Doris W. Larke
Woodruff High School
Peoria, Illinois

CHICKEN IN COCONUT MILK

1 1/4 c. milk
2 c. fresh grated coconut
1/4 c. butter
1 4-lb. chicken, disjointed
1/2 c. chopped onion
2 cardamom seed, crushed
1 bay leaf
1/2 tsp. nutmeg
1 tsp. pressed garlic
1 tbsp. crushed fresh gingerroot
1 tbsp. sugar
1 tbsp. Worcestershire sauce
1 1/2 tbsp. salt

1/2 pt. cream
1/2 c. slivered toasted almonds
2 tomatoes, cut into wedges

Heat milk; soak coconut in warm milk overnight. Strain through cheesecloth, squeezing milk out. Set aside. Melt butter in saucepan; let stand until sediment forms on bottom of pan. Pour clarified butter into skillet. Heat butter; brown chicken well on all sides. Remove chicken to large deep casserole. Saute onion in pan drippings in skillet; add cardamom seed, bay leaf, nutmeg, garlic, gingerroot and sugar. Saute for 2 minutes. Stir in Worcestershire sauce and 1/4 cup coconut milk; cook over low heat for 2 minutes. Spoon onion mixture over chicken; season with salt. Pour remaining coconut milk over chicken mixture. Bake at 275 degrees for 1 hour and 30 minutes. Stir cream into mixture before serving. Garnish with almonds and tomatoes.

Mrs. Asha Singh
Revelstoke Secondary School
Revelstoke, British Columbia, Canada

CHICKEN CONFETTI

1 4 to 5-lb. broiler-fryer
  chicken, disjointed
3 tsp. salt
Pepper
1/4 c. salad oil
1/2 c. chopped onion
1 clove of garlic, minced
2 16-oz. cans tomatoes
1 6-oz. can tomato paste
1 8-oz. can tomato sauce
2 tbsp. snipped parsley
1 tsp. basil
1 8-oz. package spaghetti

Season chicken with 1 teaspoon salt and 1/8 teaspoon pepper. Brown chicken on all sides in oil in large skillet; remove chicken from skillet. Pour off pan drippings, reserving 3 tablespoons in skillet. Add onion and garlic; saute until onion is tender. Add chicken, tomatoes, tomato paste, tomato sauce, parsley, remaining salt, basil and 1/4 teaspoon pepper. Cover skillet tightly. Simmer for 1 hour to 1 hour and 30 minutes or until chicken is tender, stirring occasionally. May add water if necessary. Cook spaghetti according to package directions; drain. Arrange spaghetti on serving platter; spoon chicken mixture over spaghetti. Yield: 4-6 servings.

Mrs. Kay Nemetz
Southern Door High School
Brussels, Wisconsin

CHICKEN CONGOLESE

1 lg. chicken, disjointed
2 tbsp. melted butter
Salt to taste
White pepper to taste
3 green peppers, cut into lg.
    strips
1/2 c. peanuts
2 med. yellow onions, sliced
2 tbsp. vegetable oil
1/2 c. peanut butter
1/4 c. mayonnaise
1/4 tsp. pepper
1/2 tsp. celery salt
1 tsp. seasoned salt

Preheat oven to 400 degrees. Brush chicken with melted butter; sprinkle with salt and white pepper. Place chicken on 11 x 14 x 2-inch baking pan, skin side up. Bake for 25 minutes. Saute green peppers, peanuts and onions in oil in large skillet until green peppers and onions are limp. Blend peanut butter, mayonnaise and remaining seasonings together. Turn chicken pieces over in baking pan; spread with peanut butter mixture. Bake for 10 minutes. Arrange green pepper mixture over chicken. Bake for 15 minutes longer or until tender.

Harriet S. Mays
Harriet Beecher Stowe School
New York, New York

CHICKEN AND COTTAGE CHEESE

1 lg. fryer, disjointed
Salt and pepper to taste
1 c. cottage cheese
1/2 c. milk

1 tsp. onion, garlic or
    seasoning salt

Season fryer with salt and pepper; arrange in baking dish. Blend cottage cheese, milk and onion salt together, using blender. Spoon cottage cheese mixture over chicken; marinate for about 1 hour. Bake in 325-degree oven until tender, turning pieces once. Fryer may be removed from dish and about 1 cup hot water added to drippings. Heat to make gravy, if desired. Yield: 4-6 servings.

Ruth Dantzler
Columbia High School
Columbia, South Carolina

CHICKEN DELUXE

1 frying chicken
Salt and pepper to taste
1 pkg. frozen spatzels
3 sm. zucchini, sliced
1 sm. onion, diced
2 tbsp. tomato sauce
Paprika to taste
Garlic powder to taste
Crushed red pepper to taste
Minced parsley to taste
1/4 c. grated Romano cheese

Cut chicken into serving pieces. Brown chicken in small amount of fat in large skillet. Cook, covered, over low heat for 15 minutes or until tender. Salt and pepper chicken; arrange in casserole. Add 1/4 cup water to pan drippings in skillet; stir well Pour over chicken. Prepare spatzels according to package directions; drain. Place spatzels over chicken. Saute zucchini and onion in small amount of fat in skillet; cook, stirring, over medium heat for 5 minutes. Add tomato sauce, salt, pepper, paprika, garlic powder, red pepper and parsley; cook, stirring, for 5 minutes longer. Pour zucchini mixture over spatzels. Add 1/4 cup water to skillet; stir, scraping up pan drippings. Pour drippings over all; sprinkle with cheese. Bake at 325 degrees for 10 minutes or until heated through.

Mrs. Florence Calderone
North High School
Youngstown, Ohio

CHICKEN DRESSING CASSEROLE

1 stewing hen
1/2 c. butter or margarine
6 c. soft bread cubes
1 c. chopped celery
1 c. grated carrots
1/2 c. chopped onion
2 c. chopped apples
1 pimento, diced
Salt and pepper to taste
Sage to taste

Place hen in large saucepan; add 4 cups water. Bring to a boil; reduce heat. Simmer, covered, until chicken is tender. Drain chicken; reserve broth. Cut chicken into serving pieces; discard skin and bones. Melt butter in heavy skillet; stir in bread cubes, celery, carrots and onion, tossing to brown lightly. Remove from heat; stir in apples and pimento. Season with salt, pepper and sage; fold in chicken. Spoon mixture into greased casserole. Pour 4 cups reserved stock over all. Bake at 350 degrees for 45 minutes. Yield: 10-12 servings.

Mrs. Robert L. Muir
Morton Junior-Senior High School
Morton, Washington

CHICKEN AND EGGPLANT

1 frying chicken with liver
1 med. eggplant
3 eggs
2 tbsp. cold water
1 tsp. crumbled oregano
1 tbsp. chopped rosemary
1 c. bread crumbs
1/4 c. butter, melted
1 oz. salt pork, diced
Flour
1/4 c. olive oil
1/4 c. heavy cream
Juice of 1 lemon
1/4 c. Parmesan cheese

Preheat oven to 400 degrees. Cut chicken into serving pieces; chop liver. Peel eggplant; cut into cubes. Beat eggs well with cold water. Mix oregano and rosemary with bread crumbs. Combine melted butter and salt pork in skillet; add chopped chicken liver. Simmer for 2 minutes on top of stove. Sprinkle chicken pieces lightly with flour, dip into egg mixture. Dredge with bread crumb mixture. Coat bottom and sides of baking pan with oil; leave remaining oil in bottom of pan. Arrange chicken pieces in pan. Sprinkle small amount of flour over eggplant cubes; stir eggplant into remaining egg mixture. Dredge with remaining bread crumbs. Ring chicken with eggplant, filling all empty spaces around chicken pieces. Add cream to liver mixture; spoon sauce over chicken mixture. Sprinkle lemon juice and cheese over top. Bake for 30 minutes; reduce oven temperature to 350 degrees. Bake for 30 minutes longer or until chicken is tender.

Mrs. LaVerne Mercer
Elbert County High School
Elberton, Georgia

CHICKEN GOULASH

4 to 6 chicken thighs
4 tbsp. butter or margarine
1 onion, sliced
2 cloves of garlic, minced
2 beef bouillon cubes
1 tbsp. flour
1 tsp. chili powder
1 lg. zucchini, sliced
1 c. cherry tomatoes
3 or 4 carrots, sliced thin

Brown chicken thighs in butter in heavy skillet. Brown onion and garlic. Add bouillon cubes to 1 cup hot water; stir in flour mixed with small amount of water and chili powder. Pour over chicken. Simmer, covered, for 30 minutes. Add onion mixture, zucchini, tomatoes and carrots. Simmer, covered, for 30 minutes more or until chicken is tender.

Marilyn Mills Anderson
North Central High School
Spokane, Washington

CHICKEN ESPANA

1/4 c. olive oil
1/4 c. butter

1   2 1/2 to 3-lb. frying chicken,
      disjointed
2 1/2 tsp. salt
1/4 tsp. coarsely ground pepper
1 c. rice
1/4 c. minced onion
1/2 c. minced green pepper
1 c. sliced fresh mushrooms
1 clove of garlic, minced
1 can tomato paste
1 No. 2 can stewed tomatoes
1/2 tsp. hot sauce

Combine olive oil and butter in skillet; heat. Brown chicken on all sides in hot oil mixture. Remove chicken from skillet. Add salt, pepper, rice, onion, green pepper, mushrooms and garlic to remaining oil mixture in skillet. Saute until rice is lightly browned. Add tomato paste, tomatoes, hot sauce and 2 1/2 cups boiling water; stir well. Add chicken to rice mixture; cover. Simmer for 30 to 45 minutes or until chicken is tender and rice is fluffy. Yield: 4-6 servings.

Linda Voelker
Cove High School
Cove, Oregon

CHICKEN MARINADA

3 lb. chicken pieces
1/3 c. oil
2 tbsp. lemon juice
1/2 tsp. oregano
1/2 tsp. seasoned salt
1/2 tsp. onion salt
1/2 tsp. garlic salt
1/2 tsp. paprika

Remove skin from all chicken pieces except wings. Combine oil, lemon juice and seasonings. Place chicken pieces in bowl; pour oil mixture over pieces. Marinate for at least 2 hours. Place chicken in broiler pan. Reserve marinade. Broil about 9 inches from source of heat for 20 to 30 minutes. Turn chicken; baste with reserved marinade. Broil for 20 to 30 minutes longer.

Marietta Fowler
Bolivar Central School
Bolivar, New York

CHICKEN HAWAIIAN

1   2 to 2 1/2-lb. frying chicken,
      disjointed
Salt and pepper to taste
Flour
Oil
1   12-oz. bottle chili sauce
1   6-oz. can frozen lemonade
      concentrate
1 med. onion, chopped
2 tbsp. Worcestershire sauce
1/8 tsp. hot sauce

Sprinkle chicken with salt and pepper; coat with flour. Brown chicken in small amount of oil in large skillet. Combine chili sauce, lemonade concentrate, 3/4 cup water, onion, Worcestershire sauce and hot sauce; blend well. Spoon sauce over chicken. Bake at 325 degrees for 1 hour; turn chicken once while baking.

Mrs. Madaline Anders
Cooper Junior High School
Fresno, California

CHICKEN MEXICALI

1   2 to 3-lb. chicken, disjointed
Flour
Oil or butter
1/2 c. diced onion
1/2 c. diced celery
1/4 c. diced green pepper
1 tsp. salt
2 tbsp. (packed) brown sugar
1 c. catsup
2 tbsp. Worcestershire sauce

Roll chicken pieces in flour to coat. Brown chicken in small amount of oil in electric frypan. Combine onion, celery, green pepper, salt, 1 cup water, brown sugar, catsup and Worcestershire sauce. Drain excess fat from chicken; pour sauce over chicken pieces. Cook in frypan at 325 degrees for 1 hour and 30 minutes or until chicken is tender. Yield: 4-5 servings.

Mrs. Gloria Thompson
Grafton Central High School
Grafton, North Dakota

CHICKEN MANDARIN CASSEROLE

1 frying chicken
1/2 c. flour
1 tsp. salt
1/4 tsp. pepper
1/3 c. oil
1 11-oz. can mandarin oranges
1/3 c. soy sauce
1/4 c. (firmly packed) brown sugar
1/2 tsp. nutmeg

Cut chicken into serving pieces. Combine flour, salt and pepper in bag; shake chicken in flour mixture. Brown chicken in oil in large skillet over medium heat; remove to a shallow casserole. Drain oranges; reserve juice. Combine soy sauce, brown sugar and nutmeg with reserved juice; pour over chicken. Bake at 350 degrees for 40 minutes; baste occasionally with pan juices. Arrange orange pieces over chicken. Bake for 20 minutes longer. May be frozen for future use. Yield: 6 to 8 servings.

Mrs. Joalene Sepke
Mt. Clemens High School
Mt. Clemens, Michigan

CHICKEN MARENGO

1 2 1/2 to 3-lb. chicken
2 tbsp. butter or margarine
1 1-lb. can tomatoes
1 4-oz. can sliced mushrooms
1 clove of garlic, minced
1 env. onion soup mix

Cut chicken into serving pieces. Brown chicken in butter in large skillet; remove chicken. Stir in tomatoes, mushrooms, garlic and soup mix; blend thoroughly. Return chicken to skillet. Simmer, covered, for 45 minutes or until chicken is tender; stir occasionally. Yield: 6 servings.

Elenor Rollins
Riverdale High School
Fort Myers, Florida

CHICKEN LUAU-STYLE

1 chicken, disjointed
Flour

1/4 c. melted margarine
1 No. 303 can crushed pineapple
1 c. shredded coconut

Coat chicken well with flour. Brown chicken in margarine in large skillet over medium heat. Drain pineapple; reserve 1/2 cup juice. Spoon pineapple over chicken; add reserved juice. Simmer, covered, for 45 minutes, basting frequently. Remove to baking dish; sprinkle with coconut. Place in broiler 5 inches from source of heat until coconut is lightly browned.

Mrs. Sandra S. Thompson
Mt. Rainer Junior High School
Mt. Ranier, Maryland

CHICKEN IN NIPPY BASTING SAUCE

1/2 c. flour
Salt
Pepper
Paprika
1 3-lb. chicken, disjointed
1/4 c. shortening or oil
1 c. sugar
1 tsp. dry mustard
1 c. cider vinegar
1 clove of garlic, pressed
3/4 c. catsup
3 tbsp. Worcestershire sauce
1 tbsp. curry powder

Combine flour, 1 1/2 teaspoons salt, 1/4 teaspoon pepper and 2 teaspoons paprika in paper bag. Place chicken pieces in bag, shaking to coat well. Heat shortening in skillet; brown chicken well on all sides. Place chicken in casserole. Combine sugar, mustard, 1 teaspoon paprika, 1 teaspoon salt, 1/8 teaspoon pepper, vinegar, garlic, catsup, Worcestershire sauce and curry powder in saucepan. Bring to a boil; simmer for 5 minutes. Pour sauce over chicken; cover. Bake at 325 degrees for 1 hour or until chicken is tender. Yield: 4-6 servings.

Mrs. Donna Hofmann
Delta Senior Secondary School
Delta, Canada

STRAWBERRY MOCHA CREAM TARTLETS

4 c. sifted all-purpose flour
2 tsp. salt
1 1/2 c. vegetable shortening
2 pt. fresh strawberries
Light corn syrup
1/2 c. strong coffee
1/2 c. sugar
6 egg yolks
1 tbsp. instant coffee powder
2 tbsp. cocoa
1 c. softened sweet butter

Combine the flour and salt in bowl. Cut in the shortening until uniform but coarse. Sprinkle with 1/2 cup water; toss with fork, then press into ball. Roll out 1/2 of the dough at a time on a lightly floured surface to a 1/8-inch thickness. Cut into 3-inch circles, then fit inside 2 1/4-inch tart pans. Prick with fork. Place on a baking sheet. Bake in a 425-degree oven for 10 minutes or until lightly browned. Cool; remove from tart pans. Brush the strawberries with corn syrup and let dry on racks. Combine the coffee and sugar; boil to the thread stage or until candy thermometer registers 234 degrees. Beat the egg yolks with the instant coffee powder and cocoa until fluffy and thick. Add the hot syrup gradually to yolks, pouring in a thin steady stream and beating constantly. Continue beating until light in color and cold, then beat in butter. Chill slightly, if necessary. Pipe a ring of the butter mixture around the inside edge of each cooled tartlet shell. Place a strawberry in each shell and chill until served. Yield: 50 servings.

Photograph for this recipe on page 101.

HERBED PINWHEELS

1 c. butter, softened
1/4 c. chopped parsley
1/2 tsp. oregano leaves
1/4 tsp. tarragon leaves
1/4 tsp. ground thyme
1/8 tsp. pepper

4 c. sifted all-purpose flour
2 tbsp. baking powder
2 tsp. salt
2/3 c. vegetable shortening
1 1/2 c. milk
1 egg

Whip the butter with parsley, oregano, tarragon, thyme and pepper; let stand for 1 hour to blend flavors. Mix the flour, baking powder and salt in a bowl; cut in shortening until mixture looks like coarse meal. Stir in the milk. Knead about 10 times on a floured board and divide the dough in half. Roll out each half into a 12 x 10-inch rectangle. Spread half the herb mixture on each rectangle; roll up each rectangle from 12-inch side and seal edge. Cut each roll into 24 1/2-inch pinwheels and place pinwheels in ungreased muffin pans. Beat the egg with 2 tablespoons water and brush over pinwheels. Bake in a 425-degree oven for 10 to 15 minutes or until golden brown.

Photograph for this recipe on page 101.

TROPICAL FRUIT BAKE

1/2 c. (packed) brown sugar
1/4 c. butter, melted
1 tsp. grated lemon rind
2 tbsp. lemon juice
1/8 tsp. nutmeg
3 bananas
1 papaya
1 c. honeydew melon balls
1 c. cantaloupe balls
Flaked coconut

Combine brown sugar, butter, lemon rind and juice and nutmeg. Peel bananas; cut in half crosswise and lengthwise. Peel papaya; discard seeds and cube fruit. Combine all fruits; divide among 6 squares of heavy-duty aluminum foil. Sprinkle brown sugar mixture over each and sprinkle with coconut. Seal foil to make tight packages. Place on grill for 10 to 15 minutes or until heated through. Yield: 6 servings.

Photograph for this recipe on page 102.

BAHAMIAN-BARBECUED CHICKEN

1/4 c. lime juice
1/4 c. honey
1/4 c. light rum
4 1/2 tsp. monosodium glutamate
1/4 c. salad oil
2 tbsp. soy sauce
1/2 tsp. dried leaf tarragon
4 broiler-fryer chickens, halved
4 tsp. salt
1 tsp. pepper
Lime slices (opt.)

Line bottom of grill with heavy-duty aluminum foil and prepare fire. Blend the lime juice and honey in a bowl. Warm the rum slightly, then ignite. Add to honey mixture when flame has burned out. Add 1/2 teaspoon monosodium glutamate, oil, soy sauce and tarragon and heat until blended. Sprinkle both sides of chickens with the salt, pepper and remaining monosodium glutamate. Place chickens, skin side up, on grate 6 inches from heat and cook, turning occasionally, for 45 minutes to 1 hour and 15 minutes depending on weight of chicken. Brush with barbecue sauce during last 30 minutes of cooking time. Chicken leg should twist easily out of thigh joint and pieces should feel tender when probed with a fork when done. Garnish chicken with lime slices.

Photograph for this recipe on page 102.

SEAFOOD CREAM WITH AVOCADO

1 lb. fresh mushrooms, sliced
1 c. sliced onion
1 c. butter or margarine
2/3 c. flour
2 1/2 tsp. salt
1 tsp. monosodium glutamate
1/2 tsp. dry mustard
1/2 tsp. pepper
1/4 tsp. thyme leaves
5 c. milk
2 c. light cream
2 eggs, slightly beaten
2 c. grated Swiss cheese
8   7-oz. cans solid white tuna
1 c. sauterne
2 tsp. grated lemon peel
Lemon juice
6   5-oz. cans lobster, drained
2/3 c. chopped toasted blanched
*   almonds*
12 ripe avocados
Watercress

Saute the mushrooms and onion in butter until lightly browned; remove with slotted spoon. Quickly stir in the flour and seasonings. Stir in the milk and cream gradually. Cook and stir until the sauce boils for 1 minute. Stir a small amount of hot sauce into eggs, then return to the saucepan. Stir the cheese into hot sauce over low heat until melted. Drain the tuna; separate into large pieces. Add sauterne, lemon peel, 2 tablespoons lemon juice, tuna, lobster, almonds, sauteed mushrooms and onion to the sauce. Heat to serving temperature. Cut the avocados in half lengthwise, twisting gently to separate halves. Whack a sharp knife directly into seeds and twist to lift out. Peel avocado halves and brush with lemon juice. Arrange on a serving platter with watercress. Garnish with lime slices. Serve hot seafood mixture over avocado halves. Garnish with buttered, toasted fine bread crumbs and sliced truffles. Yield: 24 servings.

Photograph for this recipe on page 101.

BLACK BEANS AND RICE

1   6-oz. package herb rice
1/4 c. chopped onion
1 c. cooked black beans or
*   kidney beans*
1 tomato, cut in wedges
Finely chopped parsley

Cook rice according to package directions, adding onion at beginning of cooking. Stir in part of the beans. Turn out onto a large square of heavy-duty aluminum foil. Top with tomato; add remaining beans. Fold foil over top, sealing to make a tight package. Place on grill for 10 to 15 minutes or until heated through. Sprinkle with parsley when ready to serve. Rice mixture may be cooked the day before and chilled, if desired. Yield: 6 servings.

Photograph for this recipe on page 102.

CHICKEN AND MUSHROOM DINNER IN FOIL

3/4 c. rice
1 frying chicken, quartered
2 tsp. salt.
1 8-oz. can mushrooms
2 zucchini, sliced
1 green pepper, cut in strips
1 onion, thinly sliced
1 15-oz. can tomato sauce
1/4 to 1/2 tsp. hot pepper sauce
1/2 tsp. oregano
1/2 tsp. basil
Grated Parmesan cheese

Preheat oven to 375 degrees. Cut 4 12-inch squares of heavy-duty aluminum foil. Spoon 3 tablespoons rice into center of each square. Sprinkle each chicken quarter with 1/2 teaspoon salt; place over rice. Drain mushrooms, reserving 1/4 cup liquid. Divide vegetables and mushrooms into 4 equal portions; place 1 portion over each chicken quarters. Combine tomato sauce, reserved mushroom liquid, hot pepper sauce, oregano and basil. Spoon some sauce over each chicken quarter. Seal foil; place packets on baking sheet. Bake for 1 hour or until chicken is tender. Open packets; sprinkle with cheese. Yield: 4 servings.

Ann Mary Marcero
Arthur Junior High School
Grosse Pointe, Michigan

CHICKEN PARMESAN

2 chicken breasts, halved
Butter
1 tbsp. flour
1/2 c. dry sherry
1/2 tsp. salt
1/8 tsp. pepper
1 c. heavy cream
1 tsp. grated lemon rind
1 tbsp. lemon juice
6 tbsp. grated Parmesan cheese

Brown chicken in 1/4 cup butter in skillet over medium heat; reduce heat. Cook, covered for 35 minutes or until chicken is tender. Remove chicken from pan; blend flour into pan drippings. Stir in sherry, salt, pepper and cream; blend thoroughly. Return chicken to skillet; simmer, covered, for 15 minutes. Stir in lemon rind and juice. Arrange chicken in shallow 11 x 7-inch baking dish; top with sauce. Sprinkle with Parmesan cheese; dot with 1 tablespoon butter. Brown under broiler 4 to 5 inches from source of heat. Yield: 4 servings.

Mrs. Deborah Wheeler
Cabot High School
Cabot, Vermont

CHICKEN WITH NOODLE DUMPLINGS

1 med. onion, chopped
1/2 c. chopped celery
2 to 3 tbsp. shortening
1 3 to 4-lb. fryer, cut up
4 tsp. salt
1 tsp. paprika
1/4 tsp. pepper
Flour
1 13-oz. can evaporated milk
1 can cream of mushroom soup
4 eggs, beaten
1/4 c. milk

Saute onion and celery in shortening. Season chicken with 2 teaspoons salt, paprika and pepper; add to onion mixture. Brown chicken for 10 minutes, turning occasionally. Simmer, covered, for 1 hour or until chicken is tender; remove chicken. Blend 2 tablespoons flour into onion mixture. Simmer, stirring constantly, for 5 minutes; add canned milk and soup. Simmer, stirring until smooth, for 5 minutes; remove from heat. Combine 2 cups flour, 1 teaspoon salt, eggs and milk; mix well. Bring 3 quarts water to a boil; add remaining salt. Drop dough from wet teaspoon into water; bring to a rolling boil. Cook dumplings for 10 minutes or until they rise to top of water; drain. Add dumplings to soup mixture; arrange chicken over top. Simmer until just heated through.

Grace Lamusga
Hosterman Junior High School
Minneapolis, Minnesota

CRANBERRY-ORANGE CHICKEN

1 2 1/2 to 3-lb. frying chicken,
    disjointed
1 10 1/2-oz. can beef broth
3/4 c. cranberry juice cocktail
1/4 c. butter or margarine
Salt to taste
2 med. oranges, thinly sliced
1 tbsp. cornstarch
1 tbsp. water
2 tbsp. sugar
1 tbsp. vinegar

Combine chicken neck, giblets and beef broth in medium saucepan. Simmer, covered, for 1 hour. Strain broth; add cranberry juice cocktail. Boil until liquid is reduced to 1 cup. Set aside. Brown remaining chicken pieces in half the butter in skillet. Place in 11 3/4 x 7 1/2 x 1 3/4-inch baking dish. Season chicken pieces with salt. Bake in 350-degree oven for 25 minutes. Add orange slices to chicken. Bake for 30 to 35 minutes longer. Blend cornstarch and water; stir into cranberry mixture. Cook, stirring, until sauce is thickened and bubbly. Melt remaining butter in small saucepan; stir in sugar. Cook, stirring, until mixture bubbles and is brown. Add vinegar. Stir sugar mixture into sauce; heat through. Pour over chicken. Yield: 4 servings.

Adele Olinde
Poydras High School
New Roads, Louisiana

CHICKEN WITH OYSTERS

1 clove of garlic
3 tbsp. olive oil
1 3-lb. chicken, disjointed
2 tbsp. flour
1 c. chopped oysters
1/2 tsp. salt
1 bay leaf
1/4 c. dry white wine
1/2 c. chicken stock

Saute garlic in oil in skillet until browned; remove garlic. Dredge chicken with flour; fry in garlic-flavored oil until golden. Add oys-

ters, salt, bay leaf, wine and chicken stock. Cover; simmer for 30 minutes or until chicken is tender. Yield: 4 servings.

Carole Lionberger
Irma Marsh Middle School
Fort Worth, Texas

CHICKEN PAPRIKA A LA TRISHA

8 chicken thighs
3 to 4 tbsp. melted butter
Paprika
2 med. onions
1/2 lb. small fresh mushrooms
2 chicken bouillon cubes
1/2 c. sherry
2 to 3 stalks celery with leaves
1 lg. green pepper
1 sm. can pimento strips
Flour
1 1/2 c. sour cream

Coat chicken with melted butter; sprinkle with paprika heavily. Cut onions into 1/4-inch slices; separate into rings. Place chicken pieces and onion rings in large iron skillet; brown slowly. Add mushrooms; saute for 3 to 4 minutes. Stir in 2 cups water, bouillon cubes and sherry. Additional water may be added if desired. Simmer until chicken is tender. Slice celery crosswise into 1/4-inch strips; chop green pepper coarsely. Place pimento strips, celery and green pepper over chicken mixture; cover. Steam for 5 to 7 minutes or until vegetables are crisp-tender. Make a thin smooth paste from flour and water. Add to liquid in skillet. Cook over low heat, stirring constantly, until thickened. Remove chicken mixture from heat; stir in sour cream. Serve over hot buttered noodles or rice.

Patricia Ann Harding
John F. Kennedy Junior High School
Plantsville, Connecticut

CHICKEN IN PECAN SAUCE

1 8-oz. package sm. noodles
2 2-lb. broiler-fryer chickens,
    disjointed

2 tsp. salt
1/2 tsp. crushed rosemary
1/4 tsp. pepper
3 tbsp. butter
1/2 c. finely chopped onion
4 tbsp. flour
1 3/4 c. milk
1/4 c. dry white wine
1 can cream of chicken soup
3/4 c. chopped pecans
1/4 tsp. paprika

Cook noodles in boiling salted water in saucepan until tender; drain. Place noodles in 13 x 9 x 2-inch baking dish. Season chickens with 1 1/2 teaspoons salt, rosemary and pepper. Melt butter in large skillet; brown chickens on all sides. Arrange chicken in single layer over noodles. Saute onion in pan drippings in skillet until soft. Blend in flour; stir until bubbly. Add milk and wine gradually, stirring constantly, until thickened. Cook for 1 minute longer. Stir in soup, pecans and remaining salt. Spoon sauce over chicken mixture; sprinkle with paprika. Cover dish; chill. Bake at 350 degrees for 1 hour and 15 minutes or until chicken is tender. Garnish with toasted almonds or pecans. Yield: 8 servings.

Mrs. Shirley Shepherd Allen
Redford High School
Detroit, Michigan

CHICKEN PUDDING

1   4 to 4 1/2-lb. chicken with
    giblets, disjointed
Onion salt
Celery salt
Parsley flakes
Pepper
Flour
Salt
1/3 c. butter
3 eggs
1 c. milk
2 tbsp. melted butter

Combine neck, giblets and backbone in saucepan in water to cover. Season to taste with onion salt, celery salt, parsley flakes and pepper. Cook over low heat for about 45 minutes; strain. Reserve broth. Combine 1/2 cup flour, 1 1/2 teaspoons salt and 1/4 teaspoon pepper in paper bag; shake chicken pieces in seasoned flour until coated. Melt butter in skillet; brown chicken evenly on all sides. Pour reserved broth over chicken; cover tightly. Simmer for 1 hour to 1 hour and 15 minutes or until chicken is tender. Remove chicken to 8-inch baking dish, reserving broth. Preheat oven to 450 degrees. Sift 1 1/4 cups flour and 1/2 teaspoon salt together; set aside. Beat eggs well; add milk and melted butter. Stir in flour mixture until smooth. Pour batter over chicken. Bake for 15 minutes; reduce oven temperature to 350 degrees. Bake for 20 to 25 minutes longer. Blend 1 or 2 tablespoons flour and enough water together to make a smooth paste; stir in reserved broth. Cook, stirring constantly, until slightly thickened. Serve gravy with chicken. Yield: 4-6 servings.

Mary L. Schulte
Deshler Public School
Deshler, Nebraska

CHICKEN RIESLING

1 frying chicken, cut up
1 sm. jar cocktail onions
1 sm. can mushrooms
1 clove of garlic, minced
1 bay leaf
Minced parsley to taste
1 c. Riesling
1/2 c. sour cream

Brown chicken in skillet in small amount of hot fat; arrange in casserole. Drain onions, reserving half the liquid. Combine onions, reserved liquid, mushrooms, garlic, bay leaf, parsley and Riesling; blend well. Pour sauce over chicken. Bake, covered, for 1 hour and 30 minutes or until chicken is tender. Remove chicken to heated platter. Stir sour cream into sauce in casserole. Serve with chicken.

Mrs. Beverly Romney
Montera Junior High School
Oakland, California

CHICKEN IN RED WINE SAUCE

1   3 1/2-lb. chicken with giblets
      and neck, quartered
3 bay leaves
1 tsp. salt
1/8 tsp. pepper
2 sliced onions
12 whole sm. onions
Bacon fat
1/4 c. butter
2 tbsp. chopped onion
1 lb. whole sm. mushrooms
1/4 c. cognac
2 c. Burgundy
2 tbsp. flour
1 tsp. marjoram
1/2 tsp. thyme
1 chicken bouillon cube
4 sprigs of chopped parsley
1 lg. clove of garlic

Combine chicken giblets, neck, 1 bay leaf, salt, pepper, 3 cups water and sliced onions in saucepan. Simmer for 1 hour; strain and set aside. Brown whole onions in small amount of bacon fat in skillet. Place browned onions in shallow 10-inch baking dish. Sprinkle with 2 tablespoons bacon fat. Bake at 350 degrees for 30 minutes or until barely tender. Drain on absorbent paper; set aside. Melt butter in 10-inch skillet. Brown chopped onion in butter; stir in mushrooms. Cook, stirring frequently, for 3 to 4 minutes. Remove mushrooms and chopped onions from skillet with slotted spoon. Reheat bacon fat in skillet; brown chicken over medium heat. Warm cognac in saucepan; ignite. Pour flaming cognac over chicken gradually, shaking skillet as flame dies. Place chicken in 3 to 4-quart casserole. Pour Burgundy into saucepan; boil until reduced to 1 1/2 cups. Stir flour into chicken pan drippings in skillet, scraping browned bits from side and bottom of skillet. Pour Burgundy and giblet stock into skillet. Cook, stirring constantly, until thickened. Add remaining bay leaves, marjoram, thyme, bouillon cube, parsley and garlic. Simmer for about 10 minutes. Strain sauce; pour over chicken. Bake at 350 degrees for about 30 minutes; stir onions and mushrooms into sauce. Bake for 30 minutes longer or until chicken is tender. Place chicken mixture on platter; sprinkle with additional chopped parsley. Serve over rice.

Bette R. Barben
George Dewey Junior High School
Bremerton, Washington

CHICKEN ROMANO

Flour
Salt
Pepper
1 frying chicken, disjointed
1/4 c. butter
Salad oil
3 c. chicken broth
1/4 c. wine vinegar
1 clove of garlic, pressed
1 tsp. rosemary
1 sm. can mushrooms, drained
1 c. rice
1/4 to 1/2 tsp. garlic powder
Chopped parsley

Combine enough flour to coat chicken, salt and pepper to taste. Coat chicken with seasoned flour. Combine butter and 1/2 cup salad oil in skillet; brown chicken well on all sides over medium heat. Place chicken in roasting pan. Add 1 cup chicken broth, vinegar, garlic clove, rosemary and mushrooms to pan drippings in skillet. Pour broth mixture over chicken in pan; cover. Bake at 325 degrees for 1 hour or until chicken is tender. Pour 2 tablespoons salad oil into skillet; saute rice until lightly browned. Season with garlic powder. Pour remaining broth over rice; stir in parsley. May add additional mushrooms if desired. Cover tightly; cook without removing lid for about 20 minutes over low heat. Serve rice with chicken.

Mrs. Martha Eastland
Highland Park Middle School
Dallas, Texas

CHICKEN WITH ROSEMARY

1 broiler chicken, disjointed
Salt and pepper
1 tbsp. chopped parsley
1 chopped onion

1 clove of garlic, minced
3 tbsp. salad oil
1 tbsp. butter or margarine
1/8 tsp. rosemary
2 tbsp. wine vinegar
1/3 c. water
Flour

Season chicken with salt and pepper to taste. Combine parsley, onion, garlic and 1 tablespoon oil in skillet; simmer until onion is tender. Remove vegetables from skillet with slotted spoon; set aside. Add remaining oil to skillet; brown chicken on all sides. Add butter, salt and pepper to taste and rosemary. Dilute vinegar with water; add sauteed vegetables and vinegar mixture to chicken mixture. Cover skillet; simmer for about 30 minutes or until chicken is tender, adding additional liquid if necessary. Combine small amount of flour and water, blending to smooth paste. Thicken gravy with flour mixture. May serve over cheese rice if desired.

Dorothy M. Crone
Fayetteville High School
Fayetteville, Ohio

CHICKEN SAUTE

1 3-lb. fryer, cut up
Salt and pepper to taste
5 tbsp. butter
3 med. onions, sliced
2 tbsp. flour
1/2 c. dry white wine
2 tbsp. tomato paste
1/2 lb. mushrooms, sliced thickly

Rub fryer with salt and pepper; brown in butter in skillet. Add onions. Saute until onions are golden. Stir in flour; mix well. Add wine, 1/2 cup water and tomato paste; blend thoroughly. Simmer, covered, for 30 minutes. Add mushrooms; simmer for 15 minutes longer. Add water if needed, stirring to blend well. Season to taste with additional salt and pepper, if desired. Yield: 4 servings.

Mrs. Eileen Yeakley
Martinsville Junior High School
Martinsville, Indiana

CHICKEN AND SPICE

Flour
Salt and pepper to taste
12 chicken pieces
1/2 tsp. oregano
2 tsp. paprika
1/4 tsp. tarragon
1/4 tsp. thyme
1/4 tsp. marjoram
1/2 c. cooking oil
1/2 c. butter

Combine flour with salt and pepper; roll chicken in flour mixture. Combine oregano, paprika, tarragon, thyme and marjoram; roll chicken in mixture. Refrigerate for at least six hours. Heat oil and butter in electric skillet to 325 degrees. Brown chicken in hot oil for 20 minutes, turning to brown on all sides. Arrange chicken in large shallow baking dish. Bake at 350 degrees for 25 minutes or until chicken is tender. Garnish with orange slices, pineapple, sesame seed, poppy seed and scored cucumber slices, if desired.

Beverly J. Byrne
Rocky Ford High School
Rocky Ford, Colorado

CHICKEN PARISIAN

1 No. 2 can sliced pineapple
1 3-lb. frying chicken, disjointed
2 tbsp. butter
2 tsp. seasoned salt
1 c. sour cream
2 oz. bleu cheese, crumbled
1 tbsp. snipped chives

Drain pineapple; reserve 1/2 cup syrup. Brown chicken in butter in large skillet over medium heat. Sprinkle with seasoned salt; add reserved syrup. Simmer, covered, for 30 minutes. Top chicken with pineapple slices, sour cream, cheese and chives. Simmer, covered, for 5 minutes longer or until heated through. Yield: 6 servings.

Deanna Jucht
Needles High School
Needles, California

CHICKEN SAUTERNE

2 3 1/2-lb. frying chickens,
    disjointed
6 tbsp. margarine
3 tbsp. flour
1/2 tsp. salt
1/2 tsp. paprika
1 tbsp. instant minced onion
1/4 tsp. hot sauce
1/2 tsp. Worcestershire sauce
1/2 tsp. celery salt
1/2 tsp. powdered oregano
1 c. chicken broth, strained
1 c. sauterne
1 c. light cream
1 lb. sliced cooked mushrooms
1 pkg. frozen peas

Place chickens in kettle; cover with cold water. Simmer chickens until tender. Remove skin and bones; cut into large chunks. Melt margarine in skillet; add flour, salt and paprika, blending well. Stir in minced onion, hot sauce, Worcestershire sauce, celery salt and oregano. Combine broth and sauterne; pour into flour mixture gradually. Cook, stirring constantly, until smooth and thickened. Cool slightly; stir in cream and mushrooms. Cook peas according to package directions; drain. Stir peas and chicken into sauce. Heat through. Serve over green rice if desired.

Pearl V. Johnson
Roosevelt Junior High School
Cedar Rapids, Iowa

CREAMY CHICKEN SUPREME

1 2 1/2 to 3-lb. frying chicken,
    disjointed
2 tbsp. melted butter
1 tsp. salt
1/4 tsp. pepper
1 4-oz. can mushroom pieces
3/4 c. non-dairy coffee creamer
1 tbsp. flour
1 tsp. paprika
1 tsp. Worcestershire sauce

Preheat oven to 400 degrees. Arrange chicken in shallow baking pan; brush with melted butter. Sprinkle with salt and pepper. Bake for 45 minutes. Drain mushrooms; reserve liquid. Add water to reserved liquid to measure 3/4 cup. Combine non-dairy creamer, flour, mushroom liquid, paprika and Worcestershire sauce in small bowl; blend thoroughly. Stir in mushrooms. Spoon mixture over chicken. Bake for 10 minutes longer or until tender.

Mrs. Joe Hutchison
North Side Junior High School
Humboldt, Tennessee

CHICKEN STROGANOFF ROYALE

1 c. flour
1 tbsp. salt
1 tbsp. paprika
2 tsp. poultry seasoning
1/2 tsp. pepper
2 lg. frying chickens, disjointed
1/2 c. butter
1 lb. fresh mushrooms, sliced
1/2 c. chicken broth
2 c. sour cream
Chopped parsley

Preheat oven to 350 degrees. Combine flour, salt, paprika, poultry seasoning and pepper; mix well. Coat chicken with flour mixture; reserve remaining mixture. Melt butter in skillet; brown chicken in butter over medium heat. Remove chicken to 13 x 9 x 2-inch baking dish. Saute mushrooms in remaining butter in skillet; remove from skillet. Pour pan drippings over chicken. Bake, skin side up, for 30 minutes or until tender. Arrange chicken on heated platter; keep warm. Skim 3 tablespoons fat from pan drippings; place in skillet. Blend in 3 tablespoons reserved flour mixture until bubbly; add broth gradually, stirring constantly, until smooth and thickened. Simmer for 2 minutes longer; stir in mushrooms. Simmer, stirring constantly, for 1 minute longer. Stir in sour cream; heat through. Pour sauce over chicken; sprinkle with parsley. Yield: 8 servings.

Merle Anne Jeffries
Eagle Mountain High School
Eagle Mountain, California

CHICKEN IN SUPREME SAUCE

1/2 c. flour
Salt
Pepper
1/2 tsp. paprika
1 frying chicken, disjointed
Oil
1 sm. can mushroom pieces, drained
1 c. chopped celery
1/2 c. chopped onion
1/2 tsp. rosemary
1 clove of garlic, mashed
1/2 c. beer

Combine flour, 1 teaspoon salt, 1/4 teaspoon pepper and paprika in paper bag; shake chicken pieces in seasoned flour until coated. Brown chicken in oil in skillet; remove to casserole. Combine mushrooms, celery, onion, rosemary, 1 teaspoon salt, garlic and 1/4 teaspoon pepper; stir in beer. Pour sauce over chicken. Bake at 350 degrees for 1 hour and 30 minutes or until chicken is tender.

Mrs. Colleen Weibel
Bangor High School
Bangor, Wisconsin

CHICKEN-VEGETABLE DINNER

2 chickens, quartered
Salt and pepper to taste
Flour (opt.)
1 lb. green beans, cut
4 med. potatoes, quartered
4 med. carrots, sliced
1 med. onion, sliced
2 chicken bouillon cubes

Season chicken with salt and pepper; roll in flour. Heat small amount of fat in electric skillet to 250 degrees. Brown chicken in hot fat until golden; remove from skillet. Drain off excess fat. Place vegetables in skillet; arrange chicken over vegetables. Dissolve bouillon cubes in 1 1/2 to 2 cups boiling water; pour over chicken. Simmer, covered, for 45 minutes or until tender.

Mary Ann S. Welch
Southwest Junior High School
Lakeland, Florida

CHICKEN-VEGETABLE MEDLEY

1 3 1/2 to 4-lb. stewing chicken,
*   disjointed*
Salt
Pepper
1/8 tsp. garlic powder
1/4 c. chopped parsley
4 lg. leeks
3 carrots
4 stalks celery with leaves
1 1/2 lb. fresh broccoli
1 green pepper
18 lg. button mushrooms
2 tbsp. cornstarch

Place chicken in 4-quart kettle; add 2 cups water, 1/2 teaspoon salt, 1/8 teaspoon pepper, garlic powder and parsley. Bring to a boil; cover. Reduce heat; simmer for 1 hour and 30 minutes. Chop vegetables coarsely; add vegetables and mushrooms to chicken mixture. Cook, covered, for 10 minutes over medium heat until just tender. Blend cornstarch with enough water to make a smooth paste. Stir cornstarch into chicken mixture. Cook over low heat, stirring constantly, until gravy is thickened. Season with additional salt and pepper if necessary.

Olive R. Curtis
Mount Baker Junior-Senior High School
Deming, Washington

CHICKEN TERIYAKI

1/2 c. soy sauce
1/2 c. white wine
2 tbsp. sugar
1/2 tsp. ground ginger
1/8 tsp. garlic powder
5 chicken legs, disjointed

Combine soy sauce, wine, sugar, ginger, garlic powder and 1/2 cup water; blend thoroughly. Arrange chicken in shallow baking dish. Pour sauce over chicken; marinate for at least 2 hours, turning chicken occasionally. Bake chicken in sauce at 350 degrees for 1 hour and 15 minutes, turning occasionally. Serve with rice.

Laura M. Chaney
Fernando Rivera School
Daly City, California

CHICKEN AND WILD RICE

1   2 to 3-lb. frying chicken
1 pkg. onion soup mix
1/3 c. wild rice
1/3 c. brown rice
1   2-oz. can mushroom pieces
1 tsp. salt
1 can cream of chicken soup
1/2 soup can milk

Cut chicken into serving pieces. Sprinkle soup mix into greased 5-quart casserole; sprinkle wild rice and brown rice over soup mix. Cover rice with mushrooms. Salt chicken; arrange over mushrooms. Spoon soup over chicken. Combine milk with 1/2 soup can water; pour over all. Bake, covered, at 325 degrees for 2 hours and 30 minutes or until chicken is tender. Milk or water may be added, if needed.

Lois J. Hendrickson
Sauk Rapids Senior High School
Sauk Rapids, Minnesota

CHICKEN AND YELLOW RICE CASSEROLE

1 chicken, disjointed
1/4 c. olive oil
1 clove of garlic, minced
1 1/2 tsp. salt
1 c. diced onion
1 green pepper, diced
1   1-lb. can tomatoes
1/8 tsp. pepper
1/8 tsp. saffron
1 c. packaged precooked rice
1/4 tsp. yellow food coloring
1   10-oz. package frozen peas

Brown chicken in olive oil in skillet; remove chicken. Add garlic, salt, onion and green pepper to remaining oil in skillet. Saute over medium heat until onion is golden; stir in tomatoes, pepper, saffron and 1 cup water, mixing well. Prepare rice according to package directions; stir in food coloring. Combine tomato mixture with rice and chicken. Spoon into casserole. Bake, covered, at 375 degrees for 35 minutes. Pre-

pare peas according to package directions; drain well. Stir peas into chicken mixture. Bake for 10 minutes longer. Garnish with pimento strips, if desired. May be prepared ahead of time and reheated before serving.

Mrs. Margaret Varble
Crawford Junior High School
Lexington, Kentucky

CHICKEN IN WINE

1 frying chicken, disjointed
4 tbsp. butter
4 tbsp. salad oil
1 med. onion, sliced
Salt and pepper to taste
1/2 tsp. parsley flakes
1/2 c. sauterne
1   4-oz. can mushrooms

Skin chicken pieces. Combine butter and oil in large skillet over medium heat; saute chicken with onion until browned. Season with salt and pepper; add parsley flakes and sauterne. Reduce heat; simmer, covered, for 30 minutes or until chicken is tender, turning frequently. Add mushrooms; simmer for 5 minutes longer. Arrange chicken on heated platter; pour sauce over chicken. Garnish as desired. Yield: 4 servings.

Mrs. Phyllis D. Wills
Audubon High School
Audubon, New Jersey

COMPANY CHICKEN EXOTICA

1   3-lb. frying chicken,
*   disjointed*
1/2 c. olive oil
2 c. instant rice
2 c. chopped onions
1 clove of garlic, minced
1   1-lb. can whole tomatoes
1 can chicken broth
1   4-oz. can chopped green
*   chili peppers*
1/2 tsp. saffron
1/2 tsp. crushed red pepper
2 1/2 tsp. salt
1/2 tsp. pepper

1/2 pkg. frozen green peas
1 c. pimento-stuffed olives

Brown chicken in hot olive oil in large Dutch oven or heavy roaster pan. Add rice, onions and garlic; brown slightly, stirring occasionally. Add tomatoes, broth, green chilies, saffron, red pepper, salt and pepper. Bring to a boil; cover. Bake at 325 degrees for 1 hour or until chicken is tender, adding water if necessary. Stir in 1 cup water; sprinkle frozen peas and olives over top. Bake for 20 minutes longer. Yield: 6 servings.

Mrs. Loretha Roper
Canute High School
Canute, Oklahoma

COMPANY CHICKEN WITH SAVORY RICE

5 sm. frozen chicken breasts
5 sm. frozen chicken thighs
1/2 c. flour
1/4 tsp. salt
1/4 tsp. pepper
3 tbsp. shortening
2 cans cream of chicken soup
1   4-oz. can mushrooms with liquid
2 c. instant rice
2 cans consomme

Thaw chicken pieces. Combine flour, salt and pepper in paper bag; shake chicken pieces in seasoned flour until coated. Brown chicken well in hot shortening in skillet; remove to casserole. Stir cream of chicken soup into pan drippings in skillet; add mushrooms. Pour mushroom mixture over chicken; cover. Bake at 350 degrees for 1 hour. Prepare rice according to package directions, substituting consomme for water and omitting salt. Serve rice with chicken. Yield: 10 servings.

Mrs. Bonnie Romero
Roosevelt Junior High School
Lakewood, California

COQ AU VIN

Juice of 2 limes
Juice of 1 lemon

1/3 c. dry white wine
1 clove of garlic, mashed
1 tsp. salt
1/4 tsp. tarragon
1/8 tsp. pepper
1   2 1/2 to 3-lb. frying chicken, disjointed
1/4 c. butter or margarine

Combine juices, wine, garlic and seasonings. Place chicken in bowl; pour juice mixture over pieces. Marinate for about 30 minutes at room temperature or 2 to 3 hours in refrigerator, turning occasionally. Remove chicken from marinade, reserving marinade. Place chicken in shallow casserole in 1 layer. Dot chicken with butter. Bake at 400 degrees for 45 to 50 minutes, basting every 10 minutes with reserved marinade.

Mrs. Philip Peterson
Paullina Community School
Paullina, Iowa

CHILI CHICKEN

1 frying chicken, cut up
Seasoned flour
1 c. catsup
1/4 tsp. garlic powder
1 tbsp. sugar
1 tsp. paprika
1 tsp. salt
1/2 tsp. pepper
1/2 c. finely chopped onion
1/3 c. lemon juice
1 tbsp. Worcestershire sauce
1 tbsp. chili powder

Coat chicken with flour. Brown chicken in fat in heavy skillet; arrange in shallow baking pan. Combine catsup, garlic powder, sugar, paprika, salt, pepper, onion, lemon juice, Worcestershire sauce, chili powder and 1/2 cup water in saucepan; blend thoroughly. Simmer for 10 minutes; spoon sauce over chicken. Bake, basting frequently, at 325 degrees for 45 minutes or until chicken is tender.

E. Gorek
Kamloops Senior Secondary School
Kamloops, British Columbia, Canada

CREAMED SPRING CHICKEN

1 2 1/2 to 3-lb. frying chicken,
   disjointed
1 tsp. salt
1/4 tsp. pepper
1 med. onion, minced
1 tbsp. chopped parsley
2 tbsp. flour

Place chicken in saucepan; add 1 1/2 cups of water. Season with salt and pepper; add onion. Cover pan; cook until chicken is tender. Add parsley. Make a paste with flour and 1/2 cup water; add to chicken mixture. Simmer, stirring constantly, for about 10 minutes or until thickened. Serve chicken with sauce in casserole.

Mrs. Anne Strychar
Salisbury Composite High School
Sherwood Park, Alberta, Canada

CRUMBY ORANGE CHICKEN

1 2 1/2-3 lb. broiler, quartered
3/4 c. corn flake crumbs
1/4 tsp. garlic powder
1/4 tsp. onion powder
1/4 tsp. garlic salt
1/4 tsp. onion salt
1/2 tsp. salt
1/8 tsp. pepper
1/4 c. butter or margarine
1/8 tsp. paprika
2 c. orange juice

Roll chicken in corn flake crumbs; arrange, skin side up, in 13 x 9 x 2-inch baking pan. Sprinkle remaining crumbs over chicken. Season with garlic and onion powders, garlic and onion salts, salt and pepper. Dot chicken generously with butter; sprinkle with paprika. Bake at 350 degrees for 30 minutes; pour 1 cup orange juice over chicken. Bake for 15 minutes longer; pour remaining juice over chicken. Bake for 15 minutes longer or until chicken is browned and tender. Garnish with orange slices and parsley.

Mrs. Morris Fink
Forest Park School
Springfield, Massachusetts

CRIPPLE CREEK CHICKEN

1 frying chicken, disjointed
Salt and pepper to taste
1/2 c. margarine
1/2 c. minced onion
2 cloves of garlic, minced
2 tsp. paprika
2 c. sour cream
1/2 c. Parmesan cheese
1/4 c. mayonnaise
4 c. cooked buttered noodles

Season chicken with salt and pepper. Melt margarine in small skillet; saute onion and garlic. Stir in paprika. Roll each piece of chicken in onion mixture; arrange in 11 x 15-inch shallow baking dish. Spoon remaining onion mixture over chicken. Cover loosely with aluminum foil. Bake at 375 degrees for 40 minutes. Combine sour cream, half the cheese and mayonnaise. Stir 1/3 of the sour cream mixture into the noodles. Drain liquid from chicken; add to noodle mixture, tossing well. Arrange noodles on bottom of baking dish; top with chicken. Spoon remaining sour cream mixture over chicken mixture. Top with remaining cheese. Bake at 325 degrees for 30 minutes. Yield: 6-8 servings.

Mrs. Holly Andrei
Cripple Creek-Victor High School
Cripple Creek, Colorado

DEVILED CHICKEN

1 frying chicken, cut up
2 tbsp. flour
1 c. chicken stock
1 1/2 tsp. dry mustard
2 tsp. Worcestershire sauce
2 tbsp. catsup

Brown chicken in small amount of fat in skillet. Blend flour, stock, mustard, Worcestershire sauce and catsup well. Place chicken in casserole; pour sauce over chicken. Bake at 350 degrees for 1 hour. Serve with steamed rice and green salad.

Mrs. H. B. Watson
St. Edward Public School
St. Edward, Nebraska

CURRIED CHICKEN CASSEROLE

1 chicken, disjointed
Salt and pepper to taste
1 med. onion, diced
1 can cream of mushroom soup
1 2-oz. can mushrooms
1 c. Cheddar cheese, grated
1/4 tsp. curry powder

Arrange chicken in greased 9 x 13-inch baking dish; sprinkle with salt and pepper. Combine onion, soup, mushrooms, cheese and curry powder; blend thoroughly. Spoon soup mixture over chicken. Bake at 350 degrees for 2 hours and 30 minutes or until chicken is tender.

Margaret M. Glynn
Billings West High School
Billings, Montana

DRUNK CHICKEN

Flour
1 frying chicken, disjointed
Salt
Pepper
Paprika
Cooking oil
1 can mushroom soup
1/2 soup can cooking sherry

Combine enough flour to coat chicken, salt, pepper and paprika to taste. Coat chicken well with seasoned flour. Brown chicken well in oil in skillet. Arrange chicken pieces in baking dish, skin side up. Sprinkle with additional paprika if desired. Spoon soup over chicken pieces; pour sherry over mixture. Bake at 325 degrees for about 1 hour or until chicken is tender. May serve over hot cooked rice.

Mrs. Alice Hansberger
Canton Senior High School
Canton, Illinois

ELEGANT BAKED CHICKEN

1 c. sour cream
1 clove of garlic, minced
1/4 c. chopped green pepper
1/4 c. chopped onion

1 3-oz. can chopped mushrooms,
drained
1/2 tsp. salt
2 lb. chicken pieces
1 c. cracker or dry bread crumbs

Combine sour cream, garlic, green pepper, onion, mushrooms and salt in large shallow bowl. Add chicken to mixture, turning to coat well. Chicken may be marinated overnight, if desired. Preheat oven to 350 degrees. Roll chicken in crumbs. Arrange chicken in greased 13 x 9 x 2-inch baking dish. Bake for 1 hour or until chicken is tender. Melted butter may be drizzled over chicken before baking, if desired.

Mrs. Pamela Libby
Oxford Hills High School
South Paris, Maine

FAVORITE CHICKEN CACCIATORE

1 c. flour
3 tsp. salt
1/4 tsp. pepper
2 3-lb. broiler-fryer chickens,
quartered
6 tbsp. olive oil or salad oil
1 c. chopped onion
1 clove of garlic, minced
1 2-lb. can Italian tomatoes
1/4 tbsp. sugar
1 tsp. sweet basil
1/4 to 1/2 tsp. thyme
2 med. green peppers, sliced

Combine flour, salt and pepper in paper bag. Add chickens, shaking well to coat. Heat oil in skillet; brown chickens, several pieces at a time. Remove from skillet. Saute onion and garlic in pan drippings until onion is soft. Stir in tomatoes, sugar, basil and thyme; bring to a boil. Return chickens to skillet, spooning sauce over well. Add green peppers. Cover skillet; simmer for about 1 hour and 30 minutes, basting with sauce frequently.

Mrs. Louese Spradley
Salem High School
Salem, Indiana

115

EASY MEXICAN CHICKEN MOLE

1   3 1/2 to 4-lb. chicken,
    disjointed
2 tbsp. vegetable oil
1   16-oz. can tomatoes
3/4 c. chopped onion
3/4 c. chopped green pepper
1 clove of garlic, chopped
1/4 c. unsweetened cocoa
1/4 c. (packed) brown sugar
1/4 c. raisins
1/4 c. slivered almonds
2 tbsp. light corn syrup
2 tsp. salt
2 tsp. sesame seed
2 tsp. chili powder
1/2 tsp. cinnamon
1 bay leaf, crumbled
1/4 tsp. aniseed
1/4 tsp. pepper
1/4 tsp. crushed red pepper
1/8 tsp. ground cloves
Hot cooked rice

Brown chicken in hot oil in large skillet or Dutch oven. Add water to cover; simmer for 30 minutes. Combine remaining ingredients except rice in blender container in order listed; process at medium speed until sauce is smooth. Drain broth from chicken in skillet, reserving 1 cup broth. Combine reserved broth and sauce; add to chicken. Simmer for 30 minutes. Serve over rice; garnish with sesame seed and lime slices if desired. Yield: 6 servings.

Mrs. Ella Jo Adams
Allen Senior High School
Allen, Texas

GLORIFIED ORANGE-BAKED CHICKEN

1/4 c. flour
1/2 tsp. salt
1/4 tsp. pepper
1/4 tsp. paprika
6 chicken pieces
1/4 c. oil
1/4 c. chopped onion
1/4 c. chopped celery
1/8 tsp. ginger
2 c. orange juice
1/2 c. raisins
1 c. cooked rice
Orange slices
Parsley

Mix flour, salt, pepper and paprika together. Coat each piece of chicken thoroughly with flour mixture. Brown chicken thoroughly in oil in skillet; remove to baking dish. Saute onion and celery in pan drippings until tender. Add ginger, orange juice, raisins and rice; heat through. Pour onion mixture around chicken pieces. Cover. Bake at 350 degrees for 45 minutes. Remove cover. Bake for 15 minutes longer. Remove to serving platter; garnish with orange slices and parsley.

Helen M. Young
William Byrd High School
Vinton, Virginia

GOLDEN ORANGE-CHICKEN

1/4 c. flour
1/4 tsp. salt
6 to 8 chicken legs or thighs
1/4 c. margarine
1/2 c. orange juice
2 tbsp. grated orange peel
1 tbsp. (packed) brown sugar

Combine flour and salt; coat chicken with flour mixture. Brown chicken in margarine in large skillet until golden brown. Combine orange juice, peel and sugar; mix well. Spoon orange juice mixture over chicken. Simmer, covered, for 30 minutes or until chicken is tender.

Freda H. Montgomery
Central Union High School
Fresno, California

GOURMET PICNIC CHICKEN

Flour
Salt and pepper to taste
2 chickens, halved
Shortening

8 carrots
4 potatoes, quartered
4 lg. onions, quartered
1 to 1 1/2 c. white wine

Cut heavy-duty aluminum foil into four 2-foot squares. Combine flour, salt and pepper. Coat chicken with seasoned flour. Brown chicken in hot shortening in heavy skillet. Place 1 chicken half on each square of foil. Cut carrots into 2-inch chunks. Arrange carrots, potatoes and onions around chicken on squares. Pour wine into pan drippings in skillet, mixing well. Spoon wine mixture over chicken and vegetables. Seal foil squares tightly. Bake at 300 degrees for 45 minutes or until chicken is tender. May be cooked over charcoal fire if desired.

Leslie M. Geehan
New London Junior High School
New London, Connecticut

GREEK CHICKEN

1 frying chicken, quartered
Juice of 2 lemons
1 tbsp. oregano
Salt to taste
Pepper to taste
1/4 c. melted butter

Place chicken quarters in 2-quart mixing bowl. Pour lemon juice over chicken. Add oregano; sprinkle with salt and pepper. Cover; marinate for several hours in refrigerator. Place chicken on broiler pan. Broil in oven until tender, basting with melted butter and turning several times during cooking. May be barbecued over hot coals or cooked on rotisserie. Yield: 2-4 servings.

Mrs. Connie Horn
College Park High School
Pleasant Hill, California

GREEN CHILIES WITH CHICKEN

1 broiler chicken, cut up
Flour
1 clove of garlic, minced
1 tsp. salt

1 med. onion, minced
8 to 12 green chilies
1 med. tomato
1/2 tsp. garlic salt
1/4 tsp. sweet basil
1/4 tsp. oregano

Roll chicken in flour; saute in 4 tablespoons fat in large skillet until golden brown. Add garlic, salt and small amount of water. Simmer, covered, until chicken is tender. Saute onion in 2 tablespoons fat in skillet until transparent. Roast and peel chilies; remove stems, seeds and veins. Peel tomato; mash thoroughly. Chop chilies very fine. Combine chilies and tomato; stir in garlic salt, sweet basil and oregano. Blend thoroughly. Add chili sauce to onions; bring to a boil. Pour sauce over chicken. Simmer, covered, for 1 hour longer. Serve with rice. Yield: 4-5 servings.

Mrs. Lelia C. Greenwald
Socorro High School
Socorro, New Mexico

HONEY-ORANGE CHICKEN

1 c. fine bread crumbs
1 tbsp. grated orange rind
1 tsp. salt
1/4 tsp. pepper
1 3-lb. frying chicken, disjointed
1/2 c. orange juice
1/2 c. chicken broth
1/4 c. butter or margarine
1/2 c. honey

Combine bread crumbs, orange rind, salt and pepper. Dip chicken pieces in orange juice; roll in crumb mixture. Arrange chicken pieces, skin side up, in greased shallow baking dish. Combine chicken broth, butter and honey in saucepan; heat until butter is melted. Pour butter mixture over chicken. Bake at 350 degrees for 1 hour or until chicken is tender, basting occasionally. Yield: 4 servings.

Mrs. Rita A. Hamman
French Junior High School
Topeka, Kansas

HAWAIIAN PINEAPPLE-CHICKEN

1   2 1/2-lb. fryer, disjointed
1/4 c. butter
1 No. 300 can pineapple chunks
2 tbsp. honey
1/2 tsp. ginger
1   8-oz. can tomato sauce
1/8 tsp. salt
3/4 c. chicken broth

Brown chicken in butter in large skillet over medium heat; drain off excess fat. Arrange chicken in large shallow baking dish. Drain pineapple; reserve juice. Combine honey, ginger, tomato sauce, salt and broth with reserved juice; blend thoroughly. Pour sauce over chicken. Bake, covered, at 350 degrees for 20 minutes; add pineapple. Bake for 1 hour longer; baste occasionally. Yield: 6 servings.

Mrs. Winnifred McCarthy
Camrose Composite High School
Camrose, Alberta, Canada

LEMON-BAKED CHICKEN

1 frying chicken, disjointed
1/4 c. lemon juice
3 tbsp. vegetable oil
2 tsp. parsley flakes
1 tsp. garlic salt
1 tsp. minced onion flakes

Preheat oven to 350 degrees. Remove skin from chicken; arrange in baking dish. Combine lemon juice and vegetable oil; pour over chicken. Sprinkle chicken with parsley, garlic salt and onion flakes. Cover. Bake until tender, basting occasionally.

Mrs. Joan L. Trefts
John Adams High School
Cleveland, Ohio

ITALIAN-STYLE CHICKEN CACCIATORE

1   2 1/2 to 3-lb. chicken,
     disjointed
Salt
Pepper
1/4 c. oil
2 med. onions, chopped
2 cloves of garlic, minced
1   1-lb. can whole tomatoes
1   8-oz. can tomato sauce
1 tsp. crushed oregano
2 bay leaves
1/4 c. cooking sherry

Season chicken with salt and pepper to taste. Heat oil in skillet; brown chicken over low heat until tender. Remove chicken from skillet. Saute onions and garlic in pan drippings until onions are tender. Add tomatoes, tomato sauce, 1 teaspoon salt, 1/4 teaspoon pepper, oregano and bay leaves. Return chicken to skillet; cover. Simmer for 45 minutes. Stir in sherry. Cook, uncovered, for about 20 minutes longer or until chicken is tender. Serve over hot cooked spaghetti.

Connie Granato
Escobar Junior High School
San Antonio, Texas

LO-CAL CHICKEN DELIGHT

1 frying chicken, disjointed
Melted butter
1 tsp. salt
1/4 tsp. pepper
3/4 c. non-dairy coffee creamer
1 tsp. paprika
1 tsp. Worcestershire sauce
1 tbsp. flour
1   4-oz. can mushroom pieces

Place chicken in baking dish; brush with melted butter. Bake at 400 degrees for 45 minutes. Combine salt, pepper, non-dairy coffee creamer, paprika, Worcestershire sauce and flour in small bowl. Drain liquid from mushrooms; add enough water to make 3/4 cup liquid. Add mushroom liquid to mixture in bowl; mix until blended. Add mushrooms. Spoon mushroom mixture over chicken. Bake for 25 minutes longer or until chicken is tender.

Arlene L. Carter
Horace Mann Junior High School
Omaha, Nebraska

LOT-JUI

2 green peppers
2 tbsp. oil
1/2 tsp. salt
1/8 tsp. pepper
2 c. cooked chicken breast strips
4 tbsp. cornstarch
4 tbsp. soy sauce
2 c. chicken broth
3 or 4 tomatoes, cut in wedges

Cut green peppers into strips. Heat oil in wok or electric skillet; saute green pepper strips lightly over medium heat. Add salt, pepper and chicken strips. Dissolve cornstarch in soy sauce and 1/2 cup broth. Add remaining broth to chicken mixture; bring to boiling point over high heat. Blend in cornstarch mixture, stirring constantly, until sauce thickens. Reduce heat to low; add tomatoes. Cook for 5 minutes. Serve over steamed rice or heated chow mein noodles.

Pauline E. Smith
Redbank Valley High School
New Bethlehem, Pennsylvania

MAINE MANDARIN CHICKEN

1   3 to 3 1/2-lb. broiling chicken, disjointed
1/4 c. flour
1/3 c. vegetable oil
1   8-oz. jar sweet and sour sauce
1   4-oz. can mushrooms, drained
1 lg. onion, chopped
2 c. long grain rice
2 chicken bouillon cubes
1 can mandarin oranges
2 tbsp. soy sauce

Preheat oven to 350 degrees. Coat chicken with flour; brown in hot oil in skillet on all sides. Remove chicken to baking dish; pour sweet and sour sauce and 1/2 cup water over chicken. Cover dish with aluminum foil; set aside. Saute mushrooms and onion in pan drippings in skillet. Pour rice into greased casserole. Dissolve bouillon cubes in 1 1/2 cups hot water; pour over rice. Drain oranges, reserving syrup; add reserved syrup to rice mixture. Stir in mushrooms, onion

and soy sauce; cover with aluminum foil. Place chicken mixture and rice mixture in oven. Bake for 20 minutes; remove foil from chicken mixture. Bake for 40 minutes longer. Stir oranges into hot rice mixture. Serve chicken mixture over rice mixture. Yield: 4 servings.

Judith R. Kamin
Brunswick Junior High School
Brunswick, Maine

LOUISIANA BAKED CHICKEN AND SWEET POTATOES

1 frying chicken, quartered
Salt and pepper
1/4 c. apricot preserves
1/4 c. (packed) brown sugar
2 tsp. lemon juice
2 tbsp. margarine
4 med. boiled sweet potatoes, peeled

Preheat oven to 400 degrees. Place chicken in shallow baking dish; sprinkle with salt and pepper to taste. Spread with preserves; sprinkle with brown sugar and lemon juice. Dot with margarine; cover tightly. Bake 30 minutes. Uncover; add potatoes. Baste with drippings. Bake for 30 minutes longer, basting occasionally, until chicken is tender and brown. Yield: 4 servings.

Bernadette Varnado
Pine View Junior High School
Covington, Louisiana

MARINATED SWEET-SOUR CHICKEN

11/12/2017

good

1 pkg. onion soup mix
1   10-oz. jar apricot jam
1   8-oz. bottle Russian dressing — *used Catalina*
2   3-lb. frying chickens, disjointed

Combine soup mix, jam and dressing in 5-quart oval roasting pan. Marinate chickens in jam mixture for 1 hour, turning occasionally. Cover pan. Bake at 375 degrees for 1 hour or until chickens are tender.

served w/ rice

Mrs. H. Stone
Clintondale High School
Mt. Clemens, Michigan

MUSHROOM CHICKEN WITH RICE

Flour
Salt and pepper to taste
Paprika to taste
1 2 1/2-lb. chicken, disjointed
2 cans cream of chicken soup
1 soup can milk
1 4-oz. can of mushrooms
2 tbsp. shortening
1/2 c. chopped onion
1/2 c. chopped celery
1 c. uncooked rice
3/4 c. orange juice

Combine flour, salt, pepper and paprika; dredge chicken with flour mixture. Brown chicken in fat in large skillet. Combine soup and milk; pour over chicken. Drain mushrooms; add to chicken mixture. Simmer, covered, for 45 minutes or until chicken is tender. Melt shortening in heavy saucepan. Saute onion and celery until tender. Stir in rice, orange juice, 1/2 teaspoon additional salt and 1 3/4 cup water. Simmer, covered, for 25 minutes or until liquid is absorbed. Serve rice with chicken and gravy. Yield: 4-5 servings.

Mrs. Carolyn Bryant
Hazel Green High School
Hazel Green, Alabama

PAELLA

1 2-lb. chicken, disjointed
1/2 c. olive oil
1/2 lb. chorizo sausage, sliced
1/2 c. finely chopped onions
1 tsp. minced garlic
1 med. green pepper, cut into strips
2 lg. tomatoes, chopped
3 c. uncooked rice
2 tsp. salt
Pepper to taste
1/4 tsp. ground saffron
1 c. shrimp
1 can minced clams
1/2 c. peas
1 sm. jar pimento strips
2 lemons, cut into wedges

Brown chicken in 1/4 cup olive oil in skillet; remove from skillet. Fry sausage in remaining oil in skillet; drain on paper toweling. Pour off pan drippings; add remaining olive oil to skillet over medium heat. Add onions, garlic, green pepper and tomatoes. Cook, stirring constantly, until most of liquid is absorbed. Preheat oven to 400 degrees. Combine tomato mixture with rice, salt, pepper, and saffron. Bring to a boil; remove from heat. Spoon mixture into 14-inch paella dish or large casserole. Arrange chicken and sausage over top. Bake for 30 minutes. Arrange shrimp, clams, peas and pimento over all. Bake for 15 minutes longer. Serve garnished with lemon wedges.

Mrs. Carol Mapes
Pella Community Middle School
Pella, Iowa

PARSLEY-BROILED CHICKEN

1/2 c. vegetable oil
1/4 tsp. oregano
1/2 tsp. marjoram
1/2 tsp. paprika
1/4 c. lemon juice
1 tsp. salt
1 tsp. seasoned salt
1/8 tsp. pepper
1/4 c. finely chopped parsley
1 1 1/2 to 2 1/2-lb. broiling chicken,
  split

Combine oil, oregano, marjoram, paprika, lemon juice, salt, seasoned salt, pepper and parsley; mix thoroughly. Brush chicken generously with oil mixture on both sides; arrange on broiler pan, skin side down. Broil, 10 inches from source of heat, for 20 minutes. Turn chicken, skin side up; brush with additional oil mixture. Broil for 20 minutes longer or until chicken is tender.

Mrs. Jan Gruetzmacher
Wilson Junior High School
Appleton, Wisconsin

PARMESAN CHICKEN

1/2 c. butter
3 eggs, slightly beaten
3 tbsp. milk

1 3-lb. broiling chicken,
   disjointed
1/2 c. grated Parmesan cheese
1 c. dry sherry
1/2 lb. sliced fresh mushrooms

Melt butter in electric frypan. Mix eggs and milk in small bowl. Dip chicken pieces in egg mixture, roll in cheese. Brown in butter at 365 degrees in electric frypan. Add sherry; cover. Reduce heat to simmer; cook for 45 minutes. Add mushrooms; cook for 10 minutes longer. Serve over rice. Yield: 4-5 servings.

Mrs. Sherri Day
West Anchorage High School
Anchorage, Alaska

PARTY CHICKEN

1 3 1/2-lb. chicken, disjointed
2 tbsp. chili powder
1/4 tsp. pepper
1/4 tsp. cinnamon
2 tbsp. grated onion
1 tsp. salt
1/4 c. shortening
2 c. unsweetened pineapple juice
2 c. frozen pineapple chunks,
   thawed
2 ripe bananas, sliced lengthwise
1/2 lb. seedless white grapes

Place chicken in deep kettle; add 2 cups boiling water, chili powder, pepper, cinnamon, onion and salt. Cover kettle; simmer for 1 hour. Remove chicken from broth, reserving broth. Melt shortening in skillet; brown chicken well on all sides. Arrange chicken in baking pan. Combine pineapple juice and reserved broth. Heat through; pour over chicken. Arrange pineapple chunks over chicken. Bake at 375 degrees for about 30 minutes or until chicken is tender. Remove chicken mixture to serving dish. Garnish with bananas and grapes. May thicken sauce with flour mixed with water, if desired. Yield: 6 servings.

Mrs. Mary O'Laire
Cedar Hill High School
Cedar Hill, Texas

PHILIPPINE CHICKEN ADOBO

1 onion, chopped
1/2 clove of garlic, minced
Butter
1 frying chicken, cut up
1/4 c. vinegar
1/4 c. soy sauce
1 tbsp. salt
1 tbsp. sugar
2 bay leaves
1/2 tsp. monosodium glutamate

Saute onion and garlic in small amount of butter in Dutch oven over medium heat. Add chicken; brown well on both sides. Combine vinegar, 3/4 cup water, soy sauce, salt, sugar, bay leaves and monosodium glutamate; mix well. Pour over chicken mixture; bring to a boil. Reduce heat; simmer for 2 hours or until chicken is tender and sauce is reduced to 1 cup. Serve with rice.

Mrs. Dorothy Ehm
Woodward-Granger High School
Woodward, Iowa

POLYNESIAN CHICKEN

1 13 1/2-oz. can pineapple chunks
1/2 c. margarine
1 3 to 4-lb. broiler-fryer,
   disjointed
1 7-oz. can shrimp, drained
1 sliced onion
1 sliced green pepper
1/3 c. sliced stuffed green olives
1 can tomato soup

Drain pineapple, reserving juice. Melt margarine in broiler pan; arrange fryer pieces in pan, skin side down. Bake at 425 degrees for 30 minutes, turning pieces once. Add pineapple chunks, shrimp, onion, green pepper and olives. Combine soup with reserved juice; pour over fryer mixture. Cover pan with aluminum foil. Bake for 30 minutes. Remove foil from pan. Bake for 15 minutes longer or until fryer pieces are browned.

Wendy Sue Parkinson
M. E. Ford Junior High School
Tacoma, Washington

POLLO ALLA CACCIATORE

3 tbsp. olive oil or salad oil
2 tbsp. butter
2 2-lb. broiler-fryer chickens,
*   disjointed*
1 1/2 c. sliced onion
1 clove of garlic, pressed
2 tbsp. chopped parsley
1 1-lb. can tomatoes
1 1/2 tsp. salt
1/2 tsp. dried basil leaves
1/4 tsp. pepper

Heat oil and butter in Dutch oven; add chickens, several pieces at a time. Brown well on all sides; remove from Dutch oven. Set aside. Add onion and garlic to Dutch oven; saute for about 5 minutes or until golden brown. Add parsley, tomatoes, salt, basil and pepper; mix well, mashing tomatoes with fork. Bring to boiling point; reduce heat. Simmer, uncovered, for 20 minutes. Add chicken; simmer, covered, for 45 to 50 minutes or until chicken is tender. May be served with buttered noodles, spaghetti or baked potatoes.

Charlene Merrill
Fairview High School
Fairview, Pennsylvania

QUICK CHICK

1/4 c. tarragon vinegar
1 pkg. salad dressing mix
1 frying chicken, disjointed

Combine vinegar and salad dressing mix. Brush each piece of chicken with vinegar mixture. Place chicken pieces in baking pan; cover tightly. Bake at 375 degrees for 1 hour or until chicken is tender.

Debby Purvis
Harbor High School
Santa Cruz, California

SAGED CHICKEN WITH RICE

1 c. flour
1 tsp. salt
Poultry seasoning

1 3-lb. chicken, disjointed
3 tbsp. butter
1/2 c. diced onion
1/2 c. diced celery
1 tsp. Italian salad dressing mix
1 tsp. parsley
1 c. uncooked rice
2 1/2 c. chicken broth

Combine flour, salt and 1/2 teaspoon poultry seasoning in bag; shake chicken in flour mixture to coat well. Saute chicken in small amount of fat in large skillet over medium heat for 30 minutes or until browned; remove chicken. Add butter to skillet. Saute onion and celery until tender; stir in salad dressing mix, parsley and 1/8 teaspoon poultry seasoning. Add rice and broth; blend well. Arrange chicken over rice. Simmer, covered, for 20 minutes or until chicken is tender.

Mrs. Vera Journey
Hinsdale High School South
Oswego, Illinois

SAVORY CHICKEN CASSEROLE

1 2-lb. frying chicken, disjointed
2 tbsp. shortening
1 can cream of chicken soup
1/2 soup can milk
1/4 tsp. poultry seasoning
1/4 tsp. salt
1/8 tsp. pepper
4 carrots, quartered
6 sm. onions
1 pkg. frozen lima beans

Brown chicken in shortening in skillet over medium heat; transfer to 2-quart casserole. Pour off pan drippings; discard. Blend soup, milk, poultry seasoning, salt and pepper in skillet; mix well. Add carrots, onions and lima beans. Simmer, covered, for 20 minutes; stir carefully. Pour over chicken. Bake, covered, at 375 degrees for 35 minutes; remove cover. Bake for 15 minutes longer or until chicken is tender. Yield: 4 servings.

Lois S. Gass
Line Mountain Senior High School
Herndon, Pennsylvania

SAUTEED CHICKEN WITH SHALLOTS AND ARTICHOKES

1 3-lb. frying chicken, cut up
4 tbsp. butter
4 tbsp. salad oil
1 bunch shallots or scallions
1 bay leaf
1 pkg. frozen artichoke hearts
Juice of 1/2 lemon
Salt and pepper to taste
1/2 c. chicken stock or broth

Brown chicken in butter and oil in large skillet; remove chicken. Place shallots in skillet; cook for 5 minutes. Remove from skillet. Drain excess fat, reserving 2 tablespoons in skillet. Return chicken to skillet; top with shallots and bay leaf. Simmer, covered, for 45 minutes or until chicken is tender; baste frequently with pan juices. Prepare artichoke hearts according to package directions; add lemon juice. Remove chicken from skillet; add seasonings. Add stock to pan juices; bring to a boil, stirring constantly. Arrange chicken on bed of rice on heated platter; pour sauce over chicken. Place artichoke hearts and shallots around chicken and rice. Canned artichoke hearts may be substituted for frozen.

Barbara Creede
Wisdom Lane Junior High School
Levittown, New York

SKILLET CHICKEN

1 3-lb. frying chicken
Salt and pepper to taste
Paprika to taste
1 4-oz. can mushrooms
1/4 c. red wine
1 8-oz. can tomato sauce
1/4 tsp. thyme
2 green peppers, cut in strips
1 med. onion, sliced

Cut chicken into serving pieces; sprinkle with salt, pepper and paprika. Brown chicken in small amount of fat in skillet. Drain mushrooms; reserve liquid. Stir wine, tomato sauce, liquid from mushroom and thyme into skillet. Simmer, covered, for 25 minutes. Add mushrooms, green peppers and onion. Simmer, covered, for 10 minutes longer or until chicken is tender. Serve with rice.

Mrs. Alma MacQueen
Valley Middle School
Oakland, New Jersey

SUNSHINE CHICKEN

1 frying chicken, disjointed
Salt and pepper to taste
Flour
3 tbsp. minced onion
1 6-oz. can frozen orange juice, thawed

Season chicken with salt and pepper; coat with flour. Arrange chicken in greased baking dish; sprinkle with onion. Pour orange juice over chicken. Bake, covered, at 350 degrees for 45 minutes; remove cover. Bake for 15 minutes longer or until chicken is tender and browned. Garnish with orange and lemon slices and parsley, if desired. Yield: 6 servings.

Mrs. Emely Sundbeck
Manor High School
Manor, Texas

SWEET AND SOUR CHICKEN

1 frying chicken, cut up
1/2 c. flour
1/2 c. vegetable shortening
1/2 c. white vinegar
1/2 c. (firmly packed) brown sugar
1 1/2 tsp. salt
1/4 tsp. ginger
1/8 tsp. pepper
1 med. orange, sliced
1 med. lemon, quartered

Dredge chicken in flour; brown in shortening in skillet over medium heat. Combine vinegar, sugar, salt, ginger and pepper; mix well. Pour over chicken; add orange slices and lemon wedges. Reduce heat. Simmer, covered, for 30 minutes or until tender.

Marilyn Mancewicz
Ottawa Hills High School
Grand Rapids, Michigan

123

SMOTHERED CHICKEN WITH MUSHROOMS

1 3-lb. fryer, disjointed
Salt and freshly ground pepper
   to taste
3 tbsp. butter
2 tbsp. vegetable oil
4 tbsp. minced onion
3 tbsp. flour
1 1/2 c. canned chicken broth
1/2 lb. mushrooms, thinly sliced
1/2 c. heavy cream

Season chicken with salt and pepper. Combine butter and oil in large heavy skillet over high heat. Brown chicken, turning to brown all sides. Arrange chicken in large shallow baking dish. Preheat oven to 350 degrees. Saute onion in remaining fat in skillet until tender and transparent. Stir in flour; cook, stirring constantly, until bubbly. Add broth gradually, stirring constantly until smooth and thickened; pour sauce over chicken. Bake, covered, for 20 minutes. Arrange mushrooms over chicken; baste well. Bake, covered, for 10 minutes longer or until chicken is tender. Transfer chicken to heated platter. Skim excess fat from sauce; pour into saucepan. Stir cream gradually into sauce. Simmer, stirring constantly, for 2 minutes. Season with additional salt and pepper, if desired. Pour gravy over chicken. Yield: 4 servings.

Mrs. Mary Davidson
Grant High School
Grant, Michigan

SOUTH SEAS CHICKEN

1 frying chicken, disjointed
1/4 c. oil
1 med. onion, sliced
1 4-oz. can sliced mushrooms
1 1/4 c. chicken broth
1/4 c. dark corn syrup
3 tbsp. lemon juice
1 tsp. salt
1/4 tsp. allspice
2 tbsp. cornstarch
4 green-tipped bananas

1 13 1/4-oz. can pineapple chunks,
   drained
1/2 c. green pepper strips

Brown chicken in oil in large skillet over medium heat; add onion and mushrooms. Simmer, stirring occasionally, for 3 minutes. Stir in broth, corn syrup, lemon juice, salt and allspice; blend well. Simmer, covered, for 30 minutes or until chicken is tender. Combine cornstarch with 2 tablespoons water; add to chicken mixture. Simmer, stirring constantly, until smooth and thickened. Bring to a boil; boil for 1 minute. Peel bananas; cut lengthwise and quarter. Add bananas, pineapple and green pepper to chicken mixture. Simmer, covered, for 3 minutes or until heated through. Yield: 4 servings.

Mrs. Edna Eisenhart
Bristol Junior-Senior High School
Bristol, Pennsylvania

SOY CHICKEN

1 frying chicken, disjointed
1/8 c. brown mustard
2 tsp. oregano
1/4 tsp. paprika
3/4 c. soy sauce

Skin chicken; arrange in greased 9 x 12-inch baking dish. Spread chicken with mustard; sprinkle with oregano and paprika. Pour soy sauce over all. Marinate chicken, refrigerated, for 2 hours. Bake at 350 degrees for 1 hour or until tender. Serve on heated platter with pan juices and curried rice, if desired.

Jane A. Eiden
Friendly Senior High School
Oxon Hill, Maryland

TAHITIAN CHICKEN

1 lg. frying chicken, disjointed
1 c. oil or shortening
Salt and pepper to taste
1 lg. white onion, thinly sliced
1 green pepper, thinly sliced
1 16-oz. can sliced peaches

1 sm. can pineapple chunks
1 1/2 tbsp. cornstarch
1 1/2 tbsp. soy sauce
4 1/2 tbsp. vinegar
1 sm. package slivered almonds

Brown chicken pieces in oil in skillet; season with salt and pepper. Cover skillet; cook over low heat for about 30 minutes or until chicken pieces are tender. Remove chicken pieces from skillet. Drain oil from skillet, reserving 2 to 3 tablespoons oil in skillet. Saute onion and green pepper in reserved oil in skillet until tender. Drain peaches and pineapple, reserving 1 cup peach juice and 1/2 cup pineapple juice. Combine reserved juices, cornstarch, soy sauce and vinegar. Return chicken pieces to skillet; add cornstarch mixture. Simmer, stirring, until sauce is clear and thickened. Add peach slices and pineapple. Simmer for 5 minutes longer spooning sauce over chicken mixture. Sprinkle with slivered almonds.

Mrs. Pamelia Paddock
Fountain-Fort Carson High School
Fountain, Colorado

TROPICAL CHICKEN

1 frying chicken, cut up
Salt to taste
2 c. orange juice
3/4 c. crushed pineapple
1/4 c. flaked coconut

Preheat oven to 350 degrees. Skin chicken. Brown in small amount of fat in large skillet over medium heat; sprinkle salt on both sides. Combine orange juice, pineapple and coconut; blend well. Arrange chicken in large shallow baking dish; pour sauce over chicken. Bake for 45 minutes or until chicken is tender; baste frequently. Serve chicken with sauce.

Marilynn Manning
Mountain View High School
Mountain View, Wyoming

VINEYARD CHICKEN

1 3-lb. chicken, quartered
1 c. dry white wine

1 tbsp. lemon juice
1/4 tsp. pepper
1/2 tsp. paprika
1/4 c. melted butter
1/4 c. finely chopped onion
3 tsp. salt
1/4 c. minced parsley

Place chicken, skin side down, in large shallow casserole. Combine wine, lemon juice, pepper, paprika, butter, onion, salt and parsley; blend well. Pour over chicken. Bake, covered, at 325 degrees for 1 hour. Remove cover; turn chicken skin side up. Increase oven temperature to 375 degrees. Bake for 30 minutes longer; baste occasionally. Increase oven temperature to 425 degrees. Bake for 30 minutes longer; baste frequently. Yield: 4 servings.

Mrs. Eunice Gordon
Shattuck High School
Shattuck, Oklahoma

ZIPPITY-DO CHICKEN

1/2 c. flour
1 tsp. salt
1/8 tsp. pepper
1 chicken, disjointed
1/2 c. shortening
1/2 c. mayonnaise
6 to 8 stuffed olives, sliced
1/2 pkg. onion soup mix

Preheat oven to 375 degrees. Combine flour, salt and pepper in paper or plastic bag. Add chicken; shake until coated. Remove chicken from bag; place on cookie sheet for about 30 minutes. Heat shortening in heavy skillet. Brown chicken; place in casserole. Cover. Bake for 40 minutes. Combine mayonnaise, sliced olives and soup mix; pour over chicken. Bake, uncovered, for 20 minutes longer. Remove from oven; place on serving dish. Garnish with additional stuffed olives. Yield: 4 servings.

Mrs. Lois Beguhn
Centennial Senior High School
Circle Pines, Minnesota

ALMOND-FRIED CHICKEN

1/2 c. toasted slivered almonds
2 eggs
3/4 c. milk
1 tsp. salt
Pepper to taste
1/8 tsp. garlic powder
1 tsp. herb salad mix
2 green onions, chopped
1 c. instant flour
3 chicken breasts, halved and
  boned
Oil

Chop almonds coarsely. Beat eggs in large bowl; add milk, salt, pepper, garlic powder, salad mix, green onions, almonds and flour. Coat chicken breasts with egg mixture, adding additional flour if necessary. Heat oil in skillet to 350 degrees; fry chicken breasts for about 8 to 10 minutes on each side or until golden brown.

Emilia Broome
Haydock School
Oxnard, California

AS YOU LIKE IT FRIED CHICKEN

1 3-lb. frying chicken,
  disjointed
Oil or shortening
1 med. egg
1/2 tsp. salt
1/4 tsp. pepper
1/2 tsp. soda
1/2 c. buttermilk
2 1/2 c. flour

Let chicken stand for about 30 minutes at room temperature. Pour oil into deep fat fryer; heat to 375 degrees. Beat egg, salt, pepper and soda; stir in buttermilk to make thick batter. Dip chicken pieces into batter. Place flour in paper bag; shake chicken until coated. Place chicken in hot oil; fry until golden brown and tender. Drain on absorbent paper.

Mrs. Jane S. Asbury
Jacksboro High School
Jacksboro, Tennessee

BONELESS DEEP-FRIED CHICKEN

4 chicken breasts
1 egg
3 c. chicken broth
1/2 tsp. salt
1/8 tsp. pepper
Flour
1 tsp. baking powder
Oil
2 to 3 tbsp. butter
1/4 c. heavy cream

Simmer chicken breasts in small amount of salted water until tender; remove bones and skin while still warm. Combine egg, 1 cup broth, salt and pepper in blender container; blend until mixed. Blend in 1 cup plus 2 tablespoons flour and baking powder. Dip chicken into batter. Fry in deep 325-degree oil for about 3 minutes or until browned. Drain on absorbent paper. Melt butter, blend in 2 to 3 tablespoons flour until bubbly. Add remaining chicken broth gradually; cook, stirring constantly, until thickened. Stir in cream. Serve sauce with chicken.

Mrs. Ruth Wright
Weedsport Junior-Senior High School
Weedsport, New York

FRIED CHICKEN WITH GREEN PEPPERS

1 1/4 lb. chicken breasts
3 green peppers
1 hot red pepper
1 sm. piece of gingerroot
1/2 bunch chicory or endive
1 lemon
3 tbsp. soy sauce
Saki
1/2 c. cornstarch
Peanut oil
1 tbsp. salad oil
1 tbsp. sugar
2 tbsp. water
Cooked rice

Remove skin and bones from chicken; cut into slightly larger than bite-sized pieces. Remove seeds from green peppers; cut into

1 1/4-inch pieces. Remove seeds from red pepper; cut into circular slices. Peel ginger-root; mince. Clean chicory. Cut lemon into wedges. Sprinkle chicken with 1 tablespoon soy sauce and 1/2 teaspoon saki. Let stand for 15 minutes. Dust with cornstarch, covering meat well. Heat peanut oil over medium heat; deep fry chicken for 4 minutes or until golden and done. Remove from oil; drain on paper toweling. Heat salad oil in frying pan; fry green peppers, hot red pepper and ginger-root for 30 seconds. Add fried chicken, 1 tablespoon saki, 2 tablespoons soy sauce, sugar and water. Stir constantly for 1 minute longer. Spread on platter with chicory and lemon wedges. Squeeze lemons over chicken mixture. Serve with rice. Yield: 4 servings.

JoAnne E. Suda
Norte Del Rio High School
Sacramento, California

COUNTRY-FRIED CHICKEN

1 c. flour
1 tbsp. salt
1 tsp. pepper
1 tsp. paprika
1 egg
1 c. cooking oil
3 lb. choice chicken pieces

Combine flour with the salt, pepper and paprika in small bowl; blend well. Beat egg slightly with 2 tablespoons water in shallow bowl. Dip chicken into egg mixture; coat well with flour mixture. Heat oil in large electric skillet to 375 degrees. Fry chicken, skin side down, for 15 minutes; turn chicken. Fry for 15 minutes longer or until chicken is tender and golden brown. Drain on paper toweling. Yield: 3-4 servings.

Mrs. Thelma S. Atwell
Nes Tre La Go USD No. 301 High School
Utica, Kansas

HOTCHKISS HERB CHICKEN

1 c. flour
1/4 tsp. pepper
1 tsp. salt
2 tbsp. Herb Blend

1   2 1/2 to 3-lb. frying chicken, disjointed
Salad oil

Combine flour, pepper, salt and Herb Blend in bag; shake chicken in flour mixture to coat well. Pour salad oil into skillet to 1/4-inch depth. Brown chicken on all sides over medium heat; reduce heat. Cook, covered, until chicken is tender. Remove cover; cook for 10 minutes longer. Yield: 4-6 servings.

Herb Blend

4 tbsp. marjoram
4 tbsp. rosemary
4 tbsp. oregano
4 tbsp. thyme
4 tbsp. instant minced parsley
4 tbsp. paprika
2 tbsp. dried mint
2 tbsp. basil
2 tbsp. sage
2 tbsp. chervil

Combine all ingredients; blend thoroughly. Store in airtight container. May be used in spaghetti sauce, meat loaf, salads and egg dishes.

Mary Woodruff
Hotchkiss High School
Hotchkiss, Colorado

MABEL'S FRIED CHICKEN

1   4-lb. chicken
1/2 c. cornmeal
1/2 c. flour
1/2 tsp. salt
1/4 tsp. pepper
1/2 tsp. seasoned salt
2 eggs, well beaten

Cut chicken into serving pieces. Combine cornmeal, flour, salt, pepper and seasoned salt in shallow bowl; mix well. Dip chicken into eggs; coat with cornmeal mixture. Fry chicken in hot fat in skillet over medium heat until tender and golden brown.

Maria Campo
Glenrock High School
Glenrock, Wyoming

NORTHERN-FRIED CHICKEN

1 c. flour
1 tsp. salt
1/2 tsp. pepper
1 tsp. paprika
1 lg. frying chicken, disjointed
2 tbsp. butter or margarine
1 tsp. celery seed
1 tsp. parsley flakes
1 clove of garlic, minced
2 c. milk
3 tbsp. cornstarch

Combine flour, salt, pepper and paprika; dust chicken with flour mixture. Brown chicken in butter in electric skillet. Combine 3/4 cup hot water, celery seed, parsley flakes and garlic; pour over chicken. Simmer, covered, for 30 minutes or until tender. Remove chicken to heated platter; keep warm. Add milk to pan juices. Blend cornstarch with 1/2 cup water; stir into pan juices gradually. Simmer, stirring constantly, until gravy is smooth and thickened; season to taste.

Mrs. Sharon Schultz
Owosso Junior High School
Owosso, Michigan

BAKED CRUMB CHICKEN

1   2 1/2 to 3-lb. frying chicken,
disjointed
Salt
1/4 c. margarine, melted
1 1/2 c. saltine cracker crumbs

Season chicken pieces to taste with salt; dip into melted margarine. Roll in cracker crumbs. Place chicken pieces in baking pan, skin side up. Bake at 350 degrees for 1 hour.

Effie Lois Greene
Potts Camp High School
Potts Camp, Mississippi

BUTTER-CRUSTED CHICKEN

1/3 c. butter, melted
3 tbsp. flour
1 tsp. salt

1/2 tsp. paprika
1 fryer, disjointed

Combine butter, flour, salt and paprika; brush mixture over chicken. Arrange chicken in foiled-lined shallow baking pan. Bake at 425 degrees for 20 minutes; reduce oven temperature to 350 degrees. Bake for 1 hour longer. Yield: 4-6 servings.

Mrs. D. S. Loyd
Oneonta High School
Oneonta, Alabama

CACKLE BIRD

Oil
1 c. seasoned bread crumbs
1 c. grated Romano and Parmesan
cheese
1/2 c. buttermilk
1 tbsp. prepared mustard
1 tbsp. lemon juice
1 tbsp. soy sauce
1 tbsp. Worcestershire sauce
1 tsp. garlic juice
1 tsp. paprika
1 tsp. salt
1 tsp. freshly ground pepper
2   3-lb. frying chickens,
disjointed

Line 9 x 13-inch baking pan with aluminum foil; oil foil well. Combine bread crumbs and cheeses in plastic bag. Combine buttermilk, mustard, lemon juice, soy sauce and remaining seasonings in bowl. Dip each piece of chicken in liquid mixture; shake in bag in crumb mixture. Place chicken in prepared pan, skin side up. Bake at 375 degrees for about 1 hour and 15 minutes or until chicken is golden brown.

Nancy Gowell
Northeast Intermediate School
Midland, Michigan

CHICKEN SURPRISE

1 c. corn flake crumbs
1 tsp. salt
1 tsp. sage
1 tsp. oregano
1 egg

1 tbsp. cooking oil
5 to 6 pieces chicken
Paprika to taste

Combine crumbs, salt, sage and oregano in shallow dish. Beat egg well. Add oil; beat thoroughly. Dip chicken into egg mixture; roll in crumb mixture to coat well. Place in shallow greased casserole; sprinkle with paprika. Bake at 350 degrees for 45 minutes or until tender and golden brown.

Sarah A. McCreight
Oak Hill High School
Morganton, North Carolina

CHILI OVEN-FRIED CHICKEN

3/4 c. butter or margarine
3 broiler-fryer chickens,
  disjointed
4 tsp. salt
2 c. flour
1 1/2 tsp. chili powder
1 c. milk
3 tbsp. prepared mustard
2 tsp. Worcestershire sauce
1/4 tsp. hot sauce

Line two 15 x 10 x 1-inch baking pans with aluminum foil. Divide butter between pans. Place in 425-degree oven for about 5 minutes or until butter melts. Sprinkle chicken pieces on both sides with 3 teaspoons salt. Mix flour, chili powder and remaining salt. Blend milk, mustard, Worcestershire sauce and hot sauce together. Dip chicken pieces in milk mixture; coat with seasoned flour. Place chicken, skin side down, in melted butter in baking pans. Bake in 425-degree oven for 30 minutes. Turn chicken; reverse pans on oven shelves. Bake for 20 minutes longer. Yield: 12 servings.

Mrs. Roma E. Wood
Kenesaw Public School
Hastings, Nebraska

DOROTHY'S HONEY CHICKEN

1/4 c. butter or margarine
1/2 c. honey

1/4 c. prepared mustard
1 tsp. salt
1 tsp. curry powder (opt.)
1 chicken, disjointed

Melt butter in baking pan; stir in honey, mustard, salt and curry powder. Roll chicken on both sides in honey mixture; place in single layer in pan. Bake at 375 degrees for 1 hour or until tender.

Mrs. Dorothy Soderlund
Milaca Senior High School
Milaca, Minnesota

GLAZED FRIED CHICKEN

Salt to taste
1/4 tsp. pepper
1/4 tsp. thyme
1 lg. frying chicken, quartered
1/4 c. butter, melted
4 slices bacon
1/2 c. chopped onion
1 tbsp. flour
1 tbsp. sugar
2 tsp. curry
1 chicken bouillon cube
1 c. apricot nectar
1 tbsp. lemon juice

Combine salt, pepper and thyme; coat chicken with mixture. Place chicken, skin side up, in shallow baking dish; brush with butter. Bake at 400 degrees for 45 minutes, brushing occasionally with remaining butter. Fry bacon in skillet until crisp; drain on paper toweling. Cook onion in bacon drippings until tender; blend in flour, sugar and curry powder, stirring until bubbly. Add bouillon cube and nectar. Simmer, stirring constantly, until cube is dissolved and mixture has thickened; stir in lemon juice. Spoon half the sauce over chicken. Bake for 10 minutes longer or until chicken is tender. Pour remaining sauce over chicken. Crumble bacon; garnish chicken with bacon. Yield: 4 servings.

Mrs. Alice Ketcham
Chenango Forks Junior-Senior School
Chenango Forks, New York

FRIED CHICKEN IN MILK

3/4 c. flour
4 tsp. salt
1 tsp. pepper
1/2 tsp. paprika
1   2 to 3-lb. frying chicken,
   disjointed
1/4 to 1/2 c. butter
3 to 5 c. milk

Combine flour, salt, pepper and paprika in paper bag; shake chicken pieces until coated. Melt butter in 12-inch frypan; fry chicken until golden brown on both sides. Remove frypan from heat; pour milk over chicken to cover. Bake at 350 degrees for 1 hour. May add additional salt if desired.

Susan N. Benjamin
Austin Area School
Port Allegany, Pennsylvania

HERBED OVEN-FRIED CHICKEN

2 c. finely crushed saltines
1/4 tsp. garlic salt
1/8 tsp. pepper
1 tsp. herb salad mix
1   2 1/2-lb. chicken, cut up
1/3 c. melted margarine

Combine crackers, garlic salt, pepper and herb salad mix. Dip chicken in melted margarine; roll in cracker mixture. Place pieces, skin side up, in greased baking dish; sprinkle with remaining butter and crumbs. Bake at 375 degrees for 1 hour or until tender. Yield: 4-6 servings.

Elaine Reves
Silverton High School
Silverton, Texas

HONEYED CHICKEN

1/4 c. melted butter
1 c. honey
1 tbsp. mild mustard
2 tsp. curry powder
1   2 to 2 1/2-lb. frying chicken,
   disjointed

Combine butter, honey, mustard and curry powder in bowl. Dip chicken into honey mixture; arrange in greased 10 x 8 x 2-inch baking dish. Pour remaining sauce over chicken. Bake at 425 degrees for 1 hour or until tender. Cover lightly with foil if chicken becomes too browned.

Mrs. Bessie Klassen
Abbotsford Junior Secondary School
Abbotsford, British Columbia, Canada

KRISPY CHICKEN

8 chicken pieces
2 c. crushed oven-toasted rice
   cereal
1/2 c. margarine, melted
1 1/2 tsp. salt
1 egg

Skin chicken. Combine cereal, margarine and salt. Beat egg with 2 tablespoons water. Dip chicken in egg mixture; roll in crumb mixture. Arrange pieces on ungreased baking sheet, skin side down. Bake at 350 degrees for 1 hour and 15 minutes. Yield: 4 servings.

Betty Welsh
Harlem High School
Loves Park, Illinois

OVEN-FRIED ALAGLAT CHICKEN

1   3 to 3 1/2-lb. chicken
1 tsp. smoked garlic salt
1/2 tsp. pepper
2 tsp. Italian seasoning
1/2 tsp. sweet basil
Salt to taste
2 tbsp. cranberry sauce
2 tsp. orange juice concentrate
5 tbsp. honey
1/4 c. crushed barbecued
   potato chips

Bone chicken; cut into 2-inch pieces. Place chicken in large bowl. Combine garlic salt, pepper, Italian seasoning and basil; sprinkle over chicken, tossing chicken to coat well. Arrange chicken in large shallow foil-lined baking pan; sprinkle with salt. Bake, covered lightly with foil, at 375 degrees for 30 minutes; remove foil. Bake for 30 minutes longer. Combine cranberry sauce, orange juice and honey; blend thoroughly. Brush chicken with cranberry mixture. Bake for 10 minutes longer. Transfer chicken to heated platter; sprinkle with potato chips. Garnish with pineapple and parsley, if desired.

Saralee Glatt
Woodburn Junior High School
Woodburn, Oregon

LEMON-FRIED CHICKEN

1/2 c. lemon juice
1/2 c. corn oil
1/2 tsp. garlic salt
1/2 tsp. crumbled dried thyme
1/2 tsp. crumbled dried marjoram
1 c. flour
1 tsp. grated lemon rind
1 tsp. paprika
1 tsp. monosodium glutamate
Choice pieces of 2 broiler
 chickens

Combine lemon juice with corn oil, garlic salt, thyme, marjoram, flour, lemon rind and paprika in shallow bowl. Sprinkle monosodium glutamate over chicken; coat with flour mixture. Arrange chicken in shallow foil-lined baking pan. Bake at 350 degrees for 1 hour or until chicken is tender.

Lavinia C. Miller
Eau Claire High School
Columbia, South Carolina

PARMESAN OVEN-FRIED CHICKEN

1 c. round buttery cracker crumbs
1/2 c. grated Parmesan cheese
1/4 c. finely chopped blanched
 almonds
1 tbsp. dry minced parsley
1 tsp. salt
1/8 tsp. pepper
1/2 c. butter or margarine
1/4 tsp. garlic powder
1 3 to 3 1/2-lb. frying chicken,
 disjointed

Combine crumbs, cheese, almonds, parsley, salt and pepper in shallow bowl. Melt butter with garlic powder in shallow baking dish. Dip chicken pieces into butter; dip into crumb mixture. Place chicken, skin side up, in baking dish. Let stand for 1 hour. Bake at 400 degrees for 45 minutes or until chicken is tender. Serve hot. Yield: 4 servings.

Mrs. Gladys Truitt
Warren Central High School
Bowling Green, Kentucky

PARSLIED PARMESAN CHICKEN

1 c. herb-seasoned stuffing mix,
 crushed
2/3 c. grated Parmesan cheese
1/4 c. chopped parsley
1 clove of garlic, crushed
1 2 1/2-lb. chicken, disjointed
1/3 c. melted margarine

Combine stuffing mix, cheese, parsley and garlic. Dip chicken pieces into melted butter; roll in crumb mixture. Place chicken, skin side up, in greased jelly roll pan. Sprinkle with remaining margarine and crumbs. Bake at 375 degrees for 1 hour or until chicken is tender.

Mrs. Jan Furgason
Topeka High School
Topeka, Kansas

POTATO CHIP CHICKEN

1 3-lb. frying chicken,
 disjointed
1/2 c. melted butter or
 margarine
1 lg. package potato chips,
 crumbled

Roll pieces of chicken in melted butter; shake in bag of potato chips. Place in one layer in baking pan. Bake in 350-degree oven for 1 hour. Do not turn chicken.

Mrs. Wahneita Davidson
Franklin Junior High School
Grants, New Mexico

QUICK AND EASY OVEN-BAKED CHICKEN

1/2 c. fine cracker crumbs
2 tsp. salt
1/4 tsp. pepper
1 tsp. paprika
1   3-lb. frying chicken,
* disjointed*
Cooking oil

Preheat oven to 400 degrees. Combine crumbs, salt, pepper and paprika in shallow bowl. Roll chicken in crumb mixture. Pour enough oil into bottom of 15 x 10 x 2-inch pan to coat well. Arrange chicken over oil. Bake for 30 minutes; turn chicken. Bake for 30 minutes longer or until chicken is tender and browned.

Frances Fuhrman
Eastern York County School
Wrightsville, Pennsylvania

SAUCY SKILLET CHICKEN

1/3 c. flour
1 tsp. salt
1/2 tsp. paprika
1   2 1/2 to 3-lb. chicken,
* disjointed*
1/2 c. shortening
1 env. dried chicken noodle soup mix
1 med. onion, sliced
1 c. evaporated milk
2 tsp. dried parsley flakes
1/2 tsp. poultry seasoning

Combine flour, salt and paprika in paper bag; shake chicken pieces in bag, coating well. Brown chicken in hot shortening in electric skillet; drain off drippings. Add soup mix, 1/2 cup water and onion; cover. Cook at 250 degrees for 30 to 35 minutes or until chicken is tender. Place chicken in deep serving dish. Stir milk, parsley flakes and poultry seasoning into skillet. Heat, stirring. Do not boil. Pour sauce over chicken. Yield: 4-6 servings.

Dorothy White
Sandhills Public Schools
Halsey, Nebraska

SESAME-BAKED CHICKEN

1/2 c. olive oil
1/4 c. butter or margarine
Flour
6 chicken pieces
Salt and pepper
Herb seasoning
Sesame seed
1/3 c. chopped green onion
1/2 c. white wine

Preheat oven to 275 degrees. Combine oil and butter in 9 x 13-inch baking dish; cool until slightly thickened. Combine enough flour to coat chicken, salt, pepper and herb seasoning to taste. Coat chicken well with seasoned flour; place in prepared dish, skin side down. Sprinkle with sesame seed. Bake for 40 to 45 minutes; turn pieces. Sprinkle with onion and additional sesame seed. Pour wine around chicken pieces. Bake for 30 to 35 minutes longer or until golden brown. Baste occasionally with pan drippings.

Mrs. Laura M. Studstill
Hawkinsville High School
Hawkinsville, Georgia

BAKED CHICKEN BREASTS WITH ALMONDS

3 chicken breasts, halved
2 tbsp. chopped onion
3 tbsp. lemon juice
1/2 c. mayonnaise
1 can cream of chicken soup
Slivered almonds
Crushed potato chips

Boil chicken in salted water until tender; remove skin and bones carefully. Place chicken in 6 1/2 x 12-inch baking dish. Combine onion, lemon juice, mayonnaise and soup; pour over chicken. Top with slivered almonds and crushed potato chips. Bake at 350 degrees until hot and bubbly. Serve over rice.

Helene Ramsey
Grandview Junior High School
Hickory, North Carolina

SOUTHERN-FRIED CHICKEN

1 1 to 2-lb. frying chicken
2 tsp. salt
1/2 tsp. garlic salt
1 tsp. pepper
1 c. flour
1 c. shortening

Cut chicken into serving pieces; rub with salt. Sprinkle chicken with garlic salt and pepper. Place flour in bag; shake chicken in flour to coat well. Brown chicken in shortening in heavy skillet over medium heat, turning to brown on all sides. Reduce heat. Cook, covered, until chicken is tender. Remove from pan; drain on paper toweling.

Mrs. Helen McGuire
Hobart Junior High School
Hobart, Oklahoma

ARLENE'S CHICKEN JUBILEE

1 4-oz. can sliced mushrooms
Butter
1 tsp. salt
1 chicken bouillon cube
1 c. rice
1/4 c. walnuts
6 chicken breasts, halved
1/4 c. flour
1/4 tsp. paprika
1 21-oz. can cherry pie filling
1 tbsp. lemon juice

Drain mushrooms, reserving juice. Add enough water to reserved juice to equal 1 cup liquid. Melt 1 tablespoon butter in skillet; add mushroom liquid, mushrooms, 1/2 teaspoon salt and bouillon cube. Bring to a boil; add rice and walnuts. Cover tightly; cook over low heat for about 25 minutes or until water is absorbed. Remove skin and bones from chicken breasts; pound lightly to flatten. Combine flour, remaining salt and paprika; dredge chicken in seasoned flour. Spoon 1/3 cup rice mixture in center of each chicken piece; bring up sides of meat. Secure with wooden picks. Place chicken in shallow greased baking dish. Cover lightly with alu-minum foil. Bake at 350 degrees for 1 hour or until chicken is tender. Remove to heated platter. Blend pie filling, lemon juice and 3 tablespoons water in saucepan; cook until hot. Stir in 1 tablespoon butter. Serve sauce over chicken.

Arlene V. Kain
Marietta Junior High School
Marietta, Ohio

BAKED CHICKEN BREASTS IN SAUCE

Butter
3 boned chicken breasts, skinned
1 1/2 tsp. salt
Freshly ground pepper
Garlic salt
1/4 c. chicken broth
1/4 c. dry vermouth
1 c. heavy cream
1/2 c. sliced pimento-stuffed green
  olives
5 c. boiling water
2 c. egg noodles
2 tbsp. chopped fresh parsley

Melt 1/4 cup butter in large skillet with heat-proof handle over low heat. Cut chicken breasts in half; sprinkle with 1/2 teaspoon salt, 1/4 teaspoon pepper and dash of garlic salt. Place chicken in butter; turn to coat on both sides. Remove from heat. Bake at 400 degrees for 8 to 15 minutes or until chicken is white and firm to touch. Place chicken on warm platter; cover with foil. Add chicken broth and vermouth to skillet; boil for 15 to 20 minutes or until reduced by half. Add cream; simmer, stirring constantly, until thickened. Add olives; simmer for 1 minute longer. Add remaining salt, 1 teaspoon butter and dash of pepper to boiling water; stir in noodles. Cook for 15 minutes or until tender; drain. Place on platter; place chicken on noodles. Season sauce with additional salt, if needed; pour over chicken. Garnish with parsley.

Karen Lynn Kolbe
Will C. Wood High School
Vacaville, California

BAKED CHICKEN DELIGHT

6 chicken breasts
1 c. prepared biscuit mix
Salt to taste
Ground ginger to taste
Ground cloves to taste
1 egg, beaten
Cooking oil
6 slices pineapple
1/4 c. pineapple juice
1/2 c. (packed) brown sugar
1 tbsp. butter
1 stick cinnamon
6 lime slices
3 cherries, halved

Remove skin from chicken breasts. Combine biscuit mix, salt, ginger and cloves. Dip chicken in egg, then roll in biscuit mix mixture. Brown in hot oil. Place in baking dish. Place 1 slice pineapple on each breast. Combine pineapple juice, brown sugar, ginger, cloves, butter and stick cinnamon in a small saucepan and simmer for at least 10 minutes. Bake chicken at 375 degrees for about 40 minutes, basting at least 2 times with sauce. Place a thin slice of lime and cherry on pineapple 5 minutes before baking is completed. May be prepared ahead of time and frozen.

Mrs. Ann Schroeder
Texas City High School
Texas City, Texas

BAKED ROLLED BREASTS A LA DELI

4 boned chicken breasts
1/4 lb. liverwurst
1/4 lb. sliced boiled ham
1/4 lb. sliced Swiss cheese
1/4 lb. sliced Genoa salami
2 c. prepared spaghetti sauce

Preheat oven to 400 degrees. Skin and split chicken breasts; flatten to 1/4-inch thickness. Have liverwurst at room temperature; spread thinly over chicken breasts. Place slices of ham, Swiss cheese and salami over liverwurst. Roll up each portion as tightly as possible; tie securely with polyester thread.

Arrange rolls in oblong glass baking dish. Combine spaghetti sauce with 2 cups water; pour over rolls. Bake for 1 hour and 30 minutes, turning and basting as rolls brown. Water may be added, if needed. Serve with ziti or other pasta, if desired.

Mrs. Mary E. Florio
North Salem High School and Middle School
North Salem, New York

BREASTS OF CHICKEN SUPREME

6 lg. whole chicken breasts
2 13 3/4-oz. cans chicken broth
1/2 c. minced celery
1/2 c. minced onion
1 c. minced carrot
2 tsp. salt
3 tbsp. butter
1/4 c. diced green pepper
3 tbsp. flour
2 c. light cream
1/2 tsp. powdered savory
2 tbsp. diced pimento

Place chicken breasts on trivet in large kettle. Add broth, celery, onion, carrot and salt. Cover; simmer for 1 hour and 15 minutes or until chicken is tender. Remove chicken from kettle; cool slightly. Remove skin and bones, keeping meat in 1 piece. Cover; set aside. Remove trivet from kettle. Simmer broth mixture until reduced by 1/2. Process broth mixture through food mill. Melt butter in saucepan; add green pepper. Saute until limp. Blend in flour, 1 1/2 cups broth puree and cream. Cook, stirring constantly, until smooth and thickened. Season with savory. Stir in pimento; simmer for 5 minutes longer. Arrange chicken in baking dish; cover with sauce. Cover with aluminum foil; freeze. May be taken directly from freezer and baked. Bake, covered, at 350 degrees for 1 hour, stirring occasionally. Remove cover. Bake for about 20 minutes longer. Serve over hot cooked rice. Yield: 8 servings.

Mary Alice Bird
Southwestern High School
Detroit, Michigan

RIPE OLIVE QUICHE

1 10-oz. package frozen patty
   shells
1 8-oz. package cream cheese
2 eggs
2 c. canned pitted ripe olives,
   drained
1 2-oz. can rolled anchovies
   with capers
1/2 c. grated Fontina or imported
   Swiss cheese
1/2 c. grated Parmesan cheese

Thaw patty shells in refrigerator. Knead patty shells together and roll out. Press into 10-inch fluted tart pan. Mix cream cheese with eggs; pour into pastry. Cut olives into halves and chunks. Sprinkle evenly over cheese filling. Arrange anchovies on top; sprinkle with cheeses. Bake in 400-degree oven for 40 minutes or until brown. Serve warm or cold. Yield: 20 small wedges.

Photograph for this recipe on page 135.

RIPE OLIVE RIGOLETTOS

2 c. canned pitted ripe olives
2 8-oz. packages cream cheese
1 tsp. salt
6 drops of hot sauce
2 tbsp. lemon juice
2 tbsp. tomato paste
1/2 c. mashed avocado
8 candied cherries, chopped
1 tbsp. chopped sugared ginger
1/4 c. chopped nuts
1 bunch hearts of celery
1 cucumber
1 green pepper
1 tomato
1 red onion
1 pkg. Cheddar cheese

Chop 1 1/2 cups ripe olives very fine. Cut remaining olives into halves, quarters and rings for garnish. Soften the cream cheese in a bowl. Add the chopped olives, salt, hot sauce and lemon juice and mix well. Spoon equal amounts into 3 bowls. Add tomato paste to 1 bowl, mashed avocado to 1 bowl and cherries, ginger and nuts to remaining bowl. Stuff celery with cherry mixture and press together to form bunch. Roll in waxed paper and chill. Cut the cucumber into slices. Cut green pepper and tomato into wedges, scooping out seeds and membrane. Cut the onion into wedges and separate. Cut cheese into triangles. Pipe cream cheese mixtures into canape bases with a pastry tube and garnish with reserved ripe olives. Cut celery into slices. Chill all canapes well before serving.

Photograph for this recipe on page 135.

PATE MAISON

1/2 env. unflavored gelatin
1/2 c. bouillon or consomme
Pimento
Capers
Truffles and ripe olives
1 lb. chicken livers
1/2 tsp. monosodium glutamate
2 tbsp. minced onion
6 tbsp. butter or margarine
1/2 tsp. salt
1 tsp. dry mustard
1/4 tsp. cloves
1/8 tsp. nutmeg
2 tbsp. brandy

Sprinkle gelatin over bouillon in saucepan. Place over low heat, stirring constantly, until gelatin is dissolved. Pour thin layer of bouillon mixture in bottom of 8 x 4 x 2 1/2-inch pan. Chill until slightly thickened. Press a design of pimento, capers, truffles and ripe olives into thickened bouillon. Pour remaining bouillon mixture over design and chill while preparing pate. Sprinkle chicken livers and monosodium glutamate. Saute with onion in 2 tablespoons butter for 6 to 7 minutes. Remove from heat. Turn into blender. Sprinkle with salt, dry mustard, cloves and nutmeg. Blend until smooth. Add remaining butter and brandy. Blend until smooth. Turn into prepared pan. Chill. Dip quickly into pan of hot water up to top to unmold. Loosen with sharp knife. Turn onto platter. Yield: 24 servings.

Photograph for this recipe on page 136.

LOBSTER BARQUETTES

1   10-oz. package pie crust mix
1 tbsp. butter
1   5-oz. can lobster, finely
    chopped
1 tbsp. chopped onion
1 tbsp. chopped parsley
2 tbsp. brandy
1/2 tsp. monosodium glutamate
2 tsp. lemon juice
1/3 c. warm light cream
1 egg yolk
Grated Parmesan cheese
Buttered bread crumbs

Prepare pie crust mix according to package directions. Roll dough on lightly floured board to 1/8-inch thickness. Invert 3-inch barquette molds on dough. Cut 1/3 inch around each mold with knife. Fit piece of pastry into each mold; press to bottom and sides. Trim excess around rim of mold. Prick bottom with a fork. Fill pastry shells with rice to prevent pastry from bubbling. Bake at 375 degrees for 10 to 12 minutes or until shells are golden brown. Remove rice. Cool. Melt butter in a skillet. Add lobster, onion and parsley. Cook until onion is tender but not brown. Stir in brandy. Sprinkle with monosodium glutamate and lemon juice. Combine cream and egg yolk; stir into skillet. Spoon mixture into baked barquettes. Sprinkle with Parmesan cheese and bread crumbs. Brown under broiler to serve immediately. Refrigerate until ready to serve if prepared in advance. Reheat in a 350-degree oven for 15 minutes. Brown lightly under broiler.

Photograph for this recipe on page 136.

ALMOND MUSHROOMS

18 lg. mushrooms
Monosodium glutamate
1/3 c. fine dry bread crumbs
2 tsp. lemon juice
1/8 tsp. rosemary
1 tsp. marjoram
1/4 tsp. salt
1/4 c. finely chopped almonds
1 tbsp. capers

3 tbsp. butter
3 tbsp. chopped parsley

Wash mushrooms and remove stems. Sprinkle inside of mushroom caps with monosodium glutamate. Chop stems finely; combine with bread crumbs, lemon juice, herbs, salt, almonds and capers. Spoon mixture into caps. Place in greased shallow baking pan. Dot each mushroom with butter. Bake at 350 degrees for 20 to 25 minutes. Sprinkle with parsley before serving.

Photograph for this recipe on page 136.

CRAB MEAT QUICHE

1   8-in. unbaked pie shell
2 eggs
1 c. light cream
1 tsp. monosodium glutamate
3/4 tsp. salt
Dash of cayenne pepper
3 oz. Swiss cheese, grated
3 oz. Gruyere cheese, grated
1 tbsp. flour
1   6 1/2-oz. can crab meat, flaked

Prick bottom and sides of pie shell with fork. Bake in a 450-degree oven for about 10 minutes or until delicate brown. Combine eggs, cream, monosodium glutamate, salt and cayenne pepper; beat well. Combine cheeses, flour and crab meat; sprinkle evenly in pie shell. Pour in cream mixture. Bake at 325 degrees for 45 minutes to 1 hour or until tip of knife inserted in center comes out clean. Cut into small wedges. Yield: 16 servings.

Photograph for this recipe on page 136.

VEGETABLES VINAIGRETTE

White Beans

3 c. cooked white beans
1/2 tsp. monosodium glutamate
1 onion, chopped
2 tbsp. chopped parsley
1/2 c. French dressing
1 clove of garlic, slashed

Place beans in a large bowl; add remaining ingredients. Mix well. Chill for several hours. Remove garlic before serving.

Cucumbers

3 cucumbers
1/2 tsp. monosodium glutamate
1/2 c. vinegar
2 tbsp. sugar
1 clove of garlic, slashed
Chopped dill

Peel cucumbers and slice thinly. Sprinkle with monosodium glutamate. Combine vinegar, sugar and 2 tablespoons water; pour over cucumbers. Add garlic. Sprinkle with dill. Chill. Remove garlic before serving.

Artichoke Hearts

2 1-lb. cans artichoke hearts
1 tsp. monosodium glutamate
1/2 c. French dressing
2 tbsp. lemon juice

Drain artichoke hearts and place in bowl. Sprinkle with monosodium glutamate. Add dressing and lemon juice. Marinate for several hours. Garnish with diced pimento and capers.

Photograph for this recipe on page 136.

BAKED CHICKEN DINNER

4 carrots
3 lg. potatoes
2 med. onions, cut in rings
Salt and pepper to taste
1/4 c. margarine
4 chicken breasts
1 can mushroom soup

Peel carrots and potatoes; cut as for French fries. Cut 4 squares of aluminum foil. Arrange layers of potato strips, carrot strips and half the onion rings on each piece of foil. Season with salt and pepper; place pat of margarine over each. Place chicken breast over vegetables on each square. Spread 2 to 3 tablespoons of soup over each chicken breast; top with remaining onion rings.

Sprinkle with salt and pepper. Place pat of margarine on top. Seal packets; place on baking sheet. Bake at 325 degrees for about 1 hour or until chicken is tender. Yield: 4 servings.

Mrs. Sharlott Valentine
Warren Central High School
Vicksburg, Mississippi

CANADIAN CHICKEN JUBILEE

6 sm. chicken breasts, boned
1 20 1/2-oz. can pineapple slices
1 c. finely chopped ham
2 tbsp. chopped onions
Butter
1/4 tsp. ginger
1/4 c. med. cracker crumbs
3/4 c. chicken broth
2 tbsp. vinegar
1/2 tsp. salt
1 tbsp. sugar
1 tbsp. cornstarch
1 8 3/4-oz. can pitted dark sweet cherries, drained
1/4 c. brandy

Remove skin from chicken breasts; place on cutting board, boned side up. Pound lightly until meat is 1/4-inch thick. Drain pineapple, reserving 1/2 cup syrup. Dice 4 slices pineapple. Saute diced pineapple, ham and onions in 2 tablespoons butter in skillet. Add ginger and crumbs; mix well. Stuff chicken breasts with crumb mixture; roll up as for jelly roll. Secure with skewers. Melt 1/4 cup butter in skillet; brown chicken rolls evenly over low heat. Add broth, vinegar and salt; cover. Cook over low heat for 20 minutes. Combine sugar, cornstarch and reserved syrup; stir into chicken mixture. Cook for 15 minutes or until chicken is tender. Remove chicken to serving dish. Brown remaining pineapple slices in small amount of butter; add pineapple and cherries to chicken mixture. Pour sauce into heatproof dish. Heat brandy; pour over sauce. Ignite at serving time. Spoon flaming sauce over chicken.

Mrs. Rosie Pratt
Edwin Parr Composite School
Athabasca, Alberta, Canada

BARVIEW HOUSE CHICKEN BREASTS

> 6 lg. chicken breasts
> 1 can cream of mushroom soup
> 1 1/2 c. sour cream
> 1/2 c. white wine
> 1 pkg. chicken Rice-A-Roni
> 1/2 lb. fresh mushrooms, sliced
> Paprika to taste

Split, skin and bone chicken breasts; arrange in large shallow baking dish. Combine soup, 1 cup sour cream and wine; pour over chicken. Bake, covered, at 350 degrees for 1 hour. Prepare Rice-A-Roni according to package directions; spoon into casserole. Top with chicken and mushrooms. Combine remaining sour cream with 1 cup chicken pan drippings. Pour over chicken. Sprinkle with paprika. Bake at 350 degrees for 30 minutes.

Mrs. Patricia Klessig
Millicoma Junior High School
Coos Bay, Oregon

BREASTS OF CHICKEN CORDON BLEU

> 2 boned chicken breasts, skinned
> 4 slices cooked ham
> 4 1 1/2 x 3-in. slices Swiss
>   cheese
> Flour
> 1 egg, beaten
> Bread crumbs
> 1/4 c. vegetable oil
> 2 tbsp. melted butter

Cut chicken breasts in half; place each half between pieces of plastic wrap. Flatten with wooden mallet until thin. Wrap each ham slice around slice of cheese; place on one side of chicken pieces. Fold other side over; squeeze edges together with hands. Trim off jagged edges. Dip each prepared chicken breast in flour, then in egg. Dip in bread crumbs to coat completely; shape with hands around edges, making sure all edges are sealed. Heat electric frypan to 420 degrees. Add oil; heat for 2 to 3 minutes. Saute chicken in oil for 2 to 3 minutes on each side or until golden brown. Place in greased shallow baking pan. Bake at 350 degrees for 25 minutes. Remove from pan; place on platter. Spoon butter over chicken; garnish with lemon slices and parsley.

Mrs. Marnie E. Davidson
Rosedale Junior Secondary School
Rosedale, British Columbia, Canada

BREASTS OF CHICKEN WITH HAM

> 4 chicken breasts
> Salt and pepper to taste
> 1/2 c. butter
> 1/2 lb. fresh mushrooms
> 4 1/4-in. thick baked ham slices
> 1 can cream of mushroom soup
> 1/2 c. cooking sherry
> 1/2 c. heavy cream

Bone and skin chicken breasts; stir 1 teaspoon salt into bowl of water. Soak chicken in salted water for 1 hour; drain thoroughly. Season chicken well with salt and pepper; brown chicken in butter in skillet over medium heat until golden. Remove from skillet; set aside. Saute mushrooms in pan drippings for 5 minutes. Trim ham slices to size of chicken pieces; arrange ham in shallow baking dish. Cover ham with chicken breasts. Spoon mushrooms over chicken. Combine soup, sherry and cream in skillet. Bring just to a boil, stirring constantly; pour over mushrooms. Bake, covered, at 350 degrees for 45 minutes. Serve immediately. Yield: 4 servings.

Mrs. Dorotha Hurst
Baytown Junior School
Baytown, Texas

CHICKEN ACAPULCO

> 4 whole cooked chicken breasts,
>   boned
> 3 tbsp. butter or margarine
> 3 tbsp. flour
> 1 c. sour cream
> 1 can cream of chicken soup
> 2 oz. canned diced green chilies
> 1/2 tsp. onion salt
> 2 c. shredded Jack cheese

Place chicken in 7 1/2 x 11 3/4-inch baking dish. Melt butter in medium saucepan over low heat; stir in flour until smooth. Add sour cream, stirring constantly until blended and bubbly. Do not boil. Add soup, chilies and onion salt; blend well. Pour over chicken in baking dish. Bake at 350 degrees for about 30 minutes. Sprinkle cheese over chicken mixture. Bake for 10 minutes longer or until cheese is bubbly. Yield: 6 servings.

Mrs. Betty J. Ziegler
Rosemont Junior High School
Crescenta, California

CHICKEN BREAST CASSEROLE

10 to 12 chicken breast halves
Salt to taste
1 can cream of mushroom soup
1 can Cheddar cheese soup
3/4 c. sherry
Parmesan cheese
1 sm. can mushrooms, drained

Simmer chicken in small amount of salted water until tender; drain. Combine mushroom soup, cheese soup and sherry; blend well. Layer chicken and soup mixture in greased casserole. Sprinkle Parmesan cheese over soup layers; top with mushrooms. Bake, covered, at 400 degrees for 1 hour. Sauce may be served over rice.

Montine Jackson
Moultrie Senior High School
Moultrie, Georgia

CHICKEN A LA VERONESE

4 chicken breasts
Salt to taste
2 tbsp. butter
2 tsp. orange marmalade
1/2 tsp. crumbled tarragon leaves
1/2 c. dry white wine
1/2 c. cream
2 tsp. cornstarch
1 1/2 c. seedless grapes

Bone and skin chicken breasts; sprinkle lightly with salt. Melt butter in large frying pan over medium heat; add chicken breasts.

Brown lightly on each side. Place about 1/2 teaspoon marmalade on each piece of chicken; sprinkle with 1/2 teaspoon tarragon. Pour wine over each chicken piece; cover pan. Simmer for about 20 minutes or until thickest part of meat is white. Transfer chicken to serving dish; keep hot. Add cream to pan juices; bring to a rolling boil quickly. Blend cornstarch with small amount of water; stir into sauce. Return to a boil, stirring constantly until thickened. Add seedless grapes; return to heat. Pour sauce over chicken. Serve over rice; garnish with toasted blanched almonds. One package white wine sauce mix may be substituted for wine sauce in recipe if desired. Yield: 4 servings.

Mrs. Carol J. Brottem
Truman Junior High School
Tacoma, Washington

CHICKEN BREASTS WITH GARLIC RICE

3 lg. whole chicken breasts
Flour
Salt and pepper to taste
1 can cream of mushroom soup
1/2 c. sour cream
1/4 c. cooking sherry
1 c. uncooked rice
1/2 c. butter
2 cloves of garlic, minced
1 sm. onion, finely chopped
2 cans chicken consomme
1 lg. can sliced mushrooms

Split and bone chicken breasts. Combine flour, salt and pepper; coat chicken. Arrange chicken in large shallow baking dish. Combine soup, sour cream and sherry; pour over chicken. Bake, covered, at 300 degrees for 1 hour and 30 minutes; remove cover. Bake for 30 minutes longer. Brown rice in butter in saucepan. Add garlic, onion, consomme and mushrooms; blend well. Pour rice mixture into 9 x 9-inch greased baking dish. Bake at 325 degrees for 2 hours or until liquid is absorbed. Yield: 6 servings.

Jane Bigler
Blue Valley High School
Stanley, Kansas

CHICKEN BREASTS HALA-KAHIKI

1/3 c. flour
2 tsp. salt
1/4 tsp. pepper
1/4 tsp. nutmeg
1/4 tsp. ginger
2 chicken breasts, halved
1/3 c. oil
1 med. onion, minced
1 clove of garlic, minced
1   20-oz. can sliced pineapple
3 tbsp. soy sauce
1/2 c. flaked coconut
1 bay leaf, crumbled
1 tbsp. cornstarch

Mix flour, salt, pepper, nutmeg and ginger together. Coat chicken breasts with flour mixture. Brown chicken in hot oil in skillet. Remove chicken from skillet; add onion and garlic. Cook until tender but not brown. Return chicken to skillet; Drain pineapple; reserve juice. Add reserved juice, soy sauce, coconut, bay leaf and 1 1/2 cups water. Cover; simmer for 20 minutes. Remove chicken from skillet. Blend cornstarch with 1/4 cup water. Add to mixture in skillet. Cook, stirring constantly, until thickened. Place pineapple rings in skillet; add chicken. Cover; simmer for 10 minutes. Remove chicken to heated platter; pour sauce over chicken. Top with pineapple slices. Garnish with maraschino cherries with stems.

Ohnalee M. Sholley
Northern Senior High School
Dillsburg, Pennsylvania

CHICKEN BREASTS IN HAM

4 lg. chicken breasts
1/2 tsp. minced garlic
1/2 tsp. salt
1/2 tsp. paprika
1/4 tsp. chili powder
1/4 c. flour
3 tbsp. butter
2/3 c. chicken broth or white wine
Thinly sliced baked ham

Remove skin and bones from chicken breasts; cut chicken in 1-inch wide strips.

Mix garlic, salt, paprika, chili powder and flour; dredge chicken with flour mixture. Brown in butter. Add chicken broth; cover. Simmer for 20 minutes or until chicken is tender; cool. Wrap each piece of chicken in strips of ham; skewer with cocktail picks. Refrigerate; serve cold.

Polly K. Freeze
Valley View High School
Germantown, Ohio

CHICKEN BREASTS SUPREME

3 med. chicken breasts
3/4 tsp. seasoned salt
Paprika to taste
1 chicken bouillon cube
1 c. boiling water
1/4 c. sauterne
1/2 tsp. instant minced onion
1/2 tsp. curry powder
Dash of pepper
2 tbsp. all-purpose flour
1/4 c. cold water
1   3-oz. can sliced mushrooms

Cut chicken breasts in half; sprinkle with seasoned salt and paprika. Place in 11 x 7 x 1 1/2-inch baking pan. Dissolve bouillon cube in boiling water; add sauterne, onion, curry powder and pepper. Pour over chicken; cover with foil. Bake at 350 degrees for 30 minutes. Uncover; bake for 45 minutes longer or till tender. Remove chicken to warm platter. Strain pan juices; reserve. Blend flour with cold water in saucepan; stir in reserved pan juices slowly. Cook, stirring, over low heat till sauce thickens and bubbles; cook for 3 to 4 minutes longer. Drain mushrooms; stir into flour mixture. Heat through. Spoon over chicken breasts; garnish with watercress. Yield: 6 servings.

Mrs. Merilyn O'Donnell
Cashmere High School
Cashmere, Washington

CHICKEN BREASTS IN WINE SAUCE

6 chicken breasts, split
Salt and pepper to taste
1/2 c. flour

1/2 c. butter
1 bunch green onions, sliced
1 can mushroom pieces, drained
2 tbsp. chopped parsley
1 1/2 c. dry white wine
1 bay leaf
1/2 tsp. Worcestershire sauce
1/8 tsp. marjoram
1/8 tsp. thyme

Season chicken with salt and pepper; dredge with flour. Brown chicken in butter in heavy skillet; place in large, shallow baking dish. Brown onions and mushrooms lightly in pan drippings; stir in parsley, wine, bay leaf, Worcestershire sauce, marjoram and thyme. Simmer for 10 minutes; pour over chicken. Bake, covered, at 325 degrees for 1 hour or until chicken is tender. Yield: 6 servings.

Mrs. Eunice W. Casey
Ayden-Grifton High School
Ayden, North Carolina

CHICKEN CORDON BLEU

4 1-lb. whole chicken breasts, halved
Salt
8 slices Swiss cheese
1 3-oz. package sandwich sliced ham
3 tbsp. butter
1/2 lb. fresh mushrooms, sliced
1 can cream of mushroom soup
1 soup can dry white wine
2 6-oz. packages long grain and wild rice
1 2 1/2-oz. package slivered almonds

Remove skin and bones from chicken breasts; place each piece between sheets of waxed paper. Pound with mallet into 4 x 6-inch fillets. Sprinkle each fillet with salt to taste. Place 1 slice cheese and 1 slice ham on each fillet. Roll fillets up as for jelly roll; tie rolls near each end with string. Melt butter in large skillet over medium heat. Brown rolls lightly on all sides; place in oblong baking dish. Saute mushrooms in pan drippings in skillet, adding additional butter if necessary. Combine soup and wine in blender con-tainer; blend well. Spoon soup mixture over chicken rolls; top with mushrooms. Bake at 350 degrees for 1 hour. Prepare rice according to package directions. Serve chicken rolls on bed of rice; spoon sauce and mushrooms on top. Garnish with almonds. Yield: 8 servings.

Mrs. Douglas Fogel
Milburn Junior High School
Shawnee Mission, Kansas

CHICKEN WITH LOBSTER AND TOMATO

4 chicken breasts, halved
1 1/2 tsp. salt
1/4 tsp. pepper
1/2 c. butter
2 tbsp. sherry
1/2 lb. mushrooms, sliced
2 tbsp. flour
1 1/2 c. chicken broth
1 tbsp. tomato paste
1 bay leaf, crushed
2 tbsp. chopped chives
2 10-oz. packages frozen lobster-tails
3 ripe tomatoes, peeled and quartered

Sprinkle chicken breasts with 1 teaspoon salt and 1/8 teaspoon pepper. Heat butter in skillet until foamy; add chicken breasts. Saute until golden. Spoon sherry over chicken; remove chicken from skillet. Place in shallow baking dish; cover with foil. Bake at 300 degrees for 30 minutes. Add mushrooms to skillet; saute until tender. Blend flour into pan drippings in skillet. Add broth; simmer, stirring constantly, until thickened. Add tomato paste, bay leaf, chives, remaining salt and remaining pepper. Simmer for 15 minutes. Cook lobster according to package directions; remove meat from shells. Cut meat into bite-sized pieces. Add lobster meat and tomatoes to sauce. Simmer for 5 to 8 minutes. Serve chicken breasts on heated platter; top with sauce. Yield: 6-8 servings.

Mrs. Elna P. Larson
Ondossifgon School
Ashland, Wisconsin

CHICKEN BREASTS WITH WILD RICE

4 whole chicken breasts
1 c. chopped onion
1 4-oz. can mushrooms, drained
Butter
2 c. cooked wild rice
1 tsp. salt
1/4 tsp. pepper
1 1/2 tsp. paprika

Split, skin and bone chicken breasts; pound chicken breasts between sheets of plastic wrap to 1/4-inch thickness. Saute onion and mushrooms in 2 tablespoons butter in skillet; stir in wild rice, salt, pepper and paprika blending thoroughly. Spoon 3 tablespoons rice mixture onto each half chicken breast; roll up, fastening securely with wooden picks or skewers. Arrange rolls in shallow foil-lined baking pan; brush with 4 tablespoons melted butter. Broil, brushing with additional melted butter, for 10 minutes; turn to brown on all sides. Bake at 350 degrees for 15 minutes or until tender. Remaining stuffing may be sealed in foil packet and heated with chicken. Arrange chicken on heated platter; pour pan juices over chicken. Garnish with parsley, if desired.

Mrs. Flora Hoybook
Van High School
Van, Texas

CHICKEN CANAANESE

6 chicken breasts
1 lg. purple onion, sliced
1 lg. can mushrooms
1 tsp. garlic powder
Salt and pepper to taste
1 No. 2 can pineapple chunks
1/2 c. soy sauce
1/2 c. frozen concentrate for
 imitation orange juice
1/2 c. water
1 tbsp. cornstarch

Brown the chicken breasts in a large Dutch oven in 2 tablespoons fat. Remove the breasts from the Dutch oven. Add the onion and mushrooms; saute until onion is transparent. Return the chicken to the Dutch oven; add the remaining ingredients except the cornstarch. Cover; simmer for 30 to 45 minutes or until tender, turning the chicken occasionally to coat with sauce. Remove chicken from the pan just before serving. Dissolve cornstarch in a small amount of water and stir into the pan juices. Cook until thickened. Pour sauce over the chicken and serve with brown rice.

Barbara B. McDonald
Canaan Memorial High School
Canaan, Vermont

CHICKEN AND GREEN BEANS

16 soda crackers
1 can French-style green beans,
 drained
3 whole chicken breasts, halved
1 c. grated sharp Cheddar cheese
1 can cream of chicken soup
1 can chicken broth
1/2 tsp. onion flakes
1 sm. can whole mushrooms, drained
1/4 c. slivered almonds
2 tbsp. melted butter

Crush 10 crackers. Arrange layers of beans, chicken, crushed crackers and 1/2 cup cheese in greased 1 1/2-quart casserole. Combine soup, half the broth, remaining cheese and onion flakes in saucepan; heat through. Pour over chicken mixture. Add mushrooms and almonds. Crush remaining crackers; sprinkle over almonds. Drizzle butter over crackers. Pour remaining broth over top. Bake at 350 degrees for 45 minutes. Yield: 6 servings.

Mrs. Bonnie Chenoweth
Junior High School
Black River Falls, Wisconsin

CHICKEN AND DUMPLINGS

4 meaty chicken breasts
1 3/4 tsp. salt
1/4 tsp. pepper
2 med. onions, quartered
1 c. sliced celery

3 med. carrots, cut into strips
2 chicken bouillon cubes
1 bay leaf
2 c. sifted flour
4 tsp. baking powder
1 c. milk
1/4 c. cooking oil

Soak chicken breasts in bowl of warm water mixed with 1/2 teaspoon salt for 10 minutes; drain. Sprinkle chicken with 1/4 teaspoon salt and pepper. Place chicken in 5-quart Dutch oven; add onions, celery, carrots, bouillon cubes, bay leaf and 5 cups water. Bring to a boil; reduce heat. Simmer, covered,. for 45 minutes. Remove chicken and bay leaf; discard bay leaf. Bone and skin chicken; return to Dutch oven. Combine flour, baking powder and remaining salt; add milk and oil, stirring just to moisten. Drop dough from tablespoon into hot chicken mixture. Cook over medium heat; reduce heat. Simmer, covered, for 5 minutes longer. Yield: 4-6 servings.

Mrs. Gail Jordan
L. F. Mayer Junior High School
Fairview Park, Ohio

CHICKEN ITALIANO

4 chicken breasts
1/2 c. fine bread crumbs
3 tbsp. oil
1 tbsp. flour
1 tbsp. sugar
1/2 tsp. oregano
1/4 tsp. garlic powder
1 tsp. salt
1/4 tsp. basil
1   4-oz. can mushrooms, drained
1   1-lb. can stewed tomatoes
Grated Parmesan cheese

Wash chicken; pat dry. Remove skin; coat chicken with bread crumbs. Saute in oil in skillet until golden. Remove from skillet; place in baking dish. Stir flour, sugar, oregano, garlic powder, salt and basil into oil remaining in skillet. Add mushrooms and tomatoes; simmer for 5 minutes. Pour over chicken breasts; cover. Bake in preheated

350-degree oven for 1 hour; sprinkle with Parmesan cheese. Yield: 4 servings.

Mrs. Cheryl Peters
Lakeshore High School
Stevensville, Michigan

CHICKEN WITH ORANGE RICE
Second Place

1/3 c. flour
Salt
Pepper
Paprika
Onion salt
4 chicken breasts, halved
Butter
2 cans cream of chicken soup
1 c. sour cream

Combine flour, salt, pepper, paprika and onion salt to taste; dredge chicken in seasoned flour. Melt butter in skillet; brown chicken on both sides. Remove chicken to casserole. Combine soup and sour cream; spoon over chicken. Cover. Bake at 350 degrees for 1 hour.

Orange Rice

Chopped onion to taste
1 c. chopped celery
2 tbsp. butter
1 c. rice
Grated rind of 1 orange
Juice of 2 oranges
1/2 tsp. salt
1/8 tsp. thyme
1   4-oz. can mushrooms

Saute onion and celery in butter in skillet until limp. Stir in rice and orange rind. Add enough water to orange juice to equal 2 1/2 cups liquid. Add orange liquid, salt and thyme to rice mixture. Spoon into casserole. Bake at 350 degrees for 30 minutes or until liquid is absorbed. Remove chicken from casserole. Add mushrooms to pan drippings for gravy. Serve gravy with rice and chicken. May use 1 cup diluted frozen orange juice, if desired.

Borghild Strom
Pattengill Junior High School
Lansing, Michigan

CHICKEN JAPANESE

1/2 c. soy sauce
1/4 c. corn oil
2 tbsp. parsley
2 tbsp. onion flakes
1/2 tsp. ginger
1/2 tsp. pepper
1/2 tsp. salt
8 whole chicken breasts
1 lg. can sliced mushrooms,
    drained

Combine soy sauce, oil, parsley, onion flakes, ginger, pepper and salt. Place chicken breasts and mushrooms in mixing bowl; pour marinade over chicken mixture. Cover; chill for several hours, turning chicken at least twice. Place chicken in large glass casserole. Divide mushrooms equally over chicken breasts; pour marinade over chicken mixture. Cover. Bake at 325 degrees for 30 minutes; baste. Bake for 30 minutes longer.

Mrs. Gloria Sparkman
Emerson Junior High School
San Antonio, Texas

CHICKEN AND PEPPERS MARENGO

1   16-oz. can peeled tomatoes
1   4 1/2-oz. can sliced mushrooms
4 boned chicken breasts
1 med. green pepper
1 med. sweet red pepper
3 stalks celery
2 tbsp. butter
1 clove of garlic, minced
1 pkg. onion soup mix
2 tbsp. soy sauce
2 tbsp. corn oil
1 med. sliced onion
1/2 tsp. sugar

Drain tomatoes and mushrooms, reserving juice. Cut chicken, peppers, celery and tomatoes into bite-sized pieces. Melt butter in large skillet. Brown chicken and garlic. Remove chicken from skillet. Combine soup mix and reserved juices, mixing well. Stir soup mixture into pan drippings in skillet.

Add chicken, tomatoes and mushrooms. Simmer for about 20 minutes. Combine soy sauce and oil in separate large skillet; heat. Coat skillet well with oil mixture. Add peppers, celery and onion. Cook over medium heat for 5 minutes or until just tender. Combine vegetable mixture and chicken mixture. Add sugar; simmer for 15 minutes. Serve over hot cooked rice. Yield: 4-5 servings.

Sue Moller
Windham High School
South Windham, Maine

CHICKEN IN RED WINE

3 whole chicken breasts
Flour
Salad oil
1 onion, diced
1 c. catsup
1/2 c. red wine
2 tbsp. (firmly packed) brown
    sugar
2 tbsp. lemon juice
2 tbsp. Worcestershire sauce

Split and bone chicken breasts; dredge with flour. Brown chicken in small amount of oil in large skillet. Saute onion in 2 tablespoons additional oil in medium skillet until tender; add catsup, wine, brown sugar, lemon juice and Worcestershire sauce. Simmer, stirring frequently, for 10 minutes; pour over chicken. Bake, covered, at 350 degrees for 1 hour. May be refrigerated overnight before baking, if desired.

Pearl Kaye
Weber Junior High School
Port Washington, New York

CHICKEN PUFF

4 frozen patty shells
1 1/2 tbsp. margarine
2   1-lb. chicken breasts, halved
2 c. chicken broth
1/2 box long grain and wild rice
2 tbsp. cornstarch
2 tbsp. white wine (opt.)
Salt and pepper

1/4 c. chopped onion
1/4 c. chopped green pepper
1/4 c. slivered almonds
1 sm. can mushrooms, drained
1 beaten egg

Thaw patty shells. Melt 1 tablespoon margarine in skillet; brown chicken breasts well on both sides. Pour broth into skillet; cook chicken over medium heat until tender. Cool. Remove meat from bones, reserving broth in skillet. Combine remaining margarine and 1 1/4 cups water in saucepan. Stir in rice; bring to a boil. Cover tightly; cook over low heat for about 25 minutes or until water is absorbed. Cool. Preheat oven to 425 degrees. Pour reserved broth into double boiler, stir in cornstarch. Cook over boiling water, stirring constantly, until thickened. Add wine and salt and pepper to taste. Cool. Combine chicken, rice, half the sauce, onion, green pepper, almonds and mushrooms. Roll each patty shell out on floured pastry cloth to 6-inch square. Spoon 1/4 of the chicken mixture into center of each square. Shape squares into triangles; seal edges together. Place on cookie sheet; brush with beaten egg. Bake for 15 minutes or until brown. Yield: 4 servings.

Carolyn W. Hounshell
Morton Junior High School
Morton, Illinois

CHICKEN AND RICE

1/3 c. flour
Salt
1 tsp. paprika
6 chicken breasts
1/4 c. butter
1 c. rice
2 cans chicken broth
2 tbsp. chopped parsley
1/8 tsp. curry powder
6 canned peach halves
3 tbsp. peach jam
2 tbsp. (packed) brown sugar
6 whole cloves

Sift flour, 2 teaspoons salt and paprika together; roll chicken breasts in seasoned flour.

Melt butter in skillet; brown chicken in hot butter. Remove chicken from skillet. Add rice, broth, parsley, curry powder and 3/4 teaspoon salt to pan drippings in skillet. Bring to a boil. Pour broth mixture into foil-lined 2 quart baking dish; add chicken. Cover with foil. Bake at 350 degrees for 60 minutes. Drain peach halves. Blend jam and brown sugar together; spread over peach halves. Insert clove in center of each peach half. Remove cover; place peach halves around chicken mixture. Bake for 15 minutes longer.

Mrs. Peggy Horntrop
Brookport High School
Brookport, Illinois

CHICKEN SCALLOPINI

2 whole chicken breasts
1 egg
2 tbsp. milk
1/2 c. flour
1 tsp. salt
1/4 tsp. pepper
1 c. Italian bread crumbs
2 8-oz. cans tomato sauce
1/4 c. Parmesan cheese
1/2 c. dry white wine
1 tsp. oregano
1/4 c. oil

Split chicken breasts; remove skin and bones. Place each piece of chicken between 2 sheets of waxed paper. Pound chicken gently with rolling pin until twice its original size. Beat egg with milk in shallow bowl. Combine flour, salt and pepper. Place bread crumbs on separate sheet of waxed paper. Coat chicken with flour mixture, shaking off excess. Dip into egg mixture; coat well with bread crumbs. Chill. Combine tomato sauce, cheese, wine and oregano in saucepan; simmer for about 10 minutes. Heat oil in skillet; brown chicken well on each side. Place on heated platter; pour sauce over chicken.

Mrs. Joanne Stout
S. G. Smith Intermediate School
Somerville, New Jersey

CHICKEN SALTIMBOCCA

5 boned chicken breasts
Salt and pepper to taste
1/2 lb. prosciutto, sliced thin
1/2 lb. mozzarella cheese, sliced
   thin
2 eggs, beaten
1 c. bread crumbs
1/2 c. vegetable oil
1 c. sherry

Cut chicken breasts in half; flatten as thin as possible. Season with salt and pepper. Cut prosciutto to same size as chicken; place 1 slice on each chicken breast. Cover each with 1 slice cheese. Fold chicken breast in half; secure with toothpick. Dip each piece in egg, then in bread crumbs. Cook in oil in skillet until lightly browned. Remove chicken to 3-quart casserole. Add sherry to drippings in skillet; cook for 15 seconds. Pour over chicken; cover. Bake in preheated 200-degree oven for 2 hours; remove toothpicks before serving.

Mrs. Peter Porcaro
Pascack Hills School
Montvale, New Jersey

CHICKEN SUISSE

1/2 c. wild rice
2 whole chicken breasts, halved and
   boned
Flour
Salt to taste
Pepper to taste
Paprika to taste
2 to 3 tbsp. butter or margarine
1/2 c. dry vermouth
1/2 c. grated Swiss process
   cheese
1 c. sour cream

Cook rice according to package directions. Remove skin from chicken pieces; fry until crisp. Crumble; set aside. Combine enough flour to coat chicken, salt, pepper and paprika. Dredge chicken in seasoned flour. Saute in butter in large skillet until browned. Reduce heat; cook for about 20 minutes or until meat is firm and juices run clear. Remove from skillet; keep warm. Pour vermouth into skillet, scraping up and blending in with pan drippings. Add grated cheese; stir until melted. Blend in sour cream; bring just to a simmer. Prepare bed of cooked rice on warm platter; arrange chicken pieces over rice. Ladle sauce over each chicken piece. Sprinkle crumbled chicken skin over top. Yield: 4 servings.

Mrs. Sigrid E. Hurley
Senior High School
Belle Plaine, Minnesota

CHICKEN TROPICALE

8 chicken breasts
Salt and pepper to taste
Paprika
Flour
1/4 c. melted butter
1/4 c. salad oil
1 No. 2 1/2 can pineapple slices
4 sliced green onions with tops
1/2 c. green pepper strips
1/2 c. sherry or dry white
   table wine
1 tbsp. (packed) brown sugar
1/2 c. diced blanched almonds

Sprinkle chicken with salt and pepper. Combine generous amount of paprika and flour in paper bag. Shake chicken in bag, shaking off excess. Combine butter and oil in flat baking dish; turn chicken in butter mixture until coated. Place in single layer, skin side down. Bake at 400 degrees for about 30 minutes; turn once. Drain pineapple; reserve syrup. Cut half the pineapple into bite-sized pieces; cut remaining pineapple into halves. Combine bite-sized pineapple, reserved pineapple syrup, onions, green pepper, sherry and brown sugar. Season with salt. Pour pineapple mixture over and around chicken; sprinkle with almonds. Bake at 375 degrees for about 45 minutes or until tender and brown. Baste occasionally. Serve with hot rice; garnish with remaining pineapple slices. Yield: 6-8 servings.

Mrs. Barbara Nave
Fulton High School
Knoxville, Tennessee

CHICKEN AND VEGETABLES

3 to 4 chicken breasts, split
Salt and pepper to taste
Flour
Vegetable oil
1 can cream of chicken soup
1 c. sour cream
1/2 c. sherry
1 sm. can peas and carrots,
*   drained*
Paprika

Season chicken with salt and pepper; roll in flour. Brown chicken in small amount of oil in heavy skillet; place in large shallow baking dish. Pour soup over chicken. Bake at 350 degrees for 20 minutes. Combine sour cream, sherry, peas and carrots; mix well. Pour over chicken; sprinkle with paprika. Bake for 10 minutes longer or until chicken is tender.

Mrs. Judy Vrklan
Arlington-Green Isle School
Arlington, Minnesota

CHICKEN IN RHINE WINE

3 or 4 lg. chicken breasts, halved
3 or 4 tbsp. margarine
1 can cream of chicken soup
1/2 c. Rhine wine or sauterne
Salt and pepper
1 5-oz. can water chestnuts
1/2 lb. fresh mushrooms, sliced

Remove skin and bones from chicken breasts; brown lightly in hot margarine in skillet. Place chicken in casserole. Stir soup into pan drippings in skillet; add Rhine wine gradually, stirring until smooth. Season to taste with salt and pepper. Drain and slice water chestnuts. Slice mushrooms; saute in additional butter for 3 to 4 minutes. Add water chestnuts and mushrooms to chicken. Pour sauce over chicken mixture; cover. Bake at 350 degrees for 30 minutes; uncover. Bake for 30 minutes longer.

Mrs. Sally T. Ninos
Benjamin Franklin Junior High School
Buffalo, New York

CHICKEN IN VERMOUTH SAUCE

12 boned chicken breasts,
*   halved*
1 8-oz. bottle garlic French
*   dressing*
1 1/2 cans mushroom soup
1 soup can dry vermouth
1 sm. can chopped ripe olives,
*   drained*
Cream or milk

Marinate chicken breasts in dressing overnight or for at least 5 hours, covered, in refrigerator. Drain excess dressing from chicken breasts; place in small roaster or deep pan. Bake at 400 degrees for 45 minutes. Combine soup and vermouth; mix until smooth. Pour over chicken breasts. Bake for 1 hour at 300 degrees. Remove chicken from pan; add ripe olives and small amount of cream, if needed, to sauce to thin slightly. Serve sauce in sauceboat.

Mrs. Nell Skonberg
Southern Junior High School
Louisville, Kentucky

CHICKEN IN WINE
WITH SOUR CREAM GRAVY

1/4 c. butter or margarine
4 to 6 chicken breasts
Salt and pepper to taste
1 c. white wine
1/2 c. chopped celery
1 tbsp. dried onion flakes
1 tbsp. brandy
1 c. sour cream

Melt butter in skillet; brown chicken breasts well. Combine remaining ingredients except sour cream; pour over chicken. Cover; cook for 20 to 30 minutes or until chicken is tender. Remove chicken from skillet; stir in sour cream, blending until gravy is smooth. Return chicken to skillet. One can cream of chicken soup may be substituted for sour cream if desired.

Mrs. Barbara Crabtree
Central Junior High School
Melbourne Village, Florida

CHINESE CHICKEN ROLL-UPS

4 whole chicken breasts
1/2 c. soy sauce
Salad oil
2 tbsp. molasses
1/2 tsp. ginger
1 tsp. dry mustard
1 lg. clove of garlic, minced
1 No. 2 can Chinese vegetables
1/8 tsp. onion salt
1 egg, well beaten
3/4 c. cracker crumbs
1 c. uncooked rice
Pimento strips
Lemon twists
Green pepper rings

Split, skin and bone chicken breasts; pound between sheets of plastic wrap to 1/4-inch thickness. Combine soy sauce, 3 tablespoons salad oil, molasses, ginger, mustard and garlic; blend thoroughly. Arrange chicken in shallow dish; pour sauce over chicken. Marinate for 5 minutes. Drain Chinese vegetables; combine with onion salt and 2 tablespoons marinade in plastic bag. Toss to coat vegetables thoroughly. Drain chicken on paper toweling. Place 2 tablespoons vegetable mixture in center of each piece of chicken; roll up, securing with wooden picks or skewers. Pour additional salad oil into skillet to 3/4-inch depth. Dip chicken rolls in egg; roll in crumbs. Fry in hot oil, turning to brown on all sides; arrange in casserole. Bake at 350 degrees for 45 minutes. Prepare rice according to package directions; place on heated platter. Arrange chicken rolls over rice. Garnish with pimento strips, lemon twists and green pepper rings.

Mrs. Nancy Moreno
Monroe Junior High School
Albuquerque, New Mexico

CURRIED MANDARIN CHICKEN

2 lg. whole chicken breasts,
*   split*
Salt and pepper to taste
1   11-oz. can mandarin oranges
1/2 tsp. cinnamon
1/2 tsp. curry powder
1/4 tsp. thyme
1 tbsp. raisins
1 tbsp. sliced almonds

Place chicken breasts, skin side up, on rack of broiler pan. Broil 2 inches from source of heat for 10 minutes or until skin is browned and crisp. Place chicken breasts in a shallow baking dish, skin side up. Season with salt and pepper. Drain oranges; reserve liquid. Combine reserved liquid, cinnamon, curry powder and thyme. Pour over chicken. Bake at 350 degrees for 40 minutes or until chicken is tender; add water, if needed. Add raisins, almonds and oranges. Bake for 20 minutes longer.

Wild Rice Mushroom Casserole

1 c. wild rice
1/4 tsp. thyme
1/4 tsp. basil
1/2 tsp. salt
3 chicken bouillon cubes
1/3 c. finely chopped onion
3/4 lb. fresh mushrooms; sliced
Butter
1/4 c. dry white wine

Wash wild rice thoroughly; soak for 30 minutes. Drain well. Combine wild rice, thyme, basil and salt in top of large double boiler. Combine bouillon cubes with 3 cups boiling water, stirring until cubes are dissolved; add to wild rice mixture. Cook, covered, over boiling water for 45 minutes or until rice is tender; stir occasionally. Preheat oven to 350 degrees. Place onion and mushrooms in greased 1 1/2-quart casserole; dot with butter. Season with additional salt and pepper; spoon rice mixture into casserole. Pour wine over rice. Bake for 20 minutes or until heated through; stir before serving. Serve with Curried Mandarin Chicken.

Margeret Burrow
Edmonds Junior Secondary School
Burnaby, British Columbia, Canada

BAKED CHICKEN DIVAN

2 pkg. frozen broccoli spears
2 cans cream of chicken soup

1 tsp. nutmeg
2 tsp. Worcestershire sauce
1 c. grated Parmesan cheese
4 lg. cooked boned chicken
   breasts
3/4 c. heavy cream, whipped
1/3 c. mayonnaise

Cook broccoli in boiling salted water until tender; drain. Place broccoli in oblong shallow baking dish. Combine soup, nutmeg and Worcestershire sauce; pour half the mixture over broccoli. Sprinkle with 1/3 cup cheese. Slice chicken; place over broccoli. Pour remaining soup mixture over chicken; sprinkle with 1/3 cup cheese. Bake at 400 degrees for 25 minutes. Fold whipped cream into mayonnaise; spread over chicken mixture. Sprinkle with remaining cheese. Broil for 2 to 3 minutes or until golden brown.

Mrs. Elizabeth L. Prew
Agawam High School
Agawam, Massachusetts

EASY BAKED CHICKEN BREASTS

6 med. chicken breasts, halved
Salt and pepper to taste
2 cloves of garlic, minced
4 tbsp. lemon juice
6 tbsp. Worcestershire sauce
1 c. margarine

Sprinkle chicken breasts with salt and pepper; arrange in large shallow baking dish. Sprinkle chicken breasts with garlic, lemon juice and Worcestershire sauce; dot with margarine. Bake at 250 degrees for 3 hours and 30 minutes. Pan drippings may be served over rice.

Mrs. Mary Evelyn Mitchell
Palm Beach Gardens High School
Palm Beach Gardens, Florida

CURRIED CHICKEN DIVAN

6 lg. slices cooked chicken
1 lb. broccoli, cooked
1 4-oz. can sliced mushrooms
2 tbsp. butter
2 tbsp. flour

1 c. chicken stock
Salt to taste
Dash of white pepper
1/4 tsp. curry powder
1/4 c. grated Parmesan cheese
1 beaten egg yolk

Arrange chicken in large shallow baking pan; top each slice with broccoli. Spoon mushrooms over broccoli; keep warm. Melt butter in saucepan over low heat; stir in flour until bubbly. Remove from heat; stir in chicken stock gradually. Return to heat. Bring to a boil, stirring constantly. Boil for 1 minute; stir in salt, pepper, curry powder and cheese. Remove from heat. Stir small amount of sauce into egg yolk; return to hot mixture, blending well. Bring just to a boil; pour over mushrooms. Place in broiler 6 inches from source of heat until bubbly and lightly browned. Serve immediately.

Elizabeth McClure
Greencastle High School
Greencastle, Ohio

FILLETS OF CHICKEN BREASTS

1 can button mushrooms
4 chicken breasts
2 eggs, beaten
3/4 c. fine cracker crumbs
1/2 c. melted butter or margarine
4 slices mozzarella cheese
Lemon juice to taste

Drain mushrooms; reserve liquid. Remove bone and skin from chicken breasts; fold chicken in to resemble thigh. Coat with eggs, then coat with cracker crumbs. Cook in butter until golden brown. Arrange in single layer in casserole. Place mushrooms on chicken; cover each piece of chicken with slice of cheese. Sprinkle lemon juice over top. Pour reserved mushroom liquid into casserole; cover. Bake at 400 degrees for 30 minutes. Uncover; bake for 10 minutes longer. May be served with rice pilaf, if desired.

Ann W. Stewart
McClain High School
Greenfield, Ohio

FANTASY FOWL

4 chicken breasts, skinned
Salt and pepper to taste
1/2 tsp. poultry seasoning
1/4 tsp. monosodium glutamate
1 jar marinated artichokes
1 c. white wine
1/2 c. chicken stock
1/2 lb. fresh mushroom caps

Sprinkle chicken breasts with seasonings. Drain artichokes; pour artichoke oil into electric frypan. Heat to 325 degrees. Saute chicken breasts until lightly browned. Add 1/2 cup wine and 1/2 cup chicken stock; cover tightly. Simmer for 35 to 45 minutes. Add mushroom caps, artichoke hearts and remaining wine. Simmer for 15 to 20 minutes longer. May be thickened if desired. Serve over wild rice, if desired. Yield: 4 servings.

Patricia Mundy
Perry Junior High School
Perry, Iowa

EXOTIC MANDARIN CHICKEN

3 lg. whole chicken breasts
1/3 c. flour
Salt and pepper to taste
1/4 c. cooking oil
1/2 c. sliced onion
3/4 c. diagonally sliced celery
1 clove of garlic
1 can cream of mushroom soup
1/4 c. chicken broth
1 5-oz. can sliced mushrooms, drained
1 6-oz. can water chestnuts, drained
1 7-oz. package frozen pea pods, thawed
1 11-oz. can mandarin oranges, drained

Cut chicken breasts in half. Coat chicken with flour; sprinkle with salt and pepper. Brown in hot oil in skillet. Remove chicken from skillet. Add the onion, celery and garlic; cook until tender. Remove garlic. Blend in soup and chicken broth. Return chicken to skillet and add mushrooms and thinly sliced water chestnuts. Cover; simmer for 30 minutes or until chicken is tender. Add pea pods; cover and simmer for 10 minutes. Add oranges; simmer for 5 minutes longer.

Mrs. Evelyn S. Pursley
Fairhaven High School
Fairhaven, Massachusetts

GOURMET CHICKEN

1 6-oz. package long grain and wild rice mix
3 lg. chicken breasts
Salt and pepper to taste
4 tbsp. butter
1 can cream of chicken soup
3/4 c. sauterne
1/2 c. sliced celery
1 3-oz. can sliced mushrooms, drained
2 tbsp. chopped pimento

Prepare rice mix according to package directions. Bone and split chicken breasts; season lightly with salt and pepper. Brown chicken in butter in skillet over medium heat. Spoon rice into 1 1/2-quart casserole; arrange chicken, skin side up, over rice. Add soup to pan drippings; add sauterne gradually, stirring until smooth. Add celery, mushrooms and pimento; Bring to a boil; pour over chicken. Bake, covered, at 350 degrees for 25 minutes; remove cover. Bake for 15 minutes longer or until chicken is tender. Yield: 6 servings.

Alice Lawler
Davis Hills Junior High School
Huntsville, Alabama

FRENCH CHICKEN IN ORANGE-SHERRY SAUCE

3 chicken breasts, split
1 1/2 tsp. salt
1 med. onion, sliced
1/4 c. chopped green pepper
1 c. sliced mushrooms
1 c. orange juice
1/4 c. dry sherry

1 tbsp. (firmly packed) brown sugar
1/4 tsp. pepper
1 tsp. grated orange rind
1 tbsp. flour
2 tsp. chopped parsley
Paprika
1 orange, sliced

Arrange chicken breasts, skin side up, on rack of broiler pan. Broil 2 inches from source of heat for 10 minutes or until well browned. Arrange chicken in shallow 2-quart baking dish. Sprinkle with 1/2 teaspoon salt. Add onion, green pepper and mushrooms. Combine orange juice, sherry, 1/2 cup water, brown sugar, remaining salt, pepper, orange rind and flour in small saucepan; blend well. Cook, stirring constantly, over medium heat until sauce thickens and comes to a boil; stir in parsley. Pour sauce over chickens. Bake, basting frequently, at 375 degrees for 45 minutes or until chicken is tender. Sprinkle with paprika; garnish with orange slices.

Hazel Edberg
Modesto High School
Modesto, California

DELICIOUS CHICKEN KIEV

9 med. chicken breast halves
Salt
White pepper
1/2 c. butter, chilled
1 lg. egg
1 tbsp. milk
1 c. fine dry bread crumbs
1/4 tsp. pepper
1/2 tsp. celery salt
1 tsp. paprika
Flour
3 lb. vegetable shortening

Remove skin and bones from each chicken breast. Place 1 breast, boned side up between pieces of waxed paper; pound to 1/4-inch thickness with a wooden mallet. Remove waxed paper; sprinkle with salt and white pepper. Cut butter into 9 pieces. Place 1 piece near end of cutlet; roll as for jelly roll, tucking in sides. Secure with a toothpick. Repeat with remaining breasts. Chill

for at least 1 hour. Beat egg and milk together with fork. Combine bread crumbs, 2 teaspoons salt, pepper, celery salt and paprika. Remove toothpicks; dust each stuffed breast with flour. Dip into egg mixture; roll in seasoned bread crumbs until well coated. Place on rack to dry for 20 minutes. Heat shortening in heavy 3 to 4-quart saucepan to 340 degrees. Fry 3 breasts at a time for 8 minutes. Remove with tongs; drain on absorbent paper. Yield: 9 servings.

Junia Marie Schlinkert
Willow Lake High School
Willow Lake, South Dakota

DIVINE CHICKEN KIEV

8 boned chicken breasts, halved
2 sticks cold butter
2 tbsp. minced chives or scallions
2 tbsp. minced parsley
2 tsp. lemon juice
2 eggs
2 tbsp. water
2 env. seasoned coating mix for chicken

Preheat oven to 450 degrees. Remove skin from chicken pieces; place pieces between sheets of waxed paper. Pound until meat is about 1/8 inch thick. Cut each stick of butter into 8 lengthwise pieces. Place 1 piece of butter near end of each chicken piece. Sprinkle with chives, parsley and lemon juice. Roll up each chicken piece, folding ends so butter is enclosed. Secure with picks or skewers. Beat eggs slightly with water. Dip each rolled chicken piece into egg mixture; shake off excess liquid. Coat with seasoned coating mix. Place on ungreased shallow pan, sealed side up. Bake for about 20 minutes or until browned; drain on absorbent paper. Place on heated serving platter. Chicken breasts may be prepared ahead of time and refrigerated for several hours or overnight before dipping in egg mixture and baking.

Claribel Parsons
Clarendon School
Bessemer, Alabama

NEBRASKA CHICKEN KIEV

1/2 c. softened margarine or butter
2 1/2 tsp. parsley flakes
1/2 tsp. garlic powder
4 whole chicken breasts, split and
    boned
Salt and pepper to taste
3/4 c. fine dry bread crumbs
3/4 c. Parmesan cheese
1 10 3/4-oz. can chicken gravy
1/4 c. melted margarine or butter

Combine margarine, parsley flakes and garlic powder. Form into 8 balls; freeze until firm. Pound chicken breasts with mallet; season with salt and pepper. Place 1 butter ball on each chicken breast; roll up and tuck in ends. Secure with toothpicks. Combine bread crumbs and cheese. Dip chicken breasts in gravy; roll in cheese mixture. Place in shallow 9 x 13 x 2-inch baking dish; pour melted margarine over top. Bake at 450 degrees for 25 minutes. May be frozen. Thaw completely before baking.

Mrs. Marie Mohr
Wayne-Carroll High School
Wayne, Nebraska

LEMONY PARMESAN CHICKEN

4 to 6 lg. chicken breast halves
1 egg
Cream
1 c. grated Parmesan cheese
1/2 c. flour
6 tbsp. butter
2 egg yolks
Juice of 1 lemon
Nutmeg to taste
Grated Swiss cheese

Remove skin and bones from chicken breast halves. Beat egg and 2 tablespoons cream together. Combine Parmesan cheese and flour. Heat butter in skillet. Dip each chicken piece in egg mixture; roll in flour mixture. Brown chicken in hot butter for 8 to 10 minutes on each side. Remove chicken to ovenproof dish; keep warm. Add 1 cup cream to remaining butter in pan gradually; heat gently, stirring constantly. Beat egg yolks and lemon juice together until light yellow. Add small amount of hot cream mixture to egg yolk mixture gradually, stirring constantly. Add remaining egg yolk mixture to cream mixture, stirring well. Sprinkle with nutmeg. Cook over low heat, stirring constantly, until thickened. Pour sauce over chicken; sprinkle with Swiss cheese. Broil until cheese is melted. Garnish with lemon slices.

Pat Kline
Butler High School
Louisville, Kentucky

LEMON BIRDS

10 to 12 boned chicken breasts
Softened butter
Salt
Lemon pepper
Lemon slices
1/2 c. lemon juice
1 can mushroom soup
1 sm. carton sour cream
2 tsp. chopped parsley

Form chicken breasts into firm servings; secure with picks. Rub tops with butter; sprinkle with salt and a generous amount of lemon pepper. Place 1 slice lemon on each bird. Place birds in oven cooking bag; pour lemon juice over top. Place bag in large pan; seal and puncture top according to bag instructions. Bake at 350 degrees for about 45 minutes. Heat remaining ingredients together; serve over Lemon Birds. Yield: 10-12 servings.

Mrs. Mary Nicholson
North Junior High School
Decherd, Tennessee

LINDA'S CHICKEN AMANDINE

2 whole chicken breasts
5 tbsp. butter
3 tbsp. sherry
1 clove of garlic, crushed
1/2 c. blanched almonds
1 lg. mushroom, finely chopped
1 tsp. arrowroot or potato starch
1/2 c. white wine
1/2 c. chicken stock
Salt and pepper to taste

Halve chicken breasts; remove skin and bones. Melt 4 tablespoons butter in skillet. Add chicken; cook over low heat until brown on both sides. Heat sherry; ignite. Pour over chicken; remove chicken breasts to plate. Add remaining butter, garlic, 1/4 cup almonds and mushroom to skillet; cook, stirring frequently, for several minutes or until golden brown. Blend in arrowroot until smooth; stir in wine and chicken stock. Cook over low heat, stirring constantly, until thickened; season with salt and peper. Return chicken breasts to skillet; cover. Cook over low heat for 20 minutes or until tender when tested with fork. Arrange chicken breasts on heated serving platter; pour sauce over chicken. Sprinkle with remaining almonds.

Linda M. Reichardt
Scobey High School
Scobey, Montana

MOST ELEGANT CHICKEN CASSEROLE

6 chicken breasts
1/3 c. flour
2 tsp. salt
1 tsp. paprika
1/4 c. butter
6 slices cooked ham
1 tsp. dried crumbled savory
12 celery leaves
1 c. canned sliced mushrooms
1/2 c. sauterne
1 c. sour cream

Wipe chicken breasts with damp paper towel. Combine flour, salt and paprika in paper bag; shake chicken breasts in bag, one at a time, until well floured. Brown chicken lightly in butter in electric or heavy iron skillet over medium heat. Place ham slices in 13 1/2 x 8 3/4 x 1 3/4-inch baking dish; sprinkle with savory. Place 2 celery leaves on each ham slice; cover with chicken. Add mushrooms. Pour sauterne into skillet in which chicken was browned; stir well. Mix remaining flour mixture with sour cream; stir into sauterne mixture. Pour over chicken; cover with lid or foil. Bake at 350

degrees for 1 hour. Mixing flour mixture with sour cream prevents curdling while baking.

Mrs. Myral B. Thomas
Rogers Middle School
Fort Lauderdale, Florida

PARTY CHICKEN

4 whole chicken breasts
8 slices of bacon
1   4-oz. jar dried beef
1 c. sour cream
1 can cream of mushroom soup

Split, skin and bone chicken breasts; wrap each half breast in bacon slice. Spread dried beef in shallow baking dish; arrange chicken over beef. Combine sour cream and soup; pour over chicken. Bake at 275 degrees for 3 hours. Serve over rice. May be made ahead of time and reheated before serving.

Mrs. Gerry Smith
Waco High School
Waco, Texas

PIZZA CHICKEN

3 chicken breasts, boned and halved
1 tsp. salt
1/4 c. peanut oil
1   10 1/2-oz. can pizza sauce
3 tbsp. grated Parmesan cheese
3 tbsp. onion flakes
6 slices mozzarella cheese

Sprinkle chicken with salt. Heat oil in frypan; add chicken. Cook until brown on each side. Place chicken in baking dish. Combine pizza sauce, 1/2 cup water and Parmesan cheese in small saucepan; bring just to a boil. Sprinkle onion flakes over chicken; pour sauce over top. Cover. Bake at 350 degrees for 40 minutes. Remove from oven; place mozzarella cheese slice on each breast half. Bake for 10 to 12 minutes longer or until cheese is hot and melted. Yield: 6 servings.

Mrs. Helen M. Godwin
Northwest Senior High School
Greensboro, North Carolina

155

POLYNESIAN CHICKEN-PINEAPPLE

1 ripe pineapple
2 cooked chicken breasts
1 green pepper
1 tbsp. cooking wine
1/2 c. vinegar
1/2 c. catsup
1/2 c. sugar
Pinch of garlic powder
Pinch of ginger
Cornstarch

Slice pineapple lengthwise; cut out fruit in chunks with grapefruit knife, reserving shells. Cut chicken and green pepper into chunks. Combine pineapple chunks, chicken and green pepper in large saucepan. Add 1 cup water and wine. Combine vinegar, catsup, sugar, 1/2 cup water, garlic powder and ginger; add to chicken mixture. Dissolve cornstarch in small amount of water; add to chicken mixture. Cook for 3 minutes or until thickened, stirring constantly. Serve in pineapple shells.

Mrs. Tarie M. Curtiss
Memorial Junior High School
Mentor, Ohio

ROLLED CHICKEN AND HAM

3 whole chicken breasts
Salt to taste
6 oz. natural Swiss cheese
6 thin slices boiled ham
Flour
2 tbsp. butter or margarine
1 chicken bouillon cube
1 3-oz. can sliced mushrooms,
    drained
1/3 c. sauterne
Toasted slivered almonds (opt.)

Split, skin and bone chicken breasts; flatten into cutlets 1/4 inch thick. Sprinkle chicken with salt. Slice cheese into 6 sticks. Arrange ham slice and cheese stick on each cutlet. Roll up; tie securely. Coat rolls with flour. Brown in butter in skillet over medium heat, turning until golden on all sides. Transfer rolls to 11 x 7 x 1 1/2-inch baking pan. Add

1/2 cup water, bouillon cube, mushrooms and sauterne to skillet drippings. Bring to a boil; stir well to scrape crusty bits from skillet. Pour mushroom mixture over chicken. Bake, covered, at 350 degrees for 1 hour or until chicken is tender. Arrange chicken on heated platter; remove strings. Blend 2 tablespoons flour and 1/2 cup water; add to pan drippings. Simmer, stirring constantly, until smooth and thickened. Pour small amount of gravy over chicken; garnish with almonds. Serve remaining gravy with chicken. Yield: 6 servings.

Mable P. Nichols
Marjorie Stansfield School
Haledon, New Jersey

SAILOR'S SUPREMES

3 whole chicken breasts
4 tbsp. butter or margarine
1 tbsp. lemon juice
3/4 tsp. salt
1/8 tsp. white pepper
1/4 tsp. paprika
9 oz. frozen shelled sm. shrimp
2 tbsp. flour
1/4 tsp. tarragon
1 c. heavy cream
2 tbsp. cooking sherry
1 egg yolk

Split, skin and bone chicken breasts. Melt 2 tablespoons butter in 8 x 12-inch baking pan. Dip chicken in butter; sprinkle both sides with lemon juice, salt and pepper. Arrange chicken in baking pan; tuck under edges to form meat packets. Bake, covered, at 400 degrees for 20 minutes or until chicken is tender; remove from oven. Melt remaining butter in skillet; add paprika and shrimp. Saute shrimp, stirring constantly over medium heat, for 4 minutes or until shrimp are pink. Remove shrimp with slotted spoon; keep warm. Stir flour and tarragon into skillet drippings until bubbly; reduce heat. Add cream gradually, stirring until slightly thickened; stir in sherry. Beat egg yolk. Stir small amount of hot mixture into yolk; return to hot mixture. Simmer, stirring constantly, until smooth and thickened. Drain 2 tablespoons juices from baking dish; blend well with sherry mixture. Arrange chicken on heated platter; spoon half the sauce over chicken. Arrange shrimp around chicken; garnish with parsley. Serve remaining sauce with chicken. Serve immediately. Yield: 5-6 servings.

Penelope H. Merrill
Jack Junior High School
Portland, Maine

SAM'S SURPRISE CHICKEN

2 tbsp. butter
2 tbsp. flour
1/2 c. milk
1 1/2 c. shredded sharp Cheddar
  cheese
4 slices crisp bacon, crumbled
1/4 tsp. salt
1/8 tsp. pepper
1/8 tsp. poultry seasoning
1/8 tsp. onion salt
1 clove of garlic, minced
1/8 tsp. tarragon
1/8 tsp. oregano
2 tsp. chopped fresh chives
4 whole chicken breasts
4 eggs
1/4 c. toasted slivered almonds
1/2 c. sauteed sliced mushrooms
8 slices ham or pastrami
1 c. pancake mix
1 tsp. paprika

Melt butter in medium skillet; stir in flour until bubbly. Add milk; cook, stirring constantly, until smooth and thickened. Stir in cheese, bacon, salt, pepper, poultry seasoning, onion salt, garlic, tarragon, oregano and chives; mix well. Pour cheese mixture into pie plate; chill in freezer for 30 minutes. Bone, skin and split chicken breasts; pound with mallet until 1/4 inch thick. Cut cheese mixture into 8 sections; spread evenly over chicken breasts. Scramble eggs with almonds and mushrooms; divide evenly over cheese mixture. Place ham slices over eggs. Roll as for jelly roll, tucking in sides of chicken breasts; dust lightly with additional flour. Chill, covered, for 1 hour. Combine pancake mix, paprika and 3/4 cup water; blend well. Dip rolls in batter. Fry in deep fat at 375

degrees until golden; drain. Place in baking dish. Bake at 350 degrees for 35 minutes. Serve with rice.

Joanne Ryles
Roosevelt High School
Seattle, Washington

SAN FRANCISCO CINCH

2 whole chicken breasts,
  halved
2 tbsp. flour
1/4 c. butter
1 can cheese soup
2/3 c. light cream
2 tbsp. lemon juice
1/2 tsp. dried rosemary

Coat chicken with flour. Melt butter in skillet; add chicken. Cook over medium heat until lightly browned on all sides; place in baking dish. Blend cheese soup, cream, lemon juice and rosemary; pour over chicken. Cover. Bake at 350 degrees for 45 to 60 minutes or until chicken is tender. Yield: 4 servings.

Carole Phillips
Sierra Joint Union High School
Tollhouse, California

SAUCY CHICKEN

2 tbsp. butter or margarine
2 lb. chicken breasts, halved
1 lg. clove of garlic, minced
1/8 tsp. crushed rosemary
1   10 1/2-oz. can cream of chicken
  soup
1/2 tsp. lemon juice
2 c. cooked noodles
1/3 c. chopped parsley

Melt butter in skillet; add chicken breasts, garlic and rosemary. Brown chicken well. Stir in soup and lemon juice; cover. Cook over low heat for 45 minutes to 1 hour or until chicken is tender. Toss noodles and parsley together; serve with chicken. Yield: 4 servings.

Mary E. King
Gregory High School
Gregory, South Dakota

SAUCY MANDARIN CHICKEN BREASTS

2 sm. whole chicken breasts, halved
1/4 tsp. seasoned salt
1 chicken bouillon cube
Pinch of instant minced onion
1/4 tsp. curry powder
1   4-oz. can mandarin oranges
1   2-oz. can sliced mushrooms
1 tbsp. flour

Wash and dry chicken breasts. Sprinkle with seasoned salt. Place halves in small baking dish. Dissolve bouillon cube in 2/3 cup boiling water. Add 2 tablespoons water, minced onion and curry powder. Drain mandarin oranges and mushrooms, reserving the combined liquid; set aside. Pour bouillon mixture over chicken; cover. Bake at 350 degrees for 30 minutes. Uncover; bake for 45 minutes longer or until tender. Remove chicken to platter. Blend flour and 2 tablespoons reserved liquid in saucepan. Stir in the pan juices. Cook, stirring, until bubbly. Add oranges and mushrooms to gravy and heat through. Spoon over chicken. Yield: 2 servings.

Andrea Fruit
Owen Valley High School
Spencer, Indiana

SAUTEED CHICKEN BREASTS

1/4 c. margarine
4-6 lg. chicken breasts
1 sliced onion
1 clove of garlic, minced
2 tbsp. flour
1/2 tsp. salt
1/4 tsp. pepper
1 chicken bouillon cube
1/4 c. red wine
1 sm. can sliced mushrooms,
*   drained*

Melt margarine in skillet; brown chicken well on both sides. Add onion and garlic; saute for 5 minutes. Combine flour, salt and pepper. Dissolve bouillon cube in 1 cup hot water; combine bouillon and flour mixture.

Add to chicken mixture. Cook over low heat, stirring frequently, for about 1 hour or until chicken is tender. Add wine and mushrooms; simmer for 15 minutes.

Jane T. Welton
Incarnate Word High School
San Antonio, Texas

CRUNCHY SCALLOPED CHICKEN

6 chicken breasts, boned
2 cans onion soup
1 pkg. stuffing mix
2 tbsp. butter
1 tsp. salt
1 tsp. coarsely ground pepper
1 tbsp. curry powder
1/4 c. slivered almonds

Place chicken breasts in baking dish; pour soup over chicken. Saute half the stuffing in butter in skillet until browned. Add to chicken mixture. Season with salt, pepper and curry powder. Bake at 350 degrees for 1 hour and 30 minutes. Sprinkle remaining stuffing and almonds over top. Bake for about 15 minutes longer or until stuffing is lightly browned. Yield: 6 servings.

Mrs. Wanda Roe
Pea Ridge High School
Pea Ridge, Arkansas

SESAME CHICKEN WITH RAISIN-RICE MOLDS

4 thin 1-in. wide ham strips
8 thin 1-in. wide Swiss cheese
*   strips*
4 chicken breasts, skinned and
*   boned*
1 egg
1 tbsp. water
3/4 c. dry bread crumbs
1/4 c. butter
2 tbsp. melted butter
1 tbsp. soy sauce
1/2 c. chicken broth
1 tsp. sesame seed

Place 1 ham strip and 2 cheese strips on each chicken breast. Press edges together and skewer or secure with toothpicks. Beat egg with water. Dip chicken into egg mixture, then into crumbs. Brown in butter; place in a baking pan. Combine melted butter, soy sauce and broth for sauce. Brush chicken with sauce, then sprinkle with sesame seed. Bake at 350 degrees for 45 to 50 minutes or until tender, basting frequently with sauce.

Raisin-Rice Molds

4 c. hot cooked rice
1/2 c. raisins
1/4 c. melted butter

Combine all ingredients and toss. Press into molds or custard cups. Turn out and serve at once. Garnish chicken and rice with kumquats and pineapple.

Mrs. Norman Sands
Ware County High School
Waycross, Georgia

STUFFED CHICKEN BREASTS CALABREEZE

4 boned chicken breasts
4 c. coarse fresh bread crumbs
1/4 c. finely minced onion
1/4 c. finely chopped parsley
1/4 c. chopped celery with leaves
3 tbsp. grated Romano cheese
Olive oil
Butter
1 tsp. poultry seasoning
1 tsp. sage, thyme or marjoram
1 tsp. salt
1/2 tsp. pepper
1/4 tsp. garlic salt
1/4 c. sliced fresh mushrooms
1 c. dry white wine

Split and flatten chicken breasts. Combine crumbs, onion, parsley, celery and cheese; mix well. Add equal parts olive oil and water just to moisten crumb mixture. Melt 1/3 cup butter in small skillet; stir in poultry seasoning, sage, salt, pepper and garlic salt. Brush chicken with butter mixture. Divide crumb mixture equally among chicken breasts. Roll chicken as for jelly roll; secure with heavy

thread. Add remaining butter mixture to 1/4 cup butter in heavy skillet over medium heat; brown chicken rolls, turning to brown on all sides. Add mushrooms and wine. Simmer, covered, for 10 minutes; remove cover. Simmer until chicken is tender; remove thread. Arrange on heated platter; top with mushroom sauce. Garnish with parsley.

Anita M. Filice
Emil R. Buchser High School
Campbell, California

STUFFED CHICKEN BREASTS WITH WINE

6 sm. whole chicken breasts
1 1/2 tsp. salt
1 tsp. pepper
1 6-oz. package seasoned long grain and wild rice mix
2 tbsp. salad oil
2 tbsp. margarine
1/2 c. chopped onion
1 clove of garlic, minced
3 tbsp. flour
1 13 3/4-oz. can chicken broth
1 c. dry white wine or vermouth
1/2 tsp. liquid gravy seasoning

Bone and skin chicken breasts. Sprinkle with salt and 3/4 teaspoon pepper. Prepare rice mix according to package directions. Place 1/3 cup rice mix on half chicken breast; fold other half over filling. Fasten securely with skewers. Combine salad oil and margarine in large skillet over medium heat; brown chicken on both sides in oil mixture. Arrange chicken in large shallow baking dish. Stir onion and garlic into remaining oil mixture in skillet; saute over medium heat for 5 minutes. Blend in flour; cook, stirring constantly, for 1 minute. Stir in chicken broth, wine, gravy seasoning and remaining pepper gradually, stirring constantly until sauce is smooth and thickened. Bake at 350 degrees for 50 minutes or until tender; baste occasionally with sauce.

Mrs. Sarah Blakeney
Slocomb High School
Slocomb, Alabama

STUFFED MOCK PHEASANT

2 tbsp. chopped onion
3/4 c. diced celery
4 tbsp. butter or margarine
1/2 tsp. sage
1/4 tsp. lemon pepper
2 c. cooked rice
6 boned chicken breasts
Salt
Seasoned flour
2 c. chicken broth
1 tbsp. grated onion
Pepper to taste
2 tsp. flour
2 tsp. grated orange rind
1 c. seedless white grapes

Saute chopped onion and celery in 2 table-spoons butter until tender. Add sage, lemon pepper and rice; mix thoroughly. Season inside of chicken breasts with salt; fill with rice mixture. Pull edges of breasts together; secure with round toothpicks. Dip in sea-soned flour. Cook in remaining butter in skillet until golden brown and tender, adding more butter, if necessary. Add chicken broth, grated onion, 1 teaspoon salt and pep-per; cover. Simmer for 20 minutes. Transfer chicken breasts to hot platter; keep warm. Mix flour and 1 tablespoon cold water well in small jar; stir into liquid in skillet slowly. Add orange rind; cook, stirring constantly, until thickened. Add grapes; heat thor-oughly. Pour over chicken; serve hot. Yield: 6 servings.

Mrs. Gwendolyn Webb
Ardmore High School
Ardmore, Oklahoma

STUFFED CHICKEN BREASTS MAGNIFIQUE

6 whole chicken breasts
1 c. toasted slivered almonds
1 c. chopped celery
1/2 c. chopped onion
3/4 lb. chopped fresh mushrooms
1 bunch fresh spinach, chopped
1 c. fine dry bread crumbs
2/3 tsp. sage
1/2 tsp. salt
2 egg yolks
1 c. sour cream
2 beaten eggs
1 1/2 c. crushed potato chips
1/2 c. melted margarine

Remove bones from chicken breasts; pound flat. Cut breasts in half. Toss almonds, cel-ery, onion, mushrooms, spinach, bread crumbs, sage, salt, egg yolks and sour cream together lightly. Spoon 1/2 cup of the dress-ing on each breast half; fold meat over dress-ing. Dip in beaten eggs; roll in crushed po-tato chips. Place, skin side up, in greased 9 x 13-inch baking pan. Spoon melted margarine over tops of breasts; cover with foil. Bake at 375 degrees for 50 minutes; uncover. Bake for 15 to 20 minutes longer. Yield: 12 servings.

Nancy A. Bruce
Washington Junior High School
Broderick, California

SURPRISE CHICKEN BREASTS

1 can cream of chicken soup
1 can cream of celery soup
3/4 c. evaporated milk
3/4 c. rice
6 chicken breasts
1 env. onion soup mix

Mix chicken and celery soups, milk and rice; place in greased, shallow 2-quart baking dish. Arrange chicken breasts, skin side up, on rice mixture; sprinkle onion soup over chicken. Cover with tight-fitting lid or aluminum foil. Bake at 275 degrees for 2 hours; do not re-move cover while baking. Yield: 6 servings.

Mrs. Rita Bill
Johnson Creek High School
Johnson Creek, Wisconsin

SWEET CHICKEN

4 med. chicken breasts
2 tsp. salt
1/2 c. honey
1 c. (packed) brown sugar

1 No. 2 can peach halves
2 tbsp. cornstarch

Remove skin from chicken breasts. Combine salt and enough water to cover chicken. Soak chicken for 10 minutes. Preheat oven to 350 degrees. Dip chicken into honey; roll in brown sugar. Place chicken in shallow oblong baking dish. Bake for 30 minutes. Drain peaches, reserving syrup. Pour reserved syrup into small saucepan; blend in corn-starch. Cook, stirring constantly, until thick-ened. Spoon thickened syrup over chicken. Bake for 20 minutes longer.

Germaine Philp
Morrisville High School
Morrisville, Pennsylvania

TUTTI-FRUTTI CHICKEN
Fifth Place

4 whole chicken breasts
1/2 lb. sliced ham
Butter
1 tsp. salt
1/4 tsp. pepper
1/4 c. flour
1 c. fine bread crumbs
Salad oil
1 11-oz. can mandarin oranges
1 1-lb. can pear halves
1 No. 2 can pineapple chunks
1/4 c. cornstarch
1 tbsp. soy sauce
1 4 1/2-oz. jar maraschino
   cherries
1/4 tsp. marjoram
1/4 tsp. rosemary
1/4 tsp. thyme
1/2 tsp. onion flakes
1 sm. bay leaf
1 c. uncooked rice
1/4 c. slivered almonds
1/2 c. chow mein noodles

Bone, skin and flatten chicken breasts. Split breasts; wrap each half around folded ham slice. Melt 1/2 cup butter in small saucepan; dip chicken rolls in butter. Combine salt, pepper, flour and crumbs; coat chicken well with crumb mixture. Brown chicken in small amount of oil in skillet until crisp; transfer to rack in broiler pan. Bake at 325 degrees for 20 minutes or until tender. Drain oranges; drain pears and pineapple, reserving juices. Slice pears into halves lengthwise. Combine reserved juices in large saucepan; stir in cornstarch. Cook over medium heat, stirring constantly, until clear and thickened. Stir in soy sauce and 2 tablespoons butter. Drain cherries. Fold fruits into sauce gently. Add marjoram, rosemary, thyme, onion flakes, remaining salt, 1 tablespoon butter and bay leaf to 2 1/2 cups water; bring to a boil. Add rice gradually; reduce heat. Sim-mer, covered, until rice is tender and fluffy; remove bay leaf. Arrange rice on large heated platter; place chicken over rice. Spoon fruit sauce over all. Garnish with almonds and chow mein noodles. Serve immediately. Yield: 4-6 servings.

Mrs. JoAnn M. Bailey
Elkton Middle School
Elkton, Maryland

TAYLOR-MADE CHICKEN

3 whole chicken breasts, cooked
3 tbsp. margarine
2 cloves of garlic, minced
1 lg. onion, thinly sliced
3 sm. Italian green peppers
1 sm. can sliced mushrooms
2 cans chicken gravy
1/4 c. red cooking wine
1/4 c. grated Parmesan cheese
3 c. cooked rice

Remove chicken from bone; cut into large pieces. Set aside. Melt margarine in large skil-let. Add garlic and onion; cook over low heat, stirring constantly, until lightly browned. Cut green peppers into thin rings; add to onion mixture. Cook for several min-utes or until green peppers just begin to soften. Drain mushrooms; add to onion mix-ture. Add chicken gravy and wine; simmer for 5 minutes. Place half the chicken in shal-low casserole; top with half the sauce. Add remaining chicken, then remaining sauce; sprinkle with Parmesan cheese. Bake at 400 degrees for 20 to 25 minutes; serve over rice. Yield: 5-6 servings.

Mrs. Charlene Taylor
Chelmsford Junior High School
North Chelmsford, Massachusetts

VIN ROSE CHICKEN

2 whole chicken breasts
3/4 c. Vin Rose
1/4 c. soy sauce
1/4 c. oil
1 tbsp. (firmly packed) brown sugar
1 clove of garlic, minced
2 tsp. ginger
1/4 tsp. oregano

Split chicken breasts; arrange, skin side down, in greased shallow casserole. Combine Vin Rose, soy sauce, oil, 2 tablespoons water, brown sugar, garlic, ginger and oregano in saucepan; heat through, stirring constantly. Pour sauce over chicken. Bake, covered, at 375 degrees for 1 hour and 30 minutes or until chicken is tender. Yield: 4 servings.

Gretchen Oberhauser
Mills High School
Millbrae, California

BARBECUED CHICKEN WINGS

3/4 c. soy sauce
1/2 c. sugar
1/4 c. sherry or saki
1 garlic clove, chopped
2 tsp. ginger
Chicken wings

Mix first 5 ingredients. Disjoint chicken wings; discard tips or save for soup. Place in soy sauce mixture; marinate for 2 hours. Drain wings; place in baking pan. Bake at 350 degrees for 1 hour.

Mrs. Harriet Kresel
North Central High School
Spokane, Washington

BAG OF BARBECUED CHICKEN

3 tbsp. catsup
4 tbsp. hot water
2 tbsp. vinegar
2 tbsp. butter or margarine
1 tbsp. lemon juice
3 tbsp. light brown sugar
2 tbsp. Worcestershire sauce

1 tsp. salt
1 tsp. dry mustard
1 tsp. chili powder
1 tsp. paprika
Vegetable shortening
1 3-lb. chicken, disjointed

Preheat oven to 500 degrees. Combine all ingredients except shortening and chicken in saucepan; heat to boiling point. Grease inside of a medium-size brown paper bag with vegetable shortening. Dip each chicken piece in hot sauce; place in bag. Pour remaining sauce over chicken pieces; fold top of paper bag over twice. Fasten with paper clips or staple shut. Place in shallow baking pan. Bake for 15 minutes. Reduce oven temperature to 350 degrees; bake for 1 hour longer. Do not open bag until end of cooking time.

Mrs. Virginia Claypool
Marshall High School
Marshall, Illinois

BARBECUED CHICKEN WITH RICE

1 fryer, disjointed
1/2 c. chopped onion
1/2 c. chopped celery
1/4 c. chopped green pepper
1 c. catsup
2 tbsp. brown sugar
2 tbsp. Worcestershire sauce
1 tsp. salt
1/4 tsp. pepper
Cooked rice

Brown chicken pieces; place in casserole or baking dish. Bake at 350 degrees for 15 minutes. Combine all remaining ingredients except rice in saucepan; simmer until vegetables are tender. Pour over chicken; bake for 15 minutes longer or until tender. Serve chicken and remaining sauce over rice.

Marjane Telck
Rock Springs Junior High School
Rock Springs, Wyoming

BARBECUED ROAST CHICKEN

1/4 c. pepper
1/4 c. salt
3/4 c. paprika

1/4 c. chili powder
1/4 c. garlic salt
3/4 c. monosodium glutamate
Fryer pieces

Combine first 6 ingredients. Place in container; cover with tight-fitting lid. Store in cool, dry place. Wash chicken; drain on paper towels or in colander. Place on broiler pan, skin side up; leave as mush space as possible between each piece. Place broiler pan in oven. Bake in preheated 325-degree oven for 45 minutes; sprinkle with seasoning until well coated. Turn chicken; sprinkle with seasoning until well coated. Bake for 35 to 45 minutes longer or until tender; place on warm platter to serve.

Mrs. Carol Jean Appleby
Seymour High School
Seymour, Indiana

BARBECUED CHICKEN SUPREME

1 c. cooking oil
1 1/2 c. vinegar
4 tbsp. lemon juice
6 tbsp. sugar
2 tbsp. salt
2 tbsp. Worcestershire sauce
2 tbsp. onion salt
2 tsp. hot sauce
1 tsp. dry mustard
1 tsp. chili powder
1 2 to 3-lb. fryer, disjointed

Reserve 2 tablespoons cooking oil. Combine remaining cooking oil, vinegar, lemon juice, sugar, salt, Worcestershire sauce, onion salt, hot sauce, mustard and chili powder in saucepan; bring to a boil. Remove from heat. Place chicken and reserved cooking oil in boiling water to cover; cook for 15 minutes. Remove chicken; place in shallow dish. Pour sauce over chicken; let marinate for 30 minutes. Remove chicken from sauce. Grill over hot coals for 30 to 40 minutes or until tender, basting frequently with remaining sauce. Yield: 4-5 servings.

Mrs. Mary D. Moore
Addison Central School
Addison, New York

DUM-DRUMS

3/4 c. chopped onion
3/4 c. chopped celery
1 12-oz. bottle catsup
1/4 c. water
5 tbsp. Worcestershire sauce
2 tsp. prepared mustard
2 tbsp. vinegar
1/4 c. lemon juice
1/4 c. maple-blended syrup with
   butter
1/4 c. apricot preserves
12 chicken legs
Salt and pepper to taste
Flour
1/4 c. margarine
1/2 c. vegetable shortening

Combine onion, celery, catsup, water, Worcestershire sauce, mustard, vinegar, lemon juice, syrup and preserves in saucepan; simmer, uncovered, for 30 minutes. Season chicken with salt and pepper; dredge in flour. Brown chicken evenly in margarine and shortening, turning often; place in shallow 9 x 13-inch baking pan. Pour half the sauce over chicken. Bake, uncovered, at 375 degrees for 20 minutes. Pour remaining sauce over chicken; bake for 20 minutes longer. The last 20 minutes of cooking may be completed on outdoor grill, if desired.

Mrs. Patricia Crafton
Triton Central High School
Fairland, Indiana

CHICKEN-APRICOT BARBECUE

1 12-oz. jar apricot preserves
1 8-oz. bottle Thousand Island
   dressing
1 env. dry onion soup mix
2 chickens, disjointed

Combine apricot preserves, Thousand Island dressing and onion soup mix. Place chicken in shallow pan; cover with preserves mixture. Bake, uncovered, at 350 degrees for 1 hour to 1 hour and 30 minutes.

Mrs. Barbara Deane
Glenwood Springs High School
Glenwood Springs, Colorado

LEMON BARBECUE SAUCE FOR CHICKEN

1/2 c. butter or margarine
2 lemons
1 tbsp. oregano
1/2 tsp. salt
2 cloves of garlic, minced
1/4 tsp. pepper

Melt butter in a saucepan. Squeeze lemons; add juice to melted butter. Add the remaining ingredients. Keep sauce warm; baste chicken occasionally while roasting. Yield: Sauce for 1 chicken.

Linda G. Olsen
North Central High School
Spokane, Washington

SAVORY OVEN-BARBECUED CHICKEN

1/2 c. self-rising flour
1 tsp. salt
1/4 tsp. pepper
1 fryer, disjointed
6 tbsp. butter or margarine
1/2 c. sliced or diced onion
1/2 c. diced celery
1 c. diced green pepper
1 c. catsup
1 c. water
2 tbsp. brown sugar
2 tbsp. Worcestershire sauce

Combine flour, salt and pepper. Dredge chicken pieces in flour mixture; fry in 4 tablespoons butter until golden brown. Place in casserole. Cook onion in remaining 2 tablespoons butter until clear. Add remaining ingredients; bring to a boil. Pour sauce over chicken. Bake, covered, at 325 degrees for about 1 hour. Yield: 4-6 servings.

Mrs. William Mann Nutt
Lewis County High School
Hohenwald, Tennessee

SPICY CHICKEN A LA BARBECUE

1 3 to 4-lb. chicken, disjointed
Seasoned flour
Oil
1 8-oz. can tomato sauce
1 c. water
1 sm. onion, sliced
1/2 green pepper, cut in 1/4-in. strips
2 tbsp. vinegar
2 tbsp. lemon juice
1/2 c. (packed) brown sugar
1/2 tsp. salt
Dash of pepper
3/4 tsp. dry mustard
1 tbsp. Worcestershire sauce
1/4 tsp. oregano
Dash of garlic salt
Dash of celery salt
2 tbsp. catsup

Dredge chicken in seasoned flour; fry in oil until golden. Drain chicken; place in deep casserole. Combine remaining ingredients in saucepan; bring to a boil. Let simmer for 10 minutes. Pour sauce over chicken. Bake, covered, in 350-degree oven for 45 to 60 minutes or until chicken is tender. Serve hot. Yield: 4-6 servings.

Mrs. Gwelda Anderson
Dix High School
Dix, Nebraska

CHICKEN AND DRESSING PIE

1/2 c. margarine
2 c. herb-seasoned stuffing mix
1/2 c. finely chopped celery
2 c. bite-sized cooked chicken
1/2 c. slivered almonds
1 c. chicken broth
1 recipe 1-crust pie pastry

Grease bottom and side of 9-inch pie plate with small amount of margarine. Spread stuffing mix in plate; sprinkle with celery. Place chicken evenly over celery; arrange almonds over chicken layer. Dot remaining margarine over top; pour chicken broth and 1 cup hot water over chicken mixture. Roll out pastry; cut in narrow strips. Arrange pastry strips lattice fashion over pie. Bake at 350 degrees for 30 minutes or until golden brown. Yield: 6-8 servings.

Mrs. Sybil Moore
Ware Shoals Junior High School
Ware Shoals, South Carolina

CHICKEN AND CHEESE COBBLER

1   2 1/2-lb. fryer
1 tbsp. salt
1/2 tsp. pepper
2 tbsp. flour
2 c. chicken broth
1 c. grated mild cheese
1 pkg. pie crust mix

Cut up fryer; place in enough water to cover. Add salt and pepper. Cook, covered, for 1 hour or until tender. Bone chicken; cut into large pieces. Combine flour with 1/2 cup broth; stir into remaining broth. Cook until thickened. Add chicken; let cool for 20 minutes. Mix grated cheese with pie crust mix; blend in 4 tablespoons warm water. Work dough lightly. Line well-greased 9 x 9 x 2 1/2-inch pan with 2/3 of the crust; pour in chicken mixture. Top with remaining crust, crimping to seal edges. Vent top. Bake at 425 degrees for 50 minutes. Yield: 6-8 servings.

Mrs. Euna L. Smith
Minnie Howard Middle School
Alexandria, Virginia

DIFFERENT CHICKEN PIE

1 fryer, stewed
1 c. (or more) chicken broth
1 can cream of celery soup
1 c. flour
2 tsp. baking powder
1 tsp. salt
1/2 tsp. pepper
1/2 c. melted margarine
1 c. milk

Remove chicken meat from bone; place in 2-quart Pyrex casserole. Combine chicken broth and celery soup in saucepan; bring to a boil. Pour over chicken. Beat remaining ingredients together with electric mixer; pour batter over chicken in casserole. Bake for 30 minutes at 425 degrees. May be frozen. Remove from freezer 1 hour before baking. Bake, covered, for 1 hour at 350 degrees.

Mrs. Helen B. Loftin
Denton High School
Denton, North Carolina

FAMILY CHICKEN PIE

1   3 to 4-lb. chicken
1 can peas and carrots
1/2 c. diced celery
1/2 c. diced onions
3 hard-cooked eggs, sliced
1/2 tsp. salt
1/8 tsp. pepper
2 tbsp. flour
1 recipe pastry

Boil chicken in water until tender; remove from broth, reserving broth. Remove bones; cut chicken into small pieces. Combine vegetables, eggs, salt and pepper. Combine flour and small amount of broth; stir until smooth. Add chicken and vegetable mixture to remaining chicken broth; bring to a boil. Add flour mixture; cook until thickened. Place in shallow oblong baking dish. Roll out pastry to fit baking dish; place over chicken mixture. Bake at 350 degrees for 50 minutes or until golden brown. Yield: 4-6 servings.

Lynda Herrin
Austwell-Tivoli High School
Tivoli, Texas

FRIED CHICKEN TURNOVERS

1 roasted chicken
Salt to taste
Pepper to taste
1 tbsp. butter
1 tbsp. flour
2 recipes pastry for 2-crust pies

Cut chicken into small pieces; place in saucepan. Add salt, pepper, butter, flour and 1/2 cup water. Cook, stirring, until thickened. Remove from heat and cool. Roll out pie pastry; cut around saucer to make rounds. Wet edges of each round with cold water. Place 2 tablespoons chicken mixture on 1 side of each round. Fold over and pinch edges together. Fry in deep fat until brown. May be baked in 350-degree oven until brown, if desired. Serve with a tossed salad.

Mrs. Ella Adair
Bryce Valley High School
Tropic, Utah

165

Capon, Pheasant and Quail

When hostesses want to serve a poultry dish that will win them endless praise from their guests, they frequently choose capons, pheasant or quail.

Capons are non-sexed roosters between four and seven pounds that have a generous amount of delicious white meat.

Pheasant is said to have a delightful flavor sometimes similar to venison. The young birds, which are marked by their short, round claws, are preferable because their meat is said to be more tender.

Quail has a delicate flavor. Its meat, although delicious, is usually quite dry. Basting with butter during cooking adds to the flavor and helps prevent dryness.

Enjoy trying all the great recipes in this section for these exotic flavored birds.

PAPER BAG GROUSE WITH BRUSSELS SPROUTS

6 grouse, with giblets
2 cloves of garlic, halved
1 sm. onion, chopped
10 tbsp. butter or margarine
1/2 lb. mushrooms, sliced
3/4 c. Madeira
1/2 c. chopped walnuts
1/4 tsp. rosemary leaves
1 tsp. salt
Dash of pepper
Shortening
2/3 c. chicken bouillon
2 10-oz. packages frozen California
    Brussels sprouts, halved

Chop giblets. Brown garlic in 6 tablespoons butter in saucepan; remove garlic. Saute onion and giblets in butter in saucepan for about 10 minutes. Add mushrooms, 1/2 cup Madeira, walnuts and seasonings; cook until mushrooms are tender and liquid reduced. Spoon into grouse; truss. Dot each grouse with butter, using 1 teaspoon for each; place each grouse in a small brown paper bag. Fold over ends; brush with shortening on all sides. Place in shallow roasting pan. Roast in 400-degree oven for 10 minutes. Reduce temperature to 350 degrees; roast for 1 hour and 15 minutes longer. Bring bouillon and remaining Madeira to a boil in saucepan. Add Brussels sprouts; cook until just tender. Drain; add remaining butter. Serve with grouse. Two 3-pound pheasant may be substituted for grouse, using 2 large paper bags and dotting each pheasant with 1 tablespoon butter. Yield: 6 servings.

Photograph for this recipe on page 166.

BAKED CAPON LEMONADA

2 or 3 lemons
1 3 to 3 1/2-lb. capon
Salt and pepper to taste
1 tbsp. fresh parsley, minced
1 tbsp. butter
1/2 to 3/4 tsp. fine herbs

Cut lemons into 1/8-inch slices. Rub capon cavity with salt, pepper and parsley; place butter in cavity. Sprinkle outside with herbs. Place capon, breast down, in roasting pan. Cover capon completely with lemon slices, reserving some lemon for breast side. Cover. Bake at 350 degrees for 45 minutes. Remove lemon slices; turn capon, breast side up. Cover completely with fresh lemon slices. Cover. Bake for 25 minutes. Remove cover. Bake for 20 minutes longer or until tender. Serve with small amount of pan juice. Yield: 4 servings.

Grace A. Felice
Andover High School
Bloomfield Hills, Michigan

CAPON CASSEROLE

1 lg. capon
1 12-oz. package spaghetti
2 lg. onions, diced
1 lg. green pepper, diced
1 tbsp. minced garlic
3/4 c. diced celery
2 c. tomatoes (opt.)
1 8-oz. can mushrooms, drained
1 recipe med. cheese sauce

Cook capon in boiling salted water until tender. Remove skin and bones; cut into bite-sized pieces. Cook spaghetti in capon stock according to package directions. Saute onions, green pepper, garlic and celery until tender; stir in tomatoes, mushrooms and cheese sauce. Arrange layers of spaghetti, capon and sauce in greased casserole, ending with sauce on top. Bake at 350 degrees until heated through.

Mrs. R. W. Smith
Kimmons Junior High School
Fort Smith, Arkansas

ROASTED CAPON

1 sm. capon
Imitation butter salt
Celery salt to taste
Pepper to taste
Paprika
Butter flavoring
Minced onion to taste
1 pkg. corn bread dressing mix

1 can mushroom soup
Sliced water chestnuts to taste
Chopped cooked giblets
Minced celery
Poultry seasoning to taste

Season inside of capon with imitation butter salt, celery salt, pepper, paprika and drop of butter flavoring. Sprinkle with onion. Prepare dressing mix according to package directions; add soup, water chestnuts, giblets, onion, celery and 1/2 teaspoon butter flavoring. Add poultry seasoning. Stuff capon loosely with dressing. Baked, covered, at 350 degrees for 1 hour. Remove cover. Bake for 30 minutes longer.

Mrs. J. M. Allen
Wall High School
Wall, Texas

STUFFED CAPON WITH OYSTER DRESSING

1 6 to 8-lb. capon
Salt and pepper to taste
3 tbsp. butter
1 c. chopped onions
1 c. chopped celery
1 lg. package unseasoned croutons
1/2 lb. saltine crackers, crushed
1 pt. fresh oysters
3 eggs, slightly beaten

Wipe outside of capon with damp cloth; wipe inside with dry cloth. Combine salt, pepper and 1 tablespoon butter; rub inside and outside of capon with butter mixture. Cook giblets and neck in boiling salted water until tender; strain, reserving giblets. Saute onions and celery in remaining butter. Combine croutons, crackers, sauteed vegetables, oysters, eggs and strained stock. Chop giblets; add to stuffing. Stuff capon cavity with stuffing; place in large roasting pan. Any leftover stuffing may be placed around capon. Cover. Bake at 350 degrees for 2 hours and 30 minutes. Remove cover. Bake for 30 minutes longer. May add water during baking time if necessary.

Mrs. Anna Lee Morris
Paul G. Blazer High School
Ashland, Kentucky

DOVE AND RICE

1 c. flour
2 tsp. salt
2 tsp. pepper
25 dove breasts
3 eggs, beaten
1 c. margarine
1 1/2 c. rice
1 can mushroom soup
1 can onion soup

Combine flour, salt and pepper. Dip dove breasts in egg, then roll in seasoned flour. Melt margarine in large skillet; cook dove, over medium heat, until brown. Place rice and 3 cups water in medium-sized roasting pan. Season with additional salt and pepper; mix well. Add the soups to any remaining butter in skillet. Simmer, stirring constantly, until heated through. Add to rice and stir. Place dove breasts on top; cover. Bake in 350-degree oven for 1 hour and 30 minutes.

Mrs. Aldon Prescott
Harrisburg High School
Harrisburg, Arkansas

GOOSE WITH WILD RICE STUFFING

3 c. chopped onions
2 c. chopped celery
1/2 c. chopped green olives
1 sm. can pimentos, chopped
4 tbsp. dried parsley
3 tbsp. butter
6 oz. wild rice, cooked
Salt and pepper to taste
1 tbsp. soda
1 goose

Saute onions, celery, olives, pimentos, and parsley lightly in butter. Add cooked rice and mix well. Season with salt and pepper. Rub soda into skin of goose, taking care to keep out of body cavity, then wash off completely. Stuff goose with dressing. Place a rack on a large piece of foil in a baking dish. Place goose on rack. Seal foil completely. Bake at 350 degrees for 4 hours.

Mrs. William Leadingham
Gilchrist High School
Gilchrist, Oregon

GOOSE WITH SOUR CREAM AND MUSHROOMS

1   5 to 8-lb. wild goose
Garlic salt to taste
Paprika
1 1/2 stalks celery, chopped
1 carrot, chopped
1 1/4 tsp. salt
4 tbsp. flour
1 c. onion-flavored sour cream
1   4-oz. can button mushrooms,
    drained

Wash goose inside and out and cut off neck and wing tips. Dry goose with paper towel; season with garlic salt and paprika. Place on a rack in a shallow pan. Bake, uncovered, in 325-degree oven for 1 hour or until browned. Place giblets in a saucepan; cover with water. Add celery, carrot and 1 teaspoon salt. Simmer until tender. Remove 3 tablespoons fat from goose; stir in 2 tablespoons flour. Add enough water to liquid from giblets to make 1 cup stock. Stir into flour mixture; season with remaining salt. Simmer, stirring, until thickened. Stir remaining flour into sour cream, then blend into the gravy. Place goose in roaster pan. Pour gravy and mushrooms over goose; cover. Bake for 2 hours longer. Yield: 6 servings.

Martha McMahon
Earlham Junior-Senior High School
Earlham, Iowa

ROAST GOOSE WITH APPLE STUFFING

1   8 to 10 lb. goose
1 c. minced onion
1 lg. clove of garlic, minced
1/2 lb. chicken livers, chopped
3 c. packaged bread crumbs
2 c. pared diced apple
1/4 c. brandy
1 egg, slightly beaten
1 tbsp. salt
1/4 tsp. pepper
1/4 c. chopped parsley
2 c. diced onion
1 c. diced celery
1 c. port
1   10 1/2-oz. can chicken broth
1 tsp. cornstarch

Thaw goose, if frozen. Remove fat from cavity; melt fat over low heat. Cut off wings at first joint and cut neck into 1-inch pieces. Set aside. Saute minced onion in 3 tablespoons goose fat for 2 to 3 minutes. Add garlic and goose and chicken livers. Cook for 2 minutes, stirring frequently. Cool. Place in large bowl; add bread crumbs, apple, brandy, egg, salt, pepper and parsley. Mix well. Preheat oven to 425 degrees. Stuff goose with bread mixture; force wings back under body. Skewer and lace the cavity. Tie legs together. Place, breast side up, on rack in roasting pan. Bake for 20 minutes. Reduce oven temperature to 350 degrees. Remove goose and rack from pan. Pour off all fat. Place diced onion, celery, neck pieces and wing tips in pan, then return goose. Bake for 2 hours to 2 hours and 30 minutes or for 15 minutes per pound. Remove fat from pan occasionally. Place goose on warm platter and untruss. Keep warm. Pour fat from pan; place pan on low heat. Add port. Bring to a boil; simmer for 2 minutes. Add broth and cook for 2 to 3 minutes longer. Blend the cornstarch with 1 teaspoon water. Stir into sauce. Cook, stirring, until thickened. Strain into sauceboat. Garnish platter with watercress, if desired. Yield: 6-8 servings.

Mrs. Cyndi Morris
Clifton High School
Clifton, Texas

BAKED PHEASANT WITH WILD RICE

1 pheasant
Salt and pepper to taste
Flour
Cooking oil
1   8-oz. package wild rice
1 can cream of mushroom soup
1 can cream of celery soup
1 sm. can mushrooms, drained

Cut pheasant into serving-sized pieces. Season with salt and pepper; roll in flour.

Brown well in a small amount of oil in a heavy skillet. Cook wild rice according to package directions. Combine the undiluted soups and the mushrooms with the cooked wild rice. Spoon approximately half the mixture into an oiled 2-quart baking dish. Arrange the pheasant pieces on top of rice mixture. Combine the skillet drippings with the remaining soup and rice mixture; spoon over the pheasant. Bake in 350-degree oven for 45 minutes to 1 hour or until pheasant is tender.

Mrs. Doris Sturm
Adair-Casey High School
Adair, Iowa

BRANDY AND CREAM PHEASANT

2 pheasant
4 slices bacon
2 green onions, sliced
1 clove of garlic, minced
3 tbsp. butter
1/3 c. brandy
1 1/2 c. chicken broth
3/4 tsp. salt
1/4 tsp. pepper
1 1/2 c. cream
3 tbsp. horseradish

Cover each pheasant with 2 slices bacon; truss, keeping bacon in place. Brown onions, garlic and pheasant in butter in skillet. Remove to broiler pan; pour in pan juices. Pour brandy over pheasant; ignite. Add chicken broth, salt and pepper. Bake in 375-degree oven for 35 to 45 minutes or until tender, basting frequently. Stir cream and horseradish into pan juices; bake for 15 minutes longer. Serve with cream sauce.

Mrs. Jeanette K. Cornwall
Columbia High School
Hunters, Washington

PHEASANT STROGANOFF

1 med. pheasant
Flour
1/2 med. onion, chopped

2 celery tops, chopped
Butter or margarine
1/4 lb. mushrooms
Salt and pepper to taste
1/8 tsp. basil
1/4 tsp. oregano
1/4 c. white wine

Cut breast meat from bones; cut into small pieces. Dredge in flour. Saute onion and celery in butter in large frying pan until soft; remove from pan. Add mushrooms to pan and saute; remove mushrooms. Brown pheasant on all sides; return onion, celery and mushrooms to frying pan. Season with salt, pepper, basil and oregano. Add wine and enough water to make a sauce. Cook slowly for 30 minutes or until tender. Thicken sauce with a flour and water mixture, if desired. Season to taste. May serve over rice.

Virginia Raven
Hamilton Junior High School
Stockton, California

PECAN-STUFFED PHEASANT

1/2 c. butter
1 1/3 c. dry bread crumbs
2/3 c. broken pecan meats
2 pheasant
2 tbsp. flour
3/4 tsp. salt
1/4 tsp. pepper
1/3 c. sherry

Melt half the butter; pour over bread crumbs. Add pecans; toss lightly. Stuff pheasant and truss. Combine flour, salt and pepper; sprinkle lightly over pheasant. Melt remaining butter in a heavy skillet. Brown pheasant; transfer to roasting pan. Add 1 1/2 cups hot water and sherry to browned butter; pour over pheasant. Bake, covered, in 350-degree oven for 1 hour, basting every 15 minutes. Remove cover; bake for 20 minutes longer or until crisp. Thicken pan drippings for gravy, if desired. Yield: 6 servings.

Mrs. Gertrude Collins
Sycamore High School
Sycamore, Illinois

171

PHEASANT IN WINE

1/4 c. flour
1 env. dry onion soup mix
2 pheasant, disjointed
2 13 3/4-oz. cans chicken broth
1 4-oz. can mushrooms
1 c. sauterne

Mix flour and onion soup mix together.
Dredge pheasant in flour mixture; place in
shallow baking pan. Pour broth, mushrooms
and sauterne over pheasant. Bake, covered,
at 325 degrees for 1 hour and 30 minutes to
2 hours or until tender.

Marjorie Harris
Greeley High School
Greeley, Nebraska

GOURMET PHEASANT

3 sm. pheasant
1/2 c. milk
Salt and pepper to taste
2 apples, pared, cored and sliced
2 onions, thinly sliced
2 tbsp. butter
3 c. sour cream

Brush pheasant inside and out with milk;
season with salt and pepper. Stuff cavities
with apple slices. Saute onions lightly in butter in deep flameproof casserole; brown
pheasant in onion-flavored butter. Pour sour
cream over pheasant; season lightly with salt
and pepper. Bake, covered, at 375 degrees
for 1 hour, basting every 15 minutes. Serve
hot on toast, if desired. Garnish with watercress. Yield: 3-6 servings.

Mrs. Janet H. Lee
Gunston Junior High School
Arlington, Virginia

PHEASANT EN CREME

1 pheasant
1 can cream of chicken soup
1/2 c. apple cider
4 tsp. Worcestershire sauce
3/4 tsp. salt
1/3 c. chopped onion

1 clove of garlic, minced
1 can sliced mushrooms, drained
Paprika

Preheat oven to 350 degrees. Place pheasant
in ungreased 9 x 9 x 2-inch baking dish.
Combine soup, cider, Worcestershire sauce,
salt, onion, garlic and mushrooms; pour over
pheasant. Sprinkle generously with paprika.
Bake, uncovered, for 1 hour, basting occasionally. Sprinkle generously with paprika;
bake for 30 minutes to 1 hour longer or
until fork tender. Garnish with fruit or
greenery, if desired. Yield: 2-3 servings.

Charlene Garoutte
Keokuk Junior High School
Keokuk, Iowa

VIRGINIA PHEASANT
WITH SAUCE

1/2 c. flour
1 tsp. salt
1/8 tsp. pepper
1 tsp. paprika
2 pheasant, disjointed
1/4 c. butter
1 clove of garlic, crushed
1/4 c. chopped ripe olives
1/2 tsp. Worcestershire sauce
1/2 c. white wine

Combine flour, salt, pepper and paprika;
dredge pheasant in flour mixture. Brown on
all sides in butter in skillet. Add garlic,
olives, 1/2 cup water and Worcestershire
sauce; cover tightly. Simmer for 45 minutes.
Turn pheasant; add wine. Simmer, covered,
for 45 minutes longer or until tender. Serve
hot with sauce. Yield: 6 servings.

Mrs. Wilda Carr
Holdrege Senior High School
Holdrege, Nebraska

PHEASANT A LA ORANGE

2 Valencia oranges
2 whole pheasant
3/4 c. butter
4 tbsp. chopped celery
1/2 tsp. basil

2 tbsp. parsley
2 sm. onions
1 pricked clove of garlic
2 4-oz. cans mushrooms, drained
2 c. chicken bouillon
3 to 4 tbsp. cornstarch

Slit oranges. Partially squeeze out and re-serve juice. Rub pheasant with rinds of oranges to obtain as much orange oil as pos-sible. Grate rind of 1 orange and set aside. Melt 3 tablespoons butter in heavy 8-quart Dutch oven; fry pheasant on all sides until a delicate brown. Remove from Dutch oven. Combine celery, basil, parsley and 4 table-spoons melted butter. Place 1 onion and half the celery mixture in cavity of each pheas-ant. Place rack in Dutch oven; place pheas-ant on rack, breast side up. Melt 2 table-spoons butter in Dutch oven; add 3/4 cup water and garlic. Reduce heat and cover. Brown mushrooms in 3 tablespoons butter. Add reserved orange juice and grated rind; bring to a boil. Stir in bouillon; pour into Dutch oven. Simmer, covered, for a total of 45 minutes. Place Dutch oven in 325-degree oven. Bake for 1 hour and 30 minutes or until pheasant are tender. Pour off pan juices into saucepan; return pheasant to oven to brown. Dissolve cornstarch in 1/2 cup water. Remove mushrooms from pan juices; stir in cornstarch mixture. Cook over low heat, stir-ring constantly, until thickened. Add mush-rooms; serve gravy over pheasant.

Jeannine A. Saunders
Hannibal Central High School
Hannibal, New York

WILD PHEASANT ON RICE

1 pheasant, disjointed
Salt and pepper
1 c. flour
1 c. shortening
1 pkg. brown gravy mix
1 pkg. onion gravy mix
1 c. rice
2 c. water

Season pheasant with salt and pepper; dredge in flour. Brown in shortening in skil-let; place in baking dish. Prepare brown gravy mix and onion gravy mix according to package directions; pour over pheasant. Bake, covered, at 300 degrees for 2 hours. Place rice, 1 teaspoon salt and water in saucepan; cover. Bring to a boil. Reduce heat; simmer for 14 minutes. Serve with pheasant. Pheasant may be cooked in pres-sure saucepan for 45 minutes at 15 pounds pressure. Yield: 4 servings.

Joanne Snider
Dimmitt High School
Dimmitt, Texas

PHEASANT MUSCATEL
First Place

3 1 1/2-lb. pheasant, halved
1/2 lemon
Salt and pepper to taste
1/3 c. butter
3 oranges
1 c. white raisins
1 tsp. grated lemon peel
1/3 c. muscatel
1 c. chicken broth

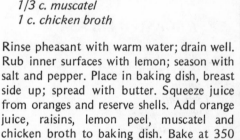

Rinse pheasant with warm water; drain well. Rub inner surfaces with lemon; season with salt and pepper. Place in baking dish, breast side up; spread with butter. Squeeze juice from oranges and reserve shells. Add orange juice, raisins, lemon peel, muscatel and chicken broth to baking dish. Bake at 350 degrees for 45 minutes, basting every 10 minutes. Chicken may be substituted for pheasant. Yield: 6 servings.

Nutted Rice in Fluted Orange Cups

2 c. chicken broth
1 c. rice
2 tbsp. butter
2/3 c. chopped pecans
2 tbsp. minced parsley
Salt to taste

Combine chicken broth and rice in saucepan; bring to a boil. Stir and cook, covered, over low heat for 14 minutes. Remove from heat. Stir in butter, pecans and parsley; season with salt. Flute reserved orange shells; spoon rice into shells. Serve with Pheasant Muscatel.

Margaret Bruce
Redwood High School
Larkspur, California

PHEASANT WITH MUSHROOM SOUP

2 pheasant, disjointed
Salt and pepper to taste
Paprika
1 c. flour
1 c. shortening
1 can mushroom soup
1 c. water

Season pheasant with salt and pepper; sprinkle with paprika. Dredge in flour. Brown slowly in hot shortening in skillet, turning once. Place pheasant in 2-quart baking dish. Cover with mushroom soup and water; cover tightly. Bake at 325 degrees for 1 hour or until tender.

Dolores Coale
Edmond Junior High School
Edmond, Oklahoma

EASY ROASTED PHEASANT

1 pheasant
3 stalks celery
1 onion
1 tsp. salt
1/8 tsp. pepper
4 bacon strips

Scald pheasant by pouring 4 cups boiling water over pheasant and into cavity. Place celery and onion in cavity; do not sew up. Sprinkle with salt and pepper; arrange bacon strips over breast. Place in roasting pan; add 1 cup water. Bake, uncovered, at 350 degrees for 2 hours or until tender, adding water, if needed. Yield: 6-8 servings.

Mrs. Edna Earl Jesse
Rossville High School
Rossville, Georgia

528
ROASTED PHEASANT IN CREAM

2 pheasant, disjointed
Salt and pepper to taste
Flour
Cooking oil
1 c. cream or half and half

Season pheasant with salt and pepper; dredge in flour. Pour in enough cooking oil to generously cover bottom of heavy skillet; brown pheasant in oil. Place browned pieces in roaster; add enough water to cover bottom of roaster. Bake, covered, in 275-degree oven for 3 hours. Stir in cream; bake for 1 hour longer, adding more cream, if needed.

Gudrun Harstad
Senior High School
Detroit Lakes, Minnesota

PHEASANT BREASTS BAKED IN WINE

4 pheasant breasts
2 c. dry white wine
2 c. sliced unpeeled red tart
    apples
Salt and pepper to taste
8 slices bacon

Bone pheasant breasts; place in shallow bowl. Pour 1 cup wine over breasts; let stand in refrigerator to marinate for 2 to 3 hours. Cover bottom of 9 x 13-inch baking dish with apple slices; place pheasant breasts on top of apples. Season lightly with salt and pepper. Place bacon strips on pheasant breasts; pour marinade and remaining wine over all. Bake, covered, for 2 hours at 325 degrees. Remove cover and bacon; bake for 20 to 30 minutes longer or until brown. Discard apples. Serve with wild rice. Yield: 4-6 servings.

Mrs. Ardith Wakefield
Eisenhower Junior High School
Darien, Illinois

TEXAS PANHANDLE QUAIL

1 c. flour
2 tsp. salt
1/2 tsp. garlic powder
1 tsp. lemon pepper
1 tsp. paprika
2 quail per person
1/2 c. butter
1 c. dry white wine
1 tbsp. minced parsley
1 tbsp. fines herbes

1 tsp. dillweed
1/4 tsp. curry powder
Salt and pepper to taste
2 tbsp. cognac
1 c. sour cream

Combine the first 5 ingredients and coat the quail with flour mixture. Brown in butter in skillet. Combine wine, parsley, fines herbes, dillweed, curry, salt and pepper. Pour over browned quail. Cover; simmer for 20 to 25 minutes,' spooning sauce over quail occasionally. Do not overcook. Remove quail and keep warm. Stir in cognac and sour cream. Blend and heat through. More wine may be added if sauce cooks down too much. Pour part of the sauce over quail and serve remaining in gravy boat.

Rebecca F. Hutchison
Travis Junior High School
Snyder, Texas

QUAIL ON THE GREEN

1/2 c. margarine
8 to 12 quail
Salt and pepper to taste
Garlic salt to taste
2 c. sour cream
2 cans cream of asparagus soup
1/2 lb. fresh mushrooms, sliced
1/2 c. sherry or brandy
Parmesan cheese
2 bunches fresh asparagus, cooked

Melt margarine in an 8 x 8 x 2 1/2-inch baking pan. Place the quail in the pan; sprinkle lightly with salt, pepper and garlic salt. Combine sour cream, soup, mushrooms and sherry and mix well. Pour about 1/4 of the sauce over the quail, then sprinkle generously with Parmesan cheese. Arrange asparagus over the top of the quail, then pour the remaining sauce over asparagus. Sprinkle with Parmesan cheese. Bake in a preheated 350-degree oven until done. Two cans asparagus, drained, may be used instead of fresh.

Meta West
Abilene School
Abilene, Kansas

QUAIL IN BROWNED RICE

4 quail
Salt and pepper
3/4 c. flour
5 tbsp. shortening
1 c. rice
1 med. onion, chopped
2 chicken bouillon cubes

Season quail with salt and pepper to taste. Place the flour in a medium-sized bag; add the quail. Shake until well coated. Melt shortening in a heavy skillet; add quail and fry until lightly browned. Remove quail from skillet; set aside. Add rice and onion to the drippings; fry until golden brown, stirring occasionally. Add bouillon cubes and 2 1/2 cups water; mix well. Season with 2 teaspoons salt and 1/2 teaspoon pepper. Place quail on top of rice mixture; cook, covered, over low heat for 20 to 25 minutes or until tender. Yield: 4 servings.

Mrs. Lela Hayek
Calallen Junior High School
Corpus Christi, Texas

SMOTHERED GUINEA HEN

Flour
Salt and pepper to taste
2 guinea hens, disjointed
Cooking oil
1 can cream of mushroom soup
1 3-oz. can mushrooms with
   liquid
1 c. sour cream
1/2 c. cooking sherry
Paprika to taste

Combine flour, salt and pepper. Dredge hens in seasoned flour. Heat oil in skillet; brown hens well on all sides. Remove to baking dish. Combine soup, mushrooms, sour cream and sherry; pour over hens. Sprinkle with paprika; cover. Bake at 350 degrees for 1 hour to 1 hour and 15 minutes or until hens are tender. Yield: 6 servings.

Mrs. Betty Rassette
Central High School
Salina, Kansas

Turkey

There's nothing better or more festive than turkey with all the trimmings. It is truly a delectable symbol for any special occasion.

Frozen turkeys are available year round, and during November and December, chilled, dressed turkeys are on the market. It is best to thaw turkey slowly in the refrigerator for one to three days. If you are more pushed for time, thaw it in its own wrap or in a plastic bag in cold water. Thawing will still take six to eight hours for a large turkey.

Recipes on the following pages will give you an invaluable resource of ideas for preparing turkey. Don't wait for a special occasion to try them out.

HARVEST DINNER

1   10-lb. turkey
Salt and pepper
1/4 c. butter or margarine
6 to 8 med. Louisiana yams
1   16-oz. jar spiced crab apples
2 tbsp. cornstarch
1/2 c. Rhine wine
1   6-oz. can unsweetened pineapple
     juice
1/2 c. dark corn syrup
1 1/2 tsp. lemon juice

Sprinkle inside of turkey with salt and pepper; place on rack in shallow roasting pan. Melt butter in saucepan; brush some on turkey. Roast in 325-degree oven for 2 hours. Cook yams in boiling, salted water until almost done; drain. Peel; cut in half. Drain crab apples; reserve syrup. Blend cornstarch and wine; stir into remaining butter. Add reserved syrup, pineapple juice, corn syrup, lemon juice and 1/4 teaspoon salt; cook, stirring constantly, until sauce boils for 30 seconds. Drain fat from roasting pan. Arrange yams around turkey; brush turkey and yams with sauce. Roast for 30 minutes longer or until meat thermometer registers 185 degrees, brushing once with sauce. Heat crab apples in remaining sauce. Arrange turkey, yams and crab apples on platter; serve with hot sauce. Two 23-ounce cans Louisiana yams may be used instead of fresh yams; bake for 15 instead of 30 minutes. Yield: 6-8 servings.

Photograph for this recipe on page 176.

DELICIOUS TURKEY CASSEROLE

1 can cream of chicken soup
1/2 c. mayonnaise
3/4 c. stock or chicken bouillon
2 tbsp. lemon juice
2 tbsp. finely chopped onion
1 c. chopped blanched almonds
1 tbsp. chopped parsley
1/2 tsp. salt
1/2 tsp. white pepper

1 c. finely chopped celery
3 hard-cooked eggs, chopped fine
2 c. chopped cooked turkey breast
1 c. cracker crumbs

Combine soup, mayonnaise, stock and lemon juice in mixing bowl; mix well. Add onion, almonds, parsley, salt and pepper; mix well. Stir in celery, eggs and turkey; place in greased 2-quart casserole. Cover with cracker crumbs. Bake at 325 degrees for 30 to 40 minutes. Yield: 6 servings.

Sarah P. Bowles
Holladay School
Holladay, Tennessee

GOODBYE TURKEY

1 can cheese soup
1 1/2 c. turkey broth
1 1/3 c. instant rice
1 pkg. frozen asparagus
2 c. cooked diced turkey
Toasted nuts or paprika

Measure 1/2 cup cheese soup; set aside. Combine remaining soup with 1 1/2 cups broth in skillet. Bring to a boil. Remove from heat. Stir in rice. Cook asparagus according to package directions; drain. Arrange asparagus and turkey over rice. Blend remaining soup with 1 tablespoon water; spoon over turkey. Cover; simmer for 5 minutes. Sprinkle with toasted nuts or paprika before serving.

Margaret W. Cyrus
Herndon High School
Herndon, Virginia

EASY TURKEY CASSEROLE

1 c. diced onion
1 c. diced green pepper
1 c. diced celery
1/2 c. margarine
1 can cream of mushroom soup
1/2 lb. Velveeta or American
     cheese, grated
1   4-oz. can mushroom stems and
     pieces

1 can water chestnuts, sliced
2 c. cubed cooked turkey
2 pkg. green noodles
Chicken broth

Saute onion, green pepper and celery in margarine in large skillet until tender. Stir in soup and Velveeta; heat through until Velveeta is melted. Stir in mushrooms, water chestnuts and turkey. Prepare noodles according to package directions, using broth in place of water; drain. Place noodles in two 1 1/2-quart casseroles. Pour turkey mixture over noodles; garnish with ripe olives, if desired. Bake at 350 degrees for 20 minutes or until heated through and bubbly. May be frozen, if desired.

Mrs. Tommie S. Preuett
Vinton High School
Vinton, Louisiana

GOURMET TURKEY

3 lb. cooked cubed turkey thighs
2 tbsp. fat
1 1/4 tsp. salt
1/8 tsp. pepper
1   8-oz. can sliced mushrooms,
   drained
3/4 c. sliced celery
1/3 c. chopped onion
3 tbsp. butter or margarine
2 chicken bouillon cubes
2 c. cooked rice
1/3 to 1/2 c. half and half

Brown turkey in fat in skillet over medium heat; season with 1 teaspoon salt and pepper. Remove turkey from skillet. Saute mushrooms, celery and onion in butter over medium heat until tender; add bouillon cubes, stirring to dissolve. Add rice, half and half and remaining salt. Spoon rice mixture into 11 x 9-inch baking pan. Arrange turkey on top. Cover with aluminum foil. Bake at 350 degrees for 45 minutes. Yield: 6 servings.

Katherine Hixon
Berthoud Junior-Senior High School
Berthoud, Colorado

ORIENTAL TURKEY CASSEROLE

1/2 c. rice
1 c. chicken broth
1 c. diced cooked celery
1   8-oz. can water chestnuts,
   drained
1 can cream of chicken soup
1/2 c. slivered almonds
3/4 c. mayonnaise
1 c. cooked diced turkey
Buttered crushed corn flakes

Preheat oven to 350 degrees. Cook rice in chicken broth until rice is tender and broth is absorbed. Cook celery in boiling salted water until crisp-tender; drain. Slice water chestnuts thinly. Combine all ingredients except corn flakes in 2-quart casserole. Top with corn flakes. Bake at 350 degrees for 40 minutes.

Mrs. Josephine Kidwell
McKinley High School
College Park, Maryland

IN A JIFFY TURKEY

1 1/2 c. chopped celery
1 sm. onion, chopped
Melted margarine
4 c. cooked cubed turkey
2 tbsp. minced parsley
1 1/2 c. mayonnaise
2 cans water chestnuts, drained
1 can cream of mushroom soup
2 c. corn bread stuffing mix
3/4 c. hot water

Saute celery and onion in 2 tablespoons margarine until onion is tender. Combine onion mixture, turkey, parsley, mayonnaise, water chestnuts and soup. Spoon turkey mixture into 9 x 13-inch baking pan. Toss corn bread stuffing mix lightly in bowl, adding water gradually. Sprinkle over turkey mixture; drizzle with 1/3 cup melted margarine. Bake at 350 degrees for 30 minutes.

Mrs. Patricia A. Gannon
Ben Franklin Junior High School
Kenmore, New York

GOBBLE-UP CASSEROLE

6 c. diced cooked turkey
3 c. bread crumbs
3/4 c. celery
1 onion, chopped
1/2 c. butter
1/2 tsp. salt
1/4 tsp. baking powder
1/4 tsp. pepper
1/2 tsp. poultry seasoning
1 egg, beaten
3/4 c. milk
1 can cream of mushroom soup

Place turkey in 9 x 13-inch baking pan. Saute bread crumbs, celery and onion in butter in skillet. Add salt, baking powder, pepper and poultry seasoning. Stir in egg and milk. Spoon mixture over turkey. Spread soup in layer over top. Bake, uncovered, at 350 degrees for 45 minutes to 1 hour. Add more liquid during baking time if necessary. Garnish with parsley.

Dianne Schiltz
Windsor Junior-Senior High School
Windsor, Colorado

CRUNCHY TURKEY STRATA

1 1/2 cans chow mein noodles
1 can water chestnuts, sliced
3 or 4 stalks celery, sliced thin
2 c. diced cooked turkey
2 cans cream of mushroom soup
1/2 soup can water
1 med. onion, minced
1/2 c. broken cashews

Spread bottom of buttered 2-quart casserole with half the noodles. Combine water chestnuts, celery, turkey, soup, water and onion; spread over noodles. Sprinkle remaining noodles on top. Bake for 40 minutes at 350 degrees. Sprinkle cashews over top; bake for 20 minutes longer. Yield: 6 servings.

Mrs. Karin Bargar
Pattengill Junior High School
Lansing, Michigan

TATER TURKEY

1 c. mayonnaise
2 tbsp. minced green pepper
2 tbsp. chopped celery
2 tbsp. chopped pimento
3 hard-boiled eggs, chopped
4 c. seasoned mashed potatoes
2 c. chopped cooked turkey
1/2 c. finely grated cheese

Combine mayonnaise, green pepper, celery, pimento and eggs for sauce. Spread half the mashed potatoes in greased 9 x 3-inch casserole. Add turkey; cover with sauce. Top with remaining mashed potatoes; sprinkle cheese over top. Bake at 350 degrees for 30 minutes or until light brown. Yield: 6-8 servings.

Mrs. R. A. Russell
John de la Howe School
McCormick, South Carolina

PARTY TURKEY CASSEROLE

5 tbsp. flour
1 tsp. salt
1/4 tsp. onion salt
1/4 c. melted butter
2 1/2 c. milk or light cream
1 1/3 c. rice
1 1/2 c. broth
1/2 c. grated cheese
1 1/2 c. cooked asparagus
2 c. cooked chopped turkey
2 tbsp. slivered almonds

Stir flour, half the salt and half the onion salt into butter over boiling water. Add milk gradually, stirring constantly. Cook, stirring, until thickened. Cook rice according to package directions; spoon into large baking dish. Combine broth and remaining salt; pour over rice. Sprinkle half the cheese over rice; top with asparagus and turkey. Spoon sauce over turkey mixture; sprinkle with remaining cheese and almonds. Bake at 375 degrees for about 20 minutes.

Mrs. Mildred W. Tate
Henderson High School
Henderson, Kentucky

MOM'S TURKEY-RICE CASSEROLE

1 c. rice
1 4-oz. can pimento, chopped
1 c. diced celery
1/2 c. chopped onion
2 c. cubed cooked turkey
1/2 c. blanched almonds, chopped
1 3/4 to 2 c. chicken broth
1 1/2 tbsp. flour
Salt and pepper to taste

Cook rice according to package directions; drain. Rinse with cold water. Combine rice and pimento. Spoon 1/3 of the rice mixture into greased 2-quart casserole. Saute celery and onion until tender. Arrange layers of turkey, onion, celery and 1/2 of the almonds over rice mixture in casserole. Spoon remaining rice mixture over layers. Combine broth, flour, and seasonings, mixing well; pour over rice mixture. Sprinkle with remaining almonds. Bake at 375 degrees for about 40 minutes. May serve with medium white sauce if desired. Yield: 6-8 servings.

Mrs. Warren F. Sims
Horace Mann School
Biwabik, Minnesota

TURKEY STRATA SUPREME

5 slices buttered white bread
2 1/2 c. diced cooked turkey or
*   chicken*
1 c. grated Cheddar cheese
3 eggs
2 c. milk
1/2 tsp. salt
1/4 tsp. pepper
1 10 1/2-oz. can cream of chicken
*   soup*
1/2 10 1/2-oz. can cream of
*   mushroom soup*
1/2 c. water
1/2 tsp. curry powder
1 c. canned mushroom caps or
*   pieces*

Remove crusts from bread; cut into 1-inch squares. Place in 8 x 8 x 2-inch oiled casserole or glass baking dish. Add layer of turkey, then layer of cheese. Repeat layers 3 times. Beat eggs slightly. Add milk, salt and pepper; blend well. Pour over cheese layer. Cover; let stand in refrigerator overnight. Remove from refrigerator; bring to room temperature before baking. Bake in preheated 325-degree oven for 1 hour. Combine soups in saucepan; add water gradually. Add curry powder; stir until smooth. Stir in mushrooms; cook over low heat, stirring frequently, until heated through. Serve over turkey. Cooked pheasant or capon may be substituted for turkey.

Mrs. EulaLee Coumbe
Hubert Olson Junior High School
Minneapolis, Minnesota

TURKEY STRATA WITH SAUCE

3 1/2 c. prepared dressing
3 c. cubed or sliced cooked turkey
1/2 c. margarine
1/2 c. flour
1/4 tsp. salt
Pepper to taste
4 c. chicken broth
6 eggs, lightly beaten
1 can cream of mushroom soup
1/4 c. milk
1 c. sour cream
1/4 c. chopped pimento

Spread dressing in 9 x 13-inch baking pan; arrange turkey on top. Melt margarine in saucepan; stir in flour and seasonings to make a smooth paste. Add broth; cook, stirring, until thick. Stir a small amount of hot mixture into eggs; return eggs to hot mixture. Pour over turkey. Bake at 325 degrees for 45 minutes or until knife inserted in center comes out clean. Let stand for 5 minutes. Combine soup, milk, sour cream and pimento in saucepan; heat thoroughly. Cut turkey into servings; serve with sour cream sauce.

Lenora Ann Hill
Charles M. Russell High School
Great Falls, Montana

TURKEY-ALMOND CASSEROLE

3 c. diced cooked turkey
1/2 c. toasted slivered almonds
1   1-lb. can cream-style corn
1   10 1/2-oz. can cream of chicken
   soup
1   6-oz. can evaporated milk
2 tbsp. instant minced onion
1/4 c. finely chopped green pepper
1/2 tsp. Worcestershire sauce
1 chicken bouillon cube
3/4 tsp. salt
2/3 c. milk
Melted butter or margarine
2 c. biscuit mix
1/4 c. sliced almonds

Place turkey in 1 1/2-quart baking dish; sprinkle with slivered almonds. Combine corn, undiluted soup, evaporated milk, onion, green pepper, Worcestershire sauce, crumbled bouillon cube and salt in saucepan. Blend well; heat to boiling point. Pour over turkey. Bake in 425-degree oven for 10 minutes. Stir milk and 1/4 cup melted butter into biscuit mix to make a soft dough; knead gently 8 to 10 times. Roll out 1/2 inch thick; cut with 2-inch cutter. Place biscuits on top of casserole; bake for 8 minutes longer. Brush tops with 2 tablespoons melted butter; sprinkle with sliced almonds. Bake for about 5 minutes longer or until lightly browned. Yield: 4-6 servings.

Mrs. Paula Calhoun
Fisher High School
Fisher, Illinois

TURKEY AND BROWN RICE CASSEROLE

3 c. cooked turkey or chicken
   chunks
3 1/2 c. cooked brown rice
1 c. chopped onion
1 c. sliced celery
1 c. chopped green pepper
3 tbsp. butter or margarine
1 can cream of mushroom soup
1/2 c. dry white wine or chicken
   broth

1   6-oz. can sliced mushrooms
1 tsp. sage leaves, crumbled
1/4 tsp. thyme leaves
1/2 tsp. salt
Dash of pepper
1   4-oz. can pimento, drained and
   chopped
1 c. herb-seasoned croutons

Preheat oven to 350 degrees. Combine turkey and rice in greased 2 1/2-quart casserole; set aside. Saute onion, celery and green pepper in 2 tablespoons butter in large skillet for 8 minutes or until tender crisp, stirring frequently. Stir in soup, wine, mushrooms, sage, thyme, salt, pepper and pimento. Pour over turkey; stir to mix well. Heat remaining butter in same skillet until melted. Toss croutons in melted butter; spoon around casserole. Bake for 40 to 45 minutes or until bubbly.

Mrs. Vivian Lund
Holmes Junior High School
Cedar Falls, Iowa

SWEET AND SOUR TURKEY

1 No. 2 can pineapple chunks
1 chicken bouillon cube
1/4 c. vinegar
1/4 tsp. prepared mustard
1 tbsp. soy sauce
1/2 tsp. salt
1/4 c. (packed) brown sugar
2 tbsp. cornstarch
2 to 3 c. cooked turkey chunks
Chow mein noodles
3/4 c. green pepper strips
1/4 c. thinly sliced onion

Drain pineapple; reserve syrup. Combine bouillon cube, vinegar, mustard, soy sauce and salt in saucepan; cook until bouillon cube is dissolved. Combine brown sugar, cornstarch and 1/2 cup reserved pineapple syrup; stir into hot liquid. Cook, stirring constantly, until thick and clear. Pour over hot turkey. Serve over chow mein noodles; top with pineapple chunks, green pepper strips and onion slices. May serve over rice, if desired.

Jill R. Olsen
Rand Junior High School
Arlington Heights, Illinois

TOSS IT TO ME

2 c. tomato sauce
1 pkg. spaghetti sauce seasoning
1 qt. cooked lasagna noodles
2 c. cooked cubed turkey
2 c. cottage cheese
8 oz. shredded Cheddar cheese
8 oz. shredded mozzarella cheese
3 sliced frankfurters

Combine tomato sauce and spaghetti sauce seasoning. Arrange layers of noodles, turkey, cheeses and tomato sauce mixture in greased casserole. Top with frankfurters. Bake at 350 degrees for 30 minutes.

Isabelle E. Moe
John Rogers High School
Spokane, Washington

TURKEY-CASHEW CASSEROLE

1 c. chopped cooked turkey
1 c. cream of mushroom soup
1 c. milk
1 1/2 c. chopped celery
1/4 lb. cashew nuts
1 tbsp. minced onion
2 c. crushed round buttery
    crackers
1/4 tsp. salt
1/4 tsp. pepper

Mix turkey, soup, milk, celery, nuts and onion together; mix crackers with salt and pepper. Arrange layers of crackers and turkey mixture in lightly greased casserole, ending with crackers on top. Bake at 350 degrees for 1 hour.

Sara Yowell
Ramay Junior High School
Fayetteville, Arkansas

TURKEY ROYALE

1 c. chopped celery
1/2 c. chopped green pepper
3 c. stuffing mix
2 c. diced cooked turkey

1/2 c. warm chicken broth
4 tbsp. pimento strips
2 cans cream of chicken soup
Melted butter
1/4 c. slivered almonds

Cook celery and green pepper in boiling salted water until crisp-tender; drain. Place 2 cups stuffing mix in greased casserole; add turkey, broth, celery and green pepper. Arrange pimento strips over vegetables; spread with soup. Toss remaining stuffing mix in small amount of melted butter; sprinkle over turkey mixture. Top with almonds. Bake at 350 degrees for 25 minutes or until heated through.

Dorothy Lindblad
Bayside Junior High School
San Mateo, California

TURKEY-CRANBERRY SQUARES

2 tbsp. butter
3/4 c. sugar
1 tsp. grated orange peel
2 c. fresh cranberries or whole
    cranberry sauce
5 c. diced cooked turkey
1 c. turkey gravy
1 c. milk
1 tsp. salt
1/4 tsp. pepper
2 tbsp. minced onion
2 c. soft bread crumbs
2 eggs, slightly beaten

Melt butter in 8 x 8-inch baking dish; stir in sugar and orange peel, blending well. Spoon cranberries over sugar mixture. Combine turkey with gravy, milk, salt, pepper, onion, bread crumbs and eggs; mix well. Pack turkey mixture over cranberries firmly. Bake at 400 degrees for 45 minutes. Invert immediately onto serving platter. Cut into squares to serve. If cranberry sauce is used, reduce sugar to 1/4 cup.

M. Christiana Gates
Middleborough High School
Middleboro, Massachusetts

TURKEY AU GRATIN

2 c. milk
2 8-oz. packages cream cheese
3/4 tsp. garlic salt
1 1/2 c. Parmesan cheese
3 10-oz. packages frozen broccoli
12 cooked 1/2-in. breast of turkey
    slices

Combine milk, cream cheese, garlic salt and cheese in double boiler. Cook, stirring, until mixture forms smooth sauce. Cover bottom of 9 x 12 x 2 1/2-inch pan with frozen broccoli. Pour 1 cup sauce over broccoli. Cover broccoli and sauce with sliced turkey; pour remaining sauce over turkey. Bake at 350 degrees for 25 to 30 minutes.

Madeline J. Bean
Centennial Junior High School
Boulder, Colorado

TURKEY-CHEESE CASSEROLE

4 c. diced cooked turkey
4 c. turkey or chicken broth
1 1/2 c. diced celery
1 c. diced process cheese
1 lg. onion, diced
1 can cream of chicken soup
1 1/2 tsp. pepper
2 tsp. salt
4 c. corn bread stuffing mix

Combine all ingredients except 1 cup corn bread stuffing mix in 3-quart casserole. Sprinkle remaining stuffing mix on top. Bake at 350 degrees for 45 minutes. Yield: 8-10 servings.

Mrs. Frances VanLandingham
Greene Central High School
Snow Hill, North Carolina

TURKEY DELIGHT

1 turkey
3 tbsp. margarine
1 med. onion, chopped
1 1/2 c. chopped celery
3 lg. eggs, beaten
1/4 c. chopped pimento
1 can mushroom soup
1 1/2 c. grated cheese
1 box round buttery crackers,
    crushed
1/2 tsp. salt and pepper

Cook turkey in boiling salted water until tender. Remove meat from bones; cut into bite-sized pieces. Chill broth until fat hardens, then remove fat from broth. Reserve 4 cups broth. Preheat oven to 350 degrees. Melt margarine in skillet; add onion and celery. Saute until onion is transparent. Combine turkey, onion mixture, reserved broth, eggs, pimento, mushroom soup, cheese, crackers, salt and pepper. Spoon into shallow 9 x 13-inch casserole. Bake, uncovered, for about 1 hour or until bubbly. Garnish with chopped parsley.

Roberta Ann Martin
Pleasant View Junior High School
Pueblo, Colorado

TURKEY SUPREME
Fourth Place

1 No. 2 1/2 can pineapple
    chunks
3 c. light cream
1 c. shredded coconut
1/2 c. butter
1/2 c. flour
2 tsp. salt
1/4 tsp. pepper
1/2 c. cashew nuts
3 c. cooked diced turkey
2 tbsp. brandy
1 recipe hollandaise sauce

Drain pineapple; reserve 1 1/2 cups juice. Combine reserved juice, cream and coconut in saucepan. Heat to scalding. Melt butter in large skillet; add flour, salt and pepper. Cook for 1 minute. Add scalded cream mixture gradually, stirring until thickened. Add cashew nuts, turkey, pineapple and brandy. Spoon into 9 x 15-inch casserole; pour hollandaise sauce over top. Broil in oven until brown. Serve at once. Yield: 8-10 servings.

Mrs. Donna N. Ray
Cascade Junior High School
Vancouver, Washington

TURKEY-CHILI CASSEROLE

1/2 c. chopped onion
2 tbsp. butter
3 cans cream of mushroom soup
1 4-oz. can chopped pimento
2 tbsp. chopped Ortega chilies
12 corn tortillas
Oil
4 c. diced cooked turkey
3 c. grated Cheddar cheese
Salt and pepper

Saute onion in butter until limp; stir in soup, pimento and chilies. Fry tortillas lightly in oil on each side. Arrange layers of tortillas, turkey, soup and cheese in greased casserole, sprinkling each layer with salt and pepper to taste. Bake at 350 degrees for 45 minutes. Yield: 12 servings.

Mrs. Ethel E. Teves
East Bakersfield High School
Bakersfield, California

TURKEY GOBBLER

1 8-oz. can oysters
1 can cream of celery soup
2 c. diced cooked turkey
1 tbsp. chopped pimento
2 tbsp. melted butter
1/2 c. coarse corn flake crumbs
1/2 c. cubed jellied cranberry sauce

Drain oysters; reserve liquid. Combine soup and reserved liquid in 1 1/2-quart casserole. Stir in turkey, pimento and oysters, mixing well. Combine butter and crumbs; sprinkle over turkey mixture. Top with cranberry sauce. Bake at 400 degrees for 20 minutes or until heated through. Yield: 5 servings.

Mrs. Ima Gean Cantrell
Dallas County High School
Plantersville, Alabama

TURKEY WITH DRESSING

4 c. cooked diced turkey
3/4 c. chopped celery
1 med. onion, chopped

3/4 c. Velveeta cheese, diced
1/4 tsp. salt
1/4 tsp. pepper
1 can mushroom soup
1 egg, beaten
2 c. cracker crumbs
2 c. turkey broth
1/3 c. dry bread crumbs
1 tbsp. melted butter

Combine turkey, celery, onion, cheese, seasonings, soup, egg, cracker crumbs and broth; mix well. Spoon turkey mixture into 2 1/2-quart greased casserole. Toss bread crumbs in melted butter; sprinkle over turkey mixture. Bake at 350 degrees for 1 hour or until set.

D. Jean Searcy
Silver Lake High School
Silver Lake, Kansas

TURKEY TETRAZZINI

4 oz. spaghetti
1 can cream of celery soup
1/2 c. milk
2 c. shredded sharp Cheddar cheese
2 c. cooked diced turkey
1 3-oz. can sliced mushrooms,
   drained
1/3 c. chopped onion
1/2 tsp. salt
1/4 tsp. pepper
1/4 c. chopped pimento
1/4 c. black olives, sliced

Break spaghetti into 2-inch pieces; cook according to package directions. Rinse with hot water. Combine soup and milk in large bowl; mix well. Add spaghetti, 1 1/2 cups cheese, turkey, mushrooms, onion, salt, pepper, pimento and olives; toss gently. Pour spaghetti mixture into lightly greased 1 1/2-quart casserole. Bake at 350 degrees for 45 minutes. Remove from oven; sprinkle remaining cheese on top. Bake for several minutes longer or until cheese melts. Yield: 6 servings.

Mrs. Jama K. Montgomery
Alexandria Junior High School
Alexandria, Indiana

185

TURKEY TEZZ

1 1/2 c. cooked spaghetti
2 c. diced cooked turkey
1/4 c. chopped pimento
1/2 c. chopped green pepper
1/4 c. chopped onion
1 can cream of mushroom soup
1/2 c. broth
1/2 tsp. pepper
1 tsp. salt
1 3/4 c. grated sharp
   Cheddar cheese

Combine all ingredients in order listed; mix thoroughly. Spoon into greased 3-quart baking dish. Bake at 350 degrees for 1 hour. May be frozen.

Mrs. William Lee
Colonial Heights High School
Colonial Heights, Virginia

TURKEY TORTILLA PIE

2 cans evaporated milk
2 cans cream of chicken soup
1 1/2 tsp. chili powder
1 doz. tortillas
4 c. diced leftover turkey
10 oz. extra sharp Cheddar cheese,
   grated

Blend milk, soup and chili powder together. Place half the tortillas, turkey, soup mixture and cheese in layers in baking dish; repeat, using remaining ingredients. Bake, uncovered, in 350-degree oven for 1 hour.

Mable B. Kirk
Ardmore High School
Ardmore, Alabama

TURKEY TORTILLA

1 pkg. flour tortillas, cut in 1-inch
   squares
3 c. cooked turkey
1/4 c. melted margarine
1/2 c. chopped onions
2 cans cream of mushroom soup

1 can Ortega sauce
1 1/2 tsp. chili powder
1 c. chicken broth
1 c. grated Cheddar cheese

Place tortilla squares and turkey in layers in deep baking dish. Combine remaining ingredients except cheese; pour over turkey. Bake in 350-degree oven for 20 minutes. Sprinkle with cheese; bake for 10 minutes longer or until cheese is melted. Yield: 6-8 servings.

Idella M. Lewis
Cotopaxi School
Cotopaxi, Colorado

TURKEY-SAUSAGE CASSEROLE

1 c. rice
1 tsp. salt
1 pkg. long grain and wild rice
1/2 lb. bulk sausage
1   13-oz. can mushrooms
2 cans cream of mushroom soup
1 tsp. Worcestershire sauce
3 c. cooked diced turkey
1/4 c. turkey or chicken broth
1/4 c. melted butter
1 to 1 1/2 c. bread crumbs

Wash rice thoroughly. Add salt to 4 cups boiling water in large saucepan; add rice gradually. Simmer, covered, for 30 minutes or until rice is tender and water is absorbed. Cook sausage in skillet over medium heat, stirring to break into bits; drain well. Stir in mushrooms, soup and Worcestershire sauce. Stir sausage mixture into rice mixture. Spoon half the rice mixture into greased 12 x 18 x 2-inch baking dish; arrange turkey over rice mixture. Top with remaining rice mixture. Pour broth over all. Combine butter with bread crumbs; arrange in 1-inch border around rice mixture. Bake at 375 degrees for 45 minutes. May be refrigerated. Bake for 55 minutes if refrigerated. Yield: 10-12 servings.

Flora Mae Doville
Southside High School
Fort Smith, Arkansas

TURKEY BALLS
IN MUSHROOM SAUCE

2 lg. eggs, beaten
3 c. finely ground cooked turkey
1 c. soft bread crumbs
1 3/4 c. turkey stock
1 tsp. instant minced onion
Pepper
1/4 tsp. ground allspice
3/4 tsp. dry mustard
1   10 1/2-oz. can cream of
*   mushroom soup*
1/4 tsp. celery salt
1/8 tsp. onion powder
1/8 tsp. garlic powder

Combine eggs, turkey, bread crumbs, 3/4 cup stock, minced onion, 1/4 teaspoon pepper, allspice and mustard in large bowl; mix well. Shape into sixteen 1 1/2-inch balls. Place in a 9 x 12-inch baking dish. Combine 1 cup stock, 1/8 teaspoon pepper and remaining ingredients in saucepan; bring almost to a boil, stirring constantly. Pour over turkey balls. Bake in a preheated 350-degree oven for 50 minutes. Garnish with parsley. Serve with rice, if desired. Yield: 8 servings.

Mary S. Debevec
Chisholm Senior High School
Chisholm, Minnesota

TURKEY TORTELLINI

2 tbsp. butter
Flour
1/2 c. evaporated milk
Salt
Pepper to taste
3 eggs
1 lb. ground turkey
Pinch of monosodium glutamate
Pinch of sugar
1/4 c. chopped parsley
Grated dry Jack cheese
Cornstarch
Melted butter

Melt butter over low heat. Stir in 3 table-spoons flour until well blended. Stir in milk and 1/2 cup water; season with salt and pep-per to taste. Cook, stirring constantly, until thickened. Cool. Place 4 cups flour on pastry board. Make a well in center; place 2 eggs and 1 teaspoon salt in well. Cut into the flour, using 2 knives, adding enough warm water gradually to make a dough. Knead until smooth; cover and let rest for at least 15 minutes. Combine turkey, monosodium glutamate, 1 teaspoon salt and sugar; saute until lightly browned. Cool. Add parsley, 1 egg, 1/2 cup cheese and sauce. Roll parts of dough on heavily floured board to a thin layer; cut into 2 1/2-inch squares. Place tea-spoon of filling in center of each square. Fold over into triangle and seal edges well with tines of fork. Pull widest points of turn-over together to form circle, being careful not to break dough. Pinch together tightly. Place on a cornstarch-covered cookie sheet. Drop into large kettle of boiling salted wa-ter. Cook for 12 to 20 minutes or until dough tests done, stirring occasionally with a wooden spoon. Drain; place in serving dish. Drizzle with generous amount of butter. Sprinkle with cheese; toss gently. Serve with tossed green salad.

Eileen Silva
Escalon High School
Escalon, California

QUICK TURKEY LOAF

4 eggs, beaten
2/3 c. milk or broth
1 tsp. salt
1 c. soft bread crumbs
2 tbsp. chopped green pepper
2 tbsp. chopped pimento
1/2 tbsp. parsley flakes
2 tbsp. melted butter
3 c. cooked turkey, in lg. pieces

Combine eggs, milk, salt, bread crumbs, green pepper, pimento, parsley, melted but-ter and turkey; mix well. Spoon into greased 7 x 4 x 4-inch loaf pan. Bake at 325 degrees for 45 to 50 minutes.

Lucille S. Brown
Narrows High School
Narrows, Virginia

TURKEY CUSTARD LOAF

2 1/2 c. coarsely ground cooked
*   turkey*
1 1/2 c. fine bread crumbs
3/4 c. turkey broth
1/2 c. diced celery
1 tbsp. finely chopped fresh parsley
*   or 1 tsp. dried parsley flakes*
2 tsp. grated onion
1/2 tsp. Worcestershire sauce
1 tsp. salt
1/8 tsp. pepper
2 tsp. lemon juice
4 lg. or 6 sm. eggs, beaten
1 c. evaporated milk

Combine turkey, crumbs, broth, celery, parsley, onion, Worcestershire sauce, salt, pepper and lemon juice. Add beaten eggs; stir in milk. Mix lightly but thoroughly; place in well-greased 8 x 5 x 3-inch loaf pan. Set in pan of hot water. Bake in 350-degree oven for about 1 hour or until loaf is firm and top is delicately browned. One chicken bouillon cube dissolved in 3/4 cup hot water may be substituted for turkey broth. Milk and eggs may be reduced by 1/2 for a drier loaf, if desired.

Mrs. Hilda B. Lye
Bloomfield Junior High School
Halifax, Nova Scotia, Canada

ORIENTAL TURKEY

1/2 c. margarine
1/2 c. all-purpose flour
1 tsp. salt
1/2 c. evaporated milk
3 c. milk
2 c. turkey stock
3 c. chopped cooked turkey
1/2 c. mushrooms
1/2 c. slivered almonds
1 c. sliced water chestnuts
1/4 c. sliced pimento
1/4 c. cooking sherry
4 c. cooked rice

Melt margarine in large saucepan; stir in flour and salt to make a smooth paste. Add milks and stock gradually, stirring constantly; cook over medium heat until thick. Stir in remaining ingredients except rice; heat thoroughly. Serve over rice. Yield: 6-8 servings.

Mrs. Betty R. Waller
Robert W. Groves School
Garden City, Georgia

KENSINGTON PANCAKES

1/4 c. butter
1/4 c. diced onion
1/4 c. flour
1 tsp. salt
2 c. milk
2 c. diced cooked turkey
1 c. chopped walnuts
1/2 tsp. curry powder
1 egg, slightly beaten
3 tbsp. shredded Cheddar cheese

Melt butter in saucepan; saute onion until tender. Blend in flour and salt; remove from heat. Add milk gradually, stirring constantly. Cook, stirring, until thickened. Pour 1 1/2 cups sauce into bowl; add turkey, walnuts and curry powder, blending well. Add egg and cheese to remaining sauce in pan. Bring to a boil, stirring constantly until cheese melts.

Pancakes

6 eggs, slightly beaten
2 to 3 tbsp. water
1/4 tsp. salt
1/4 c. flour

Beat eggs, water and salt together; add flour gradually, beating well. Pour batter by 1/4 cupfuls onto lightly greased hot griddle. Brown delicately on each side. Remove from griddle. Spread 1/2 cup turkey filling in line down center of each pancake. Fold one edge over; fold remaining edge up. Place in ovenproof baking dish. Spoon cheese sauce over pancakes. Bake at 325 degrees for about 10 minutes.

Linda Adams
Millersburg High School
Millersburg, Pennsylvania

SWEET POTATO-TURKEY PIE

1   18-oz. can sweet potatoes
2 tbsp. melted butter
1/4 tsp. nutmeg
1/4 tsp. allspice
1/2 tsp. salt
1/2 c. chopped onion
2 tbsp. butter
2 cans cream of mushroom soup
2 c. cooked diced turkey
1   10-oz. package frozen mixed
*   vegetables, partially thawed*

Mash sweet potatoes; beat in butter, spices and salt. Line 9-inch pie plate with sweet potato mixture, building up edge about 1/2 inch high. Cook onion in butter in skillet until almost tender; add soup and turkey. Break up frozen vegetables; stir into soup mixture. Spoon into prepared shell. Bake in 350-degree oven for 30 minutes. Garnish with fresh tomato poinsettia and parsley. Yield: 6 servings.

Mrs. Beverly Berkebile
Urey Middle School
Walkerton, Indiana

TURKEY-CASHEW PIE

1/2 c. coarsely diced celery
2 c. chicken broth or 1 can
*   consomme*
3 c. cooked diced turkey
1/4 c. diced green onion tops
1 c. cashew halves
1 tbsp. parsley flakes
2 tbsp. soy sauce
1 tbsp. Worcestershire sauce
1 tsp. salt
1/2 tsp. white pepper
1 pkg. refrigerator biscuits

Cook celery in chicken broth for 5 minutes. Stir in turkey, onion tops, cashews and seasonings; bring to a boil. Pour into greased casserole; place biscuits on top. Bake at 400 degrees for 10 to 12 minutes or until biscuits are browned. Yield: 4 servings.

Mrs. Ruth H. Methvin
Fall River High School
McArthur, California

OVEN-SMOKED TURKEY

1   10 to 12-lb. turkey
1/4 c. salad oil
1/2 c. salt
2 tbsp. liquid smoke
1 c. vinegar
1/4 c. pepper
2 tsp. finely chopped parsley

Preheat oven 350 degrees. Rinse turkey; pat dry with paper towels. Make a paste of salad oil and salt; rub 1/4 cup of the mixture into inside and neck cavities. Truss turkey; brush with additional oil. Place on roaster rack, breast side up. Bake for 1 hour. Combine remaining salt paste, liquid smoke, vinegar, pepper and parsley. Baste turkey with vinegar mixture. Bake for 3 hours and 30 minutes longer or until turkey is tender, basting with vinegar mixture every 30 minutes. Let turkey stand for at least 15 minutes before carving.

Mrs. Ruth H. Burch
Foster Junior High School
Tulsa, Oklahoma

ROASTED TURKEY HEN

1   10 to 12-lb. turkey hen
Melted butter
Salt
3 stalks celery, chopped
1 lg. green pepper, diced
Cooked diced giblets

Rub turkey inside and out with butter; season with salt, using 1/4 teaspoon per pound. Add small amount of water to 1/2 cup melted butter. Saturate a cheesecloth folded in 2 thicknesses large enough to cover turkey. Pour 1/2 cup water into roasting pan; add celery and green pepper. Place turkey in pan; cover with prepared cheesecloth. Place lid on pan. Bake at 300 degrees for 4 hours, basting frequently and keeping cheesecloth moistened. Remove cheesecloth from turkey. Bake, uncovered, for 30 minutes longer. Remove turkey from pan; thicken gravy. Stir giblets into gravy.

Willa Fuqua
Belpre High School
Belpre, Ohio

TURKEY ENCHILADA

1 2-lb. butter-basted boneless
   turkey roast
1 tbsp. butter
1/4 c. minced onion
1 clove of garlic, pressed
1 tsp. dehydrated parsley
1 tsp. leaf oregano
1/8 tsp. cayenne pepper
2 tsp. chili powder
1/2 tsp. salt
1 tsp. sugar
1 6-oz. can tomato paste
1 tsp. vinegar
1 tbsp. flour

Cook turkey according to package directions. Reserve drippings. Melt butter in skillet; saute onion and garlic until tender. Add parsley, oregano, cayenne pepper, chili powder, salt, sugar, tomato paste and vinegar. Simmer for 3 minutes, stirring occasionally. Add enough water to reserved drippings to measure 1 cup liquid. Mix flour into liquid until smooth; add to tomato mixture. Simmer for 5 minutes, stirring occasionally. Serve sauce with turkey roast.

Esther Engelhardt
Mt. Pleasant Community School
Mt. Pleasant, Iowa

TURKEY CORNETS

12 slices bacon
1 sm. onion, finely chopped
3 c. cooked rice
2 c. cooked frozen spinach,
   well drained
2 tbsp. lemon juice
1/2 tsp. salt
12 slices baked breast of turkey
2 c. mushroom soup
1 c. sour cream

Fry bacon until crisp; drain and crumble. Saute onion in bacon drippings, then stir in bacon, rice, spinach, lemon juice and salt. Place 1/2 cup spinach mixture on one side of turkey slice; roll up jelly roll fashion. Arrange in baking pan; cover lightly with foil. Bake at 350 degrees for 10 minutes or until

heated through. Combine soup and sour cream; heat thoroughly. Serve each cornet with 1/4 cup sauce over top.

Mrs. Ruth Wingo
Kaufman High School
Kaufman, Texas

TURKEY ROLL-UPS

3/4 c. diced fresh mushrooms
2 stalks celery, diced
1 med. onion, chopped
3 tbsp. butter
1 1/2 c. chicken stock
Salt and pepper to taste
1/2 tsp. sage
Pinch of thyme
Pinch of sweet basil
1 tbsp. chopped parsley
White wine (opt.)
5 c. soft bread crumbs
4 1/4-in. thick slices fresh
   turkey breast steaks
4 slices bacon

Saute mushrooms, celery and onion in butter in heavy skillet until tender. Add chicken stock; simmer for 5 minutes. Remove from heat; add salt, pepper, sage, thyme, basil, parsley and 1/3 cup wine. Pour over bread crumbs; mix thoroughly. Add more stock or water if needed. Pound turkey steaks until 1/8-inch thick and about 6 inches square. Place about 1 cup stuffing on each steak; fold turkey around stuffing. Wrap strip of bacon around each turkey roll; secure with a wooden pick. Place in well-buttered casserole. Spoon any remaining stuffing around turkey rolls. Pour 1/4 cup wine over all; cover. Bake at 325 degrees for 1 hour to 1 hour and 30 minutes or until tender. May place in broiler to brown bacon, if desired. Yield: 4 servings.

Claudia R. Fay
Skykomish High School
Skykomish, Washington

TURKEY AND RICE SALAD

1 1/2 env. unflavored gelatin
1/2 tsp. salt

Dash of pepper
Dash of paprika
1 1/2 c. cooked diced turkey
1 c. cold cooked rice
3/4 c. minced celery
2 tbsp. chopped green pepper
1 tbsp. pickle relish
1/4 c. chopped pecans
2 tbsp. chopped stuffed olives
2/3 c. mayonnaise
2/3 c. heavy cream, whipped

Soften gelatin in 2 cups cold water; add salt, pepper and paprika. Stir over hot water until dissolved. Add turkey and remaining ingredients. Pour into 8 x 8 x 2-inch pan. Chill until set. Cut into squares; serve on lettuce. Garnish with 1 tablespoon snipped parsley. Yield: 6 servings.

Hazel F. Gibson
Roosvelt High School
Roosvelt, Oklahoma

TURKEY-STUFFED TOMATO

2 c. diced cooked turkey
1 c. celery
1 hard-cooked egg, diced
1 c. salad dressing
Salt and pepper to taste
4 lg. tomatoes
1/2 c. slivered almonds
Paprika

Combine turkey, celery, egg, salad dressing and seasonings. Chill for 2 hours. Hollow out each tomato; spoon 1 cup turkey mixture into each tomato. Top with almonds; sprinkle with paprika. Serve on lettuce leaves.

Cathy R. Lobe
North Central High School
Spokane, Washington

ESTELLE'S TURKEY SALAD SPECIAL

1/2 lb. fresh mushrooms
2 tbsp. olive oil
1 pkg. frozen peas
1 c. sour cream

4 c. diced cooked turkey
2 c. sliced celery hearts
1/4 c. drained capers
3/4 c. mayonnaise
Salt and pepper to taste
3 red pimentos
1/2 med. cucumber, sliced

Saute mushrooms for 8 to 10 minutes in olive oil; cool. Chill well. Cook frozen peas in boiling water until just tender; cool. Add sour cream to turkey; let stand in refrigerator for 1 hour to moisten, turning turkey 2 or 3 times. Combine turkey mixture, celery, capers, mushrooms, mayonnaise, salt, and pepper. Spoon salad into center of oblong platter; garnish with peas, thin strips of pimento and cucumber slices. May add asparagus spears, tomato wedges, radish roses, additional cucumber slices and sliced celery hearts if desired.

Mrs. Estelle B. Nickell
Morgan County High School
West Liberty, Kentucky

TURKEY-HAM IMPERIAL

2 tbsp. unflavored gelatin
1/2 c. chicken bouillon
3/4 c. mayonnaise
3/4 tbsp. lemon juice
1 1/2 c. diced cooked turkey
3/4 c. diced smoked ham
3/4 c. minced celery
2 tbsp. chopped green pepper
1/2 c. chopped almonds
3/4 c. whipped cream
Salt and pepper to taste

Soften gelatin in bouillon; dissolve over boiling water. Combine gelatin mixture, mayonnaise, lemon juice, turkey, ham, celery, green pepper, almonds, whipped cream and seasonings. Pour into oiled mold. Chill for 6 hours or until set. Unmold on serving tray. Garnish with cherry tomatoes and cucumber slices.

Mrs. Barbara Chausow
Niles North High School
Skokie, Illinois

TURKEY CURRY

1/2 c. finely chopped onion
1/2 c. finely chopped celery
1/3 c. flour
2 c. turkey broth or 1 No. 2 can
  chicken broth
1 8-oz. can tomato sauce
1 8-oz. can water
1/2 tsp. Worcestershire sauce
1 1/2 tsp. curry powder
Salt and pepper to taste
4 c. diced cooked turkey

Brown onion and celery lightly in 1/4 cup hot fat. Stir in flour and turkey broth; cook until thick. Add tomato sauce, water, Worcestershire sauce, curry powder, salt, pepper and turkey; heat thoroughly. Serve in ring mold of rice, if desired. Yield: 8 servings.

Mrs. Edith Blasi
Bowie Junior High School
Odessa, Texas

LUCKY SEVEN SANDWICH

4 slices rye bread
4 slices Swiss cheese
8 slices tomato
8 crisp lettuce leaves
8 slices crisp bacon
4 to 8 slices cooked breast of
  turkey
Thousand Island Dressing

Place 1 slice rye bread for each sandwich on luncheon plate. Top with 1 slice Swiss cheese, 2 tomato slices, 2 lettuce leaves, 2 strips bacon and 1 or 2 turkey slices. Top each sandwich with generous portion of Thousand Island Dressing; serve with extra dressing. Yield: 4 sandwiches.

Thousand Island Dressing

2 eggs
1/2 tsp. mustard
1/4 tsp. salt
3 tsp. sugar
2 tbsp. vinegar
Dash of paprika
Dash of red pepper
2 c. salad oil
1 1/2 c. catsup
1 sm. can pimento, finely chopped
1 sm. onion, finely grated
1/2 c. sweet pickle relish,
  drained

Beat eggs until thick; add mustard, salt, sugar, vinegar, paprika and red pepper. Add salad oil, drop by drop, beating constantly, until all oil is used and dressing is thick. Add catsup gradually; stir in pimento, onion and pickle relish. Store in covered jar in refrigerator for several hours before using. Yield: 1 quart.

Norma Gay Whitlow
Hill High School
Winston-Salem, North Carolina

TURKEY SOUFFLE SANDWICH

6 to 8 slices white bread
2 c. cooked turkey
1/2 c. chopped onion
1/2 c. chopped green pepper
1/2 c. chopped celery
1/2 c. mayonnaise
3/4 tsp. salt
1/8 tsp. pepper
2 beaten eggs
1 1/2 c. milk
1 can cream of mushroom soup
1/2 c. shredded Cheddar cheese

Cube 2 slices bread; place in greased casserole. Combine turkey, vegetables, mayonnaise and seasonings; spoon over bread in casserole. Trim crusts from remaining bread; arrange over turkey mixture. Combine eggs and milk; pour over turkey mixture. Chill for 2 hours or overnight. Spoon soup over top; sprinkle with cheese. Bake at 325 degrees for 1 hour and 15 minutes. Yield: 6-8 servings.

Janet C. Wellman
Central Middle School
Montevideo, Minnesota

Index

COLOR ILLUSTRATIONS

PHOTOGRAPHY CREDITS: Florida Citrus Commission; American Lamb Council; National Kraut Packers Association; California Strawberry Advisory Board; Proctor & Gamble Company: Crisco Division; International Tuna Fish Association; Accent International; Olive Administrative Committee; Spanish Green Olive Commission; National Cherry Growers & Industries Foundation; Brussels Sprouts Marketing Program; Louisiana Yam Commission; Best Foods, a Division of CPC International Inc.

Complete Your Cooking And Entertainment Library With Favorite Recipes Of Home Economics Teachers

Blue Ribbon Poultry Cookbook — This year's award winning Blue Ribbon cookbook focuses on the delights of chicken, pheasant, turkey, duck . . . making everyday dinner — Sunday dinner!

Blue Ribbon Pies and Pastries — Smell fresh baked apple pie or taste a fluffy chiffon pie. Here are over 500 award winning recipes for every pie and pastry imaginable. Cream pies, turnovers, eclairs, custard pies, tarts and tassies, and many more . . . all promise you a fantastic dessert every time.

Meats Cookbook — The way to a man's heart? Nothing beats beef, lamb, pork, veal . . . or any other meat dish. Plain or fancy, mouth watering main dishes for every occasion and taste are included in this valuable recipe book. **Desserts Cookbook** — Flaming crepes to frosted cakes . . . desserts are the crowning complement to every meal. And this marvelous book contains hundreds of tempting desserts . . . sure to bring smiles of delight from young and old alike.

Casseroles Cookbook — From poultry to sirloin tips, hundreds of delicious and timesaving casseroles. Mix and match vegetables, meats, pasta, seasonings . . . and come up with a scrumptious meal -- all in one dish. Fun to prepare and a breeze to serve.

Holiday Cookbook — Delicious, festive meals for all those special holiday events. Recipes are included for not only Christmas, Thanksgiving and New Year's Eve and Day . . . but for Halloween, Fourth of July, St. Patrick's Day . . . every exciting occasion.

Quick and Easy Cookbook — The perfect answer to all those last minute meals -- for families on the go! Hundreds of recipes to make delicious desserts, dinners, suppers and snacks in a snap. Sure to be a real family favorite!

All-Purpose Cookbook — Desserts, main meals, salads, snacks . . . recipes for every meal imaginable. This happy combination cookbook makes meal planning and preparation fun and easy, and guarantees success -- every time! **Money-Saving Cookbook** — You can prepare delicious and appealing meals -- for dollars less with these nifty, budget-pleasing recipes. This is the perfect answer to high prices . . . and a valuable addition to any cooking library.

Americana Cookery — Yankee Pot Roast, Southern Pecan Pie, New England Clam Chowder . . . favorite American dishes that the whole family will enjoy. Handed down by families through the years . . . these are foods that best reflect our great heritage.